AF361323

CASANOVA IN THE ENLIGHTENMENT

From the Margins to the Centre

THE UCLA CLARK MEMORIAL LIBRARY SERIES

CASANOVA IN THE ENLIGHTENMENT

FROM THE MARGINS TO THE CENTRE

Edited by Malina Stefanovska

Published by the University of Toronto Press in association with the UCLA Center for Seventeenth- and Eighteenth-Century Studies and the William Andrews Clark Memorial Library

© The Regents of the University of California 2021
utorontopress.com

ISBN 978-1-4875-0664-3 (cloth)
ISBN 978-1-4875-3458-5 (EPUB)
ISBN 978-1-4875-3457-8 (PDF)

Library and Archives Canada Cataloguing in Publication

Title: Casanova in the Enlightenment : from the margins
to the centre / edited by Malina Stefanovska.
Names: Stefanovska, Malina, editor.
Series: UCLA Clark Memorial Library series ; 30.
Description: Series statement: UCLA Clark Memorial Library series ;
30 | Includes bibliographical references and index.
Identifiers: Canadiana (print) 20200253387 | Canadiana (ebook)
20200253514 | ISBN 9781487506643 (cloth) | ISBN 9781487534585
(EPUB) | ISBN 9781487534578 (PDF)
Subjects: LCSH: Casanova, Giacomo, 1725–1798. Mémoires.
Classification: LCC D285.8.C4 C37 2021 | DDC 940.2/53092 – dc23

This book has been published with the help of a grant from the UCLA Center
for Seventeenth- and Eighteenth-Century Studies.

University of Toronto Press acknowledges the financial assistance to its
publishing program of the Canada Council for the Arts and the Ontario Arts
Council, an agency of the Government of Ontario.

Funded by the Financé par le
Government gouvernement
of Canada du Canada | Canadä

Contents

Acknowledgments vii

Introduction 3
MALINA STEFANOVSKA

Part I: Libertine Traces

1 "Triompher par la force": Sexual Violence and Its
Representation in Casanova's *History of My Life* 17
RAPHAËLLE BRIN

2 The Writer of Dux: Casanova's Dialogue with
His Ladies from Autobiography to Correspondence 35
BRUNO CAPACI

3 Casanova and the Undifferentiated Body 54
MLADEN KOZUL

Part II: Emerging Sociabilities

4 Negotiating Sociabilities in Casanova's *History of My Life* 71
CLORINDA DONATO

5 Casanova, Mercury, Mercurio 91
MALINA STEFANOVSKA

Contents

6 Casanova, the Love of Paris 105
PIERRE SAINT-AMAND

7 Paris in Three Movements 120
CHANTAL THOMAS

Part III: Representational Shifts and Legacies

8 Rewriting, Revolution, Melancholy:
Two Versions of the First Stay in Paris 129
JEAN-CHRISTOPHE IGALENS

9 Casanova, from Man to Myth 141
MICHEL DELON

10 *Fellini's Casanova*: The Story of a Man Who
Was Never Born 150
CHRISTOPHER B. WHITE

Contributors 161

Index 165

Acknowledgments

The editor is grateful to the Department of French and Francophone Studies of UCLA, the Department of Italian of UCLA, and the UCLA Center for Seventeenth- and Eighteenth-Century Studies/William Andrews Clark Memorial Library for their support in organizing the initial conference on Casanova, as well as in shaping its results into a book. The project was helped by the Dean of Humanities and would not have been possible without the "little hands" of any publishing effort: translation into English by Jennifer Curtiss Gage, William Hamlet, and Thomas Wynn, copy editing by Allison Van Deventer, and indexing by Ellan Hawman. Finally, I am grateful to my husband Henry Schellhorn, who put up with such a formidable – even though virtual – rival in my time and affections.

CASANOVA IN THE ENLIGHTENMENT

From the Margins to the Centre

Introduction

MALINA STEFANOVSKA

For all the good and bad reasons that motivate readers, this moment is perfect for rereading Casanova. And since our times are rife with sexual scandals and questioning, let us start with the – oh, so sweet! – forbidden pleasures that make us keep on reading his sulphurous autobiography, the *History of My Life.*

A libertine, a serial seducer, or at least an outstanding narrator capable of endowing his name with such an archetypal meaning, Casanova has aged rather well. The slight erotic titillation that he was able to create despite his respect for eighteenth-century decorum has a timeless appeal. Yet even though the *History of My Life* has often been read as libertine literature, and may well be one of those books that according to Rousseau should be read with only one hand – the other being occupied elsewhere – it never slips into pornography.[1] While in the past, commentary on Casanova was male territory, recent scholarship has shown that "the man who loved women" can also be an object of female interest.[2] Literature, after all, has always been about "*le plaisir du texte,*" as French literary theorist Roland Barthes argued, and it may take today's generation of post-feminist readers to admit to pleasure's plasticity and its many facets of identification.

But the pleasure brought by reading his life story[3] goes well beyond the sexual and the sensual. Casanova's ability to create a detailed, complex, and multifaceted material universe is inimitable. This adventurer and exile criss-crossed the entire European continent, from England to Spain, from France to Germany, from Italy to Russia, Poland, parts of today's Estonia, to Cyprus, and even Constantinople. He brought to life with equal success Venetian casinos, imperial balls in Saint Petersburg, coffee houses in London, the gambling dens of Spa, theatres where he met beautiful women, literary gatherings where he sparred with men of letters or women poets, and royal courts he visited. Casanova named and described a multitude of real individuals, from princes to valets, from prostitutes to queens; he noted and analysed the customs and characters of many nations. He even documented in detail his finances (including his gambling gains and losses in scores of currencies), his bodily maladies and their cures, the food he ate and the wine he drank in good company. Casanova is thus to be counted among the outstanding witnesses of his century, an ethnographer of sorts who covers domains as varied as food, sex, marriage customs, morals, politics, clothes, jewellery, language, and even transportation, as he listed the many types of carriages he travelled in. In particular, he touched on crucial ideas of his age, in philosophical discussions that blend science, religion, and free-thinking; libertine perspectives and – last but not least – a novel impetus to write about the self, ushered in by Rousseau's *Confessions*.

In all these respects, the *History of My Life* is much more than a mere description or travelogue. As should be the case in a true autobiography, hardly any aspect or sentiment that makes up a full human existence is passed over in it, from the highest to the lowest: romantic dreams, passionate or casual sex, witty conversations, fits of melancholy, joy, despair, bouts of venereal disease, thoughts of suicide, remorse, material misery, and fear of aging. And one should note that Casanova's was not a run-of-the-mill existence. As an adventurer and a cosmopolitan, he crossed the boundaries between languages and cultures, as well as those between the high nobility, the popular classes, and the underworld. Duels, jail stints (including one spectacular escape), meetings with royalty, orgies, the utmost poverty and extraordinary wealth, elaborate scams and experiments in high finance – these are just a few of his life experiences. His precarious status on the margins of the good society of his time gave him a privileged position from which he managed to dream up and live an absolutely unique life, and then to write it.

Writing, indeed, is what brings him to the core of the Enlightenment and of his century. Just as varied as Casanova's life, his works situate him squarely at the centre of that effervescence that characterized the Enlightenment's encyclopedic spirit. Their number and variety substantiate his important position in its various circles of sociability. A member of several poets' academies, a lover of antiquity, a student of science, a translator, and a playwright, he was a bona fide member of the Republic of Letters, cultivating relationships with notable men and women of letters, artists and art critics, erudite scholars, physicians, and natural scientists.

A few examples among the many in the *History of My Life* illustrate these relationships: during his first stay in Paris, Casanova was welcomed by a friend's mother, Silvia Balletti, a famous actress and muse to Marivaux. In her house, he met several men of letters: Crébillon the Elder,[4] with whom he established a lasting friendship; and the fashionable Claude-Henri de Fusée, abbé de Voisenon, who then introduced him to Bernard Le Bovier de Fontenelle, a founding figure of the Enlightenment and a "grand poète, profond physicien" (great poet, profound physicist; 1:641). Other members of the Republic of Letters he knew included the prolific playwright Antoine-Alexandre-Henri Poinsinet; the novelist and playwright Françoise de Graffigny; and the well-known economist and scholar abbé Ferdinand Galiani. Through Crébillon, Casanova also met Jean Le Rond d'Alembert, the famous mathematician and Diderot's co-editor of the *Encyclopédie*, whose acquaintance he cultivated. During his second stay in Paris, after escaping the Leads, the French statesman and diplomat François-Joachim de Pierre, Abbé de Bernis, whom Casanova knew in Venice, introduced him to the royal minister Étienne-François de Choiseul and helped him obtain the privilege of running the royal lottery. But the influence of Parisian circles radiated still wider: his brother, the painter Francesco Giuseppe Casanova, led him to the artist Anton-Raphael Mengs, well-known in his century, who in turn acquainted him with the art critic Johan Joachim Winckelmann in Rome. In Switzerland, after visiting Voltaire and sparring with him on literature, he called upon the fashionable physician Johann Friedrich von Herrenschwand, whom he knew from Paris, and paid a three-day visit to Albrecht Haller, a famous physician and natural scientist with whom he began a long-lasting epistolary friendship. Such examples abound.

It is clear that Casanova's aspirations, beyond following his "demon" and indulging his senses, were of the intellectual sort. A prolific author in both French and Italian, as well as a translator and scholar of antiquity, he produced such works as a translation of Homer into Italian (and partly into Venetian) verse,[5] several plays, among which a parodic transposition of a Racinian tragedy into Italian comedy,[6] a detailed (and incorrect) mathematical proof,[7] and several works of historiography.[8] The projects in which he was trying to spark interest among various European rulers included reforming the Julian calendar, creating a system for manufacturing silk from silkworms, and populating the Spanish Sierra Morena with colonies of Swiss immigrants. All were jotted down, at times in detail. His medical interests were put to work in the satirical pamphlet *Lana Caprina*, in which he mocked physicians' theory that female thinking is influenced by the uterus.[9] He even claimed to have made some money on it. That, unfortunately, was far from being the case with *Icosameron,* a voluminous work of utopian science fiction that narrated a journey to the centre of the earth, which he published at his own expense in the hope of becoming famous.[10] The same mix of science, ideas, and imagination characterizes the writings found among his manuscripts: more than thirty dialogues and meditations on religion;[11] various texts on language and neologisms, including a proposal for a linguistic lottery;[12] a critical essay on the bestselling author Bernardin de Saint-Pierre;[13] and much more.

When all his efforts failed to bring him the fame and wealth he dreamed of, in his old age, living out his life at the isolated summer estate of Count Waldstein (Wallenstein) in Dux (today's Dushcov, in the Czech Republic) as his protégé and librarian, Casanova set out to write, in secret, the *History of My Life,* with which he was finally to enter the literary pantheon. He penned it over more than ten years, in French, a language he had learned and adopted as an adult, claiming that writing at his desk thirteen hours a day helped him escape madness. He left it to be published posthumously.

This unique autobiographical narrative, although it was at first available to readers only in a highly expurgated version, earned him a legendary stature and appeal, that arguably dwarfs the myth of Don Juan (one that he himself actually helped perfect if, as scholars believe, he participated in writing the libretto for Mozart's *Don Giovanni.*) The numerous artistic, cinematographic, and literary representations of Casanova testify to his lasting legacy in European culture. Casanova scholarship, moreover, has recently experienced a renewal. The recent acquisition by the French Bibliothèque Nationale of the original manuscript of his autobiography, hitherto inaccessible to the public, was followed by an important exhibition, "Casanova and His Times" in 2010, a spate of literary and historical studies, and two major new editions of the *Histoire de ma vie* in French, one of which is the famous Pléiade collection by Gallimard.[14] In the English-speaking world, however, Casanova scholarship lags behind. It consists principally of biographies, well researched but presented in a traditional format, that focus on his life rather than on his works.[15] A recent publication, *Casanova: The Seduction of Europe,* testifies to a new interest in connecting Casanova to the European culture of his times.[16]

Despite Casanova's marginalization both in his lifetime and in subsequent literary history, in most of which he has been treated as the archetypal libertine writer, today he is finally receiving his due as an author: his output, from his philosophical dialogues to his scientific musings and memoirs, expresses the crucial ideas of his century, as well as revealing their inherent tensions. After significant rehabilitation in the past decade, he can finally claim a central position in the Enlightenment republic of letters. Casanova's religious ideas, spelled out in all their inconsistencies and hesitations in the Preface of the *History of My Life*, as well as in several dialogues unpublished in his lifetime, can be taken as an example. Living the life of a sinner, riding the coat-tails of chance, dabbling in alchemy, using magic for profit (but also believing in it a little!), he simultaneously proclaimed his faith in Providence and in a Higher Being. This is also how recent studies depict the Enlightenment, in which progressive thought and the praise of reason often went hand-in-hand with outlandish beliefs.[17]

Our endeavour thus arises from a renewed interest in the pan-European and trans-disciplinary perspectives in which Casanova lived and wrote. Based on the premise that the *History of My Life* needs to be re-evaluated, the following chapters gather recognized scholars and younger voices from the United States and Europe. Their contributions highlight several essential new directions in Casanova scholarship: the relationship to violence and its representation (Brin); issues of uncertain sexual and gender identity, including the transformation of inherited Renaissance medical views on the human body (Kozul); the representation and negotiation of circles and networks of sociability and of patterns of communication among persons, sciences, and areas of knowledge (Capaci, Donato, Stefanovska); and the evolving image of Paris as a European capital of the eighteenth century (Saint-Amand, Thomas).[18] The contributors also advance new perspectives in Casanova scholarship, stemming from the publication of the original manuscript of the *History of My Life* (Igalens), bringing together European literary representations of the "Casanova myth" (Delon), or building on his cinematographic representations and their critique (White).

The opening chapters focus on the body and gender, interrogating previous interpretations and showing how a new understanding of medicine, gender, or sexual violence can modify the traditional readings focused on Casanova's libertine ideas. Raphaëlle Brin reads episodes in the *History of My Life* from a feminist perspective and argues that Casanova's stance on seduction is informed by the implicit ideology of his times regarding female sexuality and male "prowess." Bruno Capaci provides a detailed reading of the rarely discussed letters sent to Casanova by his female correspondents, demonstrating the subtle but significant differences between epistolary and autobiographical discourse and the inevitable self-fashioning of any autobiographer, even the most sincere. Mladen Kozul undermines the seducer myth, which is anchored in a rarely disputed vision of the libertine's libido, and shows its tensions through Casanova's images of the sexually undifferentiated body and its fluids in light of the "humoral theory" that nourished eighteenth-century medicine.

The second part of the book broadens its perspective from libertine themes to Casanova's involvement in Enlightenment sociabilities and networks. Unlike Sade, this author did not develop his erotic imagination in monomaniacal isolation: he was an active agent in numerous networks of sociability, from academies of poets to epistolary relations with scientists and erudite scholars, circuits of Freemasonry, and the theatre circles of his time. The four chapters in part II are dedicated to this newly emphasized interdisciplinarity, which throws new light on Casanova studies and on Enlightenment scholarship. Clorinda Donato reads the *History of My Life* as a rich, encyclopedic cross-section of European sociability. As a highly informed member of Europe's itinerant republic of letters, Casanova described its distinct cultural aspects, such as the very open structure of the *conversazione*, the role of Masonic sociability, and the "somber and scientific" regional sociability of Berne in the 1760s. As a nexus in which all the forms of eighteenth-century life – exchange, travel, scientific pursuits, musical appreciation, journalistic awareness, correspondence networks, sexual networks, Masonic networks, and conversation – come together, the *History of My Life* is a true showcase of "how the Enlightenment worked." Malina Stefanovska, focusing on mercury as a metal and a figure, explores the symbiotic relationship between Casanova and this highly charged mythological, literary, and scientific symbol. Since mercury/Mercurio designates the metal used in medicine to cure syphilis, as well as a love messenger and go-between – in reference to the ancient myth of Mercury/Hermès – the theme of mercury/Mercurio in the *History of My Life* highlights Casanova's self-fashioning as a mediator between people, literary genres, and languages. In this light, Pierre Saint-Amand reads the account of Casanova's first stay in Paris as a novel of initiation into the libertine perspective on family and marriage. Positioning himself as a "candid" newcomer to the city, Casanova describes his gradual education in the manners and morals of the French capital, as well as his "enlightenment" about the various marital "arrangements" that ensure the family transmission of heritage even within a libertine lifestyle. Casanova's account of Paris is placed in parallel with a typical libertine novel, as well as in contrast with Rousseau's bestselling proto-romantic *Julie ou la nouvelle Héloïse*. Chantal Thomas, for her part, contrasts the different representations of Paris that stemmed from Casanova's three stays there over his lifetime. His first account emphasizes the young man's wish to acquire linguistic and social know-how and carefully avoids "the cold gaze of the libertine," transforming his whims into love stories, or at least into amorous moments. In his second stay, Casanova, at the peak of his capacities, takes the Parisian stage with utmost playfulness. In his third stay, however, the aging adventurer finds himself considerably less capable of charming audiences or of rebounding after a love affair. Yet although he fails to win acceptance into high society and is eventually expelled from Paris as a dangerous element, this unruly and indomitable part of himself is precisely what enables him to decipher the theatre of appearances that constitutes society.

The last three chapters of the book highlight tectonic shifts in Casanova scholarship, elicited by recent publication events as well as by his fictional and artistic representations in the media. Jean-Christophe Igalens, who recently co-authored a new edition of the *History of My life*, highlights how the publisher's editorial decision to place two successive versions of the same narrative side-by-side enables the reader to "confront two modes of organization for a single, narrated period." In a close reading based on Casanova's rewriting of the first draft of a part of his manuscript, Igalens detects a shift in its general mood: it becomes more suited to the "melancholic temperament" that Casanova attributes to himself and more consistent with his views on the French Revolution, which had occurred in the meantime. Through this close reading, Igalens discusses the subtle ways the historical present has tended to modify the representation of the past. Michel Delon examines the notorious "Casanova myth" in fictional writings that he inspired over time, by such literary figures as Guillaume Apollinaire, Arthur Schnitzler, Marina Tsvetaeva, and Sándor Márai. Delon places the legend of Casanova in opposition to the Don Juan myth, arguing that it is central to "mittel-Europa" with its gilded decadence, from the Venetian carnival to the high society of Vienna and Prague. Authors who fictionalize Casanova, whether treating him as a comedic symbol (through his return as an aged libertine) or as an imaginary interlocutor, use him to work through their own obsessions or tragedies, all the more successfully on account of his proverbial lightness and playfulness in the face of life's hardships. Rather than the hackneyed "libertine myth," Casanova thus represents in Delon's interpretation a founding "myth of modernity, defined as the mourning for all transcendence." Finally, Christopher B. White aptly highlights a seminal reappropriation that contributed to fleshing out Casanova's myth, Fellini's *Casanova*. According to White's interpretation, this "dark, funereal work," which shatters the seducer myth and creates "the story of a man who was never born, the adventures of a zombie, a mournful marionette without personal ideas," showcases Fellini's cinematographic creation as a polemical act that attempts to "cancel" a literary work by transferring it to a filmic medium. Paradoxically, this visceral antagonism toward his hero is precisely what enabled Fellini to create an inimitable masterpiece.

As is to be expected, the interpretations below evince certain tension between them: the place of "Casanova in the Enlightenment" entails indeed different ways of reading and understanding both this author and the Enlightenment at large. Some contributors see Casanova as "the living embodiment of the *esprit des Lumières*" (Capaci), or underline his active role in the European circulation of knowledge and its sociabilities (Donato, Saint-Amand). Others insist on his conflicted status and legacy both in terms of gender (Brin, Capaci, Kozul), or as a legend (White, Delon). Others, yet, underline inevitable deformations in his autobiographical narrative, due to memory lapses, literary influences, or a libertine perspective in matters of sex and love (Brin, Thomas, Saint-Amand, Igalens). Thus, one identical episode from the *History of My Life* may be dubbed a rape or an innocent moment of pleasure. This is not surprising, since several contributions stress in Casanova's identity an instability, inherent to any autobiographical enterprise (Capaci, Igalens), which produces a "figure that exists beyond borders and fixed identities" (Delon). Such tensions are telling of different perspectives: was the eighteenth century a period of Enlightenment, radical or otherwise, a shift in scientific paradigms, or – as Casanova represents it – a willed Carnival of libertine recollections, forever lost after 1789? And from which perspective are "we" entitled to judge it today? The authors here do not offer solutions, only individual choices that colour their interpretations. Perhaps the last word when dealing with such a myth is to show how it continually evolves and how it becomes endowed with a substantial – if debatable – historicity.

Our ambition, mirrored in the structure and organization of this book, was consequently to re-evaluate the status of Casanova as both an Enlightenment author and a mythical figure of our contemporary culture and to showcase how new scholarship on the global eighteenth century, cultural and gender studies, memory and autobiographical acts inflects our critical perspective. By bringing American scholars into a dialogue with Europe, where numerous recent publications testify to a robust interest in this author,[19] the contributions in this volume appeal to a readership interested in topics ranging from the European Enlightenment to libertine literature, eighteenth-century sociability, and early modern autobiography. Given the legendary status of this book's protagonist and hero, they will also appeal to any appreciative reader.

References to *History of My Life* in this study are generally to the Gallimard edition and are marked in the text by the volume and page, as are those to the Laffont edition, used by Jean-Christophe Igalens. The English translation by Willard Trask, Giacomo Casanova (Chevalier de Seingalt), *History of My Life*, vol. 1–12 (New York: Harcourt, Brace and World, 1966; repr. Baltimore, MD: Johns Hopkins University Press, 1996), is provided, with volume and page. Where there are two versions of the manuscript, Casanova's first version, occasionally referred to by the contributors and included in both French editions has been translated into English by the editor, as it is not included in Trask's translation. When quoted, his unpublished manuscripts are designated by their archival numbers and letters.

NOTES

1 As was the case with Jean Baptiste de Boyer, Marquis d'Argens, an erudite scholar of Greek and Hebrew to whom Casanova paid a visit in Provence, but also a libertine to whom the pornographic novel *Thérèse philosophe* (1748) is attributed. Libertine literature has been the object of many studies: in particular Dominique Hölzle, *Le Roman libertin au XVIIIe siècle* (Oxford: Voltaire Foundation, 2012); Patrick Wald Lasowski, *Le Grand dérèglement. Le roman libertin du XVIIIe siècle* (Paris: Gallimard, 2008); Jean Goldzink, *Le Vice en bas de soie ou le roman du libertinage* (Paris: José Corti, 2001); the issue of *Yale French Studies* on "Libertinage and Modernity," #94 (New Haven, CT: Yale University Press, 1998). Most of these studies, however, focus primarily on fiction.

2 Lydia Flem, *Casanova ou l'exercice du bonheur* (Paris: Seuil, 1995), translated by Katherine Temerson as *Casanova: The Man Who Really Loved Women* (New York: Farrar, Straus and Giroux, 1997). See also Chantal Thomas, *Casanova. Un voyage libertin* (Paris: Denoël, 1985); and Marie-Françoise Luna, *Casanova mémorialiste* (Paris: Champion, 1998).

3 Casanova usually called *History of My Life* his memoirs, as the term
   autobiography did not yet exist. We shall refer to it with both designations, as
   well as in its abbreviated form, *History*.

4 Prosper Jolyot de Crébillon, a well-known author of tragedies, known as
   Crébillon the Elder, was so taken by Casanova's translation of his tragedy in
   Italian verse that the young man recited to him on the spot that he offered
   to tutor him in French.

5 *Dell'Iliade di Omero, tradotta in ottava rima da Giacomo Casanova Viniziano,*
   3 vols. (Venice, 1775–8); in Venetian dialect, ed. Carlo Odo Pavese (Venice:
   Edizioni della Laguna, 2005).

6 This play, *La Moluccheide,* has disappeared, as did *Les Thessaliennes, ou
   Arlequin au Sabbat,* a first play co-written with Le Prévost d'Exmes and
   staged at the Comédie Italienne in Paris. Among those that survived is *Le
   Polémoscope ou la calomnie démasquée par la présence d'esprit,* written in 1791.

7 *Solution du problème déliaque démontré e par J. Casanova de Seingalt ...*
   (Dresden, 1790).

8 *Confutazione della storia del governo veneto d'Amelot de la Houssaie* (Amsterdam,
   1769); *Istoria delle turbolenze della Polonia ...* (Gorizia, 1774); *Di aneddoti
   viniziani militari ed amorosi del secolo decimoquarto ...* (Venice, 1782).

9 *Lana Caprina: Epistola di un licantropo* (Bologna, 1772).

10 *Icosameron, ou Histoire d'Édouard, et d'Élisabeth qui passèrent quatre-vingts-un
   ans chez les Mégamicres habitans aborigènes du Protocosme dans l'intérieur de notre
   globe,* 5 vols. (Prague: Schönfeld, 1787).

11 *Le philosophe et le théologien,* 18 dialogues (State Archives of Prague, Marr.
   1.3); and *Rêve. Dieu. Moi* (State Archives of Prague, fol. 389–488, Marr.
   1.1.d), both published in the 1993 edition of *Histoire de ma vie* (Laffont, ed.
   F. Lacassin), 1:1108–1256, and 1:1278–1334.

12 *A Léonard de Snetlage, docteur en droit de l'Université de Goettinge ...* (1797).

13 Jacques Casanova de Seingalt, *Examen des* Études de la Nature *et de "Paul
   et Virginie" de Bernardin de Saint-Pierre,* ed. Marco Leeflang and Tom Vitelli
   (Utrecht: 1985).

14 Jacques Casanova de Seingalt, *Histoire de ma vie* (Paris: Gallimard, 2014–15),
   and Casanova, *Histoire de ma vie,* vols. 1–2 (Paris: Laffont, 2013–16),
   vol. 1–3.

15 John Masters, *Casanova* (New York: Bernard Geis Associates, 1969); James
   Rives Childs, *Casanova: A Biography Based on New Documents* (London:
   Allen and Unwin, 1961); Derek Parker, *Casanova* (Gloucestershire: Sutton,
   2002); Judith Summers, *Casanova's Women: The Great Seducer and the Women
   He Loved* (London: Bloomsbury Publishing, 2011); Laurence Bergreen,
   Casanova, The World of a Seductive Genius (New York: Simon and Schuster,

2016); and Ian Kelly's *Casanova: Actor Spy Lover Priest* (London: Hodder and Stoughton, 2008).

16 *Casanova, the Seduction of Europe*, ed. F. Ilchman, C.D. Dickerson III, and Th. Michie (Boston: Museum of Fine Art Press, 2018), a beautifully illustrated coffee-table book, includes essays by historians, art historians, and literary scholars. It was published in conjunction with a fine arts exhibition, organized jointly by the Boston Museum of Fine Arts, the Kimbell Art Museum, Fort Worth, Texas, and the Legion of Honor Museum of San Francisco in 2017–18.

17 *Let There Be Enlightenment: The Religious and Mystical Sources of Rationality*, ed. A. Matytsin and D. Edelstein (Baltimore, MD: Johns Hopkins University Press, 2018) provides a useful overview of the recent "revisionist" scholarship on the Enlightenment and its inextricable relationship with religion; Robert Londen, *The World We Want: How and Why the Ideals of the Enlightenment Still Elude Us* (Oxford: Oxford University Press, 2007), argues that "the Enlightenment was fundamentally religious rather than anti-religious" (132).

18 This book is the result of an international conference organized in 2016 by the UCLA Center for Seventeenth- and Eighteenth-Century Studies, and its Departments of French and Francophone Studies, and of Italian.

19 See, among others, Branko Aleksic, ed., *Giacomo Casanova:. Propos littéraires* (Paris: Alain Baudry et Co., 2011); Giorgio Ficara, *Casanova e la malinconia* (Turin: Einaudi, 1999); Cyril Francès, *Casanova, la mémoire du désir* (Paris: Garnier, 2014); *Casanova Enlightenment Philosopher*, ed. Ivo Cerman, Oxford Studies in the Enlightenment (Oxford: Oxford University Press, 2016); Jean-Christophe Igalens, *L'écrivain en ses fictions* (Paris: Garnier, 2011); Bruno Rosada, *Casanova e il suo contrario* (Treviso: Matteo Editore, 2012); Guillaume Simiand, *Casanova dans l'Europe des aventuriers* (Paris: Garnier, 2017); Sophie Rothé, *Casanova en mouvement. Des attraits de la raison aux plaisiairs de la croyance* (Paris: Le manuscrit, 2016).

PART I

LIBERTINE TRACES

"Triompher par la force": Sexual Violence and Its Representation in Casanova's *History of My Life*

RAPHAËLLE BRIN

A small handful of readers and critics excepted, most have sought to portray Casanova as the "tender and joyful lover"[1] celebrated by Apollinaire in one of his later works. The "sexual myth"[2] seems to have been founded in large part on an irenic conception of gender relations and on the gleeful image of a sexuality devoid of dangers or consequences – and, ideally, of violence. Numerous studies have underlined the distinction between Casanova's amorous ethics and those of the libertine, from which the *History of My Life* is to be distanced.

Nevertheless, a small handful of readings question the aforementioned myth: thus, Fellini's quasi-hallucinated vision that reduces Casanova to nothing more than a grotesque alpha male obsessed with his sexual prowess, or Françoise Giroud's reflections that call for a "feminist"[3] reading of the *History of My Life,* condemning the univocal apprehension about Casanova's adventures. If these analyses often lean toward caricature – Fellini himself admits to having forged a "hysterical"[4] reading of the text – they still allow us to pay attention to what seems to be overlooked in the public and critical interpretations of Casanova: the question of sexual violence, and especially its narrative staging and discursive theorization.

Indeed, a more attentive reading of the *History of My Life* is needed to stress the recurring sexual violence – both real and imagined – within the story. Interestingly enough, while most of the episodes studied can be said to belong to the "libertine" stratum of these memoirs, and while they must be repositioned in a historical context that was relatively insensitive to the question of rape, they are unexpectedly written against the grain of a narration that is generally presumed to make erotic cooperation and partners' reciprocity the basis for a lovers' ethos. These episodes' integration into the storyline seems, then, to rely on various discursive strategies to attenuate their violence. With the noted exception of La Charpillon's adventures, the staging of brutality in the *History of My Life* is therefore systematically veiled by the narration, and accounts of rape are wrapped into amusing, good-humoured acts.

Casanova's Love Ethics, or: The Refusal of Violence

Showcasing the violent episodes' dissonant character in the story's general economy entails the study of Casanova's ethics of love, as it is theorized and illustrated in the *History of My Life*. Certainly, the Venetian's own *savoir-vivre* in matters of love seems based on a rejection of violence and on a refusal of the objectification of women as passive creatures surrendered to men's pleasures. Drawing from the difficulty of constructing a feminine *subject* – a difficulty that lies at the heart of the ancien régime discourse on rape, according to Georges Vigarello[5] – and from the social constraints imposed on feminine desire, many dialogues insist on the necessity of erotic emancipation and assert the equality of the sexes through the mutual aspiration to pleasure.

His lover's "submission" to brute force or her passivity in the sexual act are, in Casanova's eyes, a form of prostitution that he fervently rejects. Generally speaking, while Casanova does not ignore other types of brutality (namely, financial domination), he never ceases to stress the necessity of *shared* pleasure. Cruelty, rape, and the suffering of the desired partner accordingly seem incompatible with proper sentimental etiquette. On numerous occasions, the Venetian declines to take an abusive advantage, in this way expressing his horror of sexual violence. Perversity and the suffering of the other bear no value for Casanova: far from being elements that enhance pleasure, as they are for Sade, they deprive the subject of any access to pleasure. Rebuffing the image of the "seducer" along with its aggressive undertones, Casanova prefers to portray himself as the benefactor of his *belles*; the generosity and tenderness of the lover triumph over the brute's instinct for possession. Violence is then criticized not in the name of moral principles, but rather because it infringes on erotic refinement and threatens to drown pleasure in seriousness and tragedy.

Given this context, the only acceptable violence seems to be what arises from codified and consensual erotic cooperation. Masculine violence is but a ploy: it must be read as a "simulacrum"[6] that, when perceived as such by the partner, allows her to consent to her own desire while respecting social conventions. Its use rests on a sharp awareness of roles and situation; the woman is invited to pretend to cede to violence.

Nonetheless, the ill-defined limits of these social and amorous conventions allow the masculine hero any and all "impertinences." Casanova has no trouble taking advantage of what Georges Vigarello has called the "certainty of consent."[7] Indisputably, many of his encounters blur the line between seduction and rape, between the use of force and consent.

A particular scene testifies to Casanova's difficulty in seeing violence as exercised *against* women. It is found at the end of the adventures between him and the second "M.M.," a young nun who has come to Aix to birth her child and with whom Casanova falls instantly in love. Her character is a variation on the "Sleeping Beauty," a recurring theme in libertine and sentimental literature of the eighteenth century. However, as Jean-Christophe Igalens explains in a recent article, while this "feigned sleep" – of which we find many instances in the *History of My Life* – is customarily destined to "conciliate a feminine erotic initiative ... and social conventions which do not recognize its legitimacy," the scene obscures the device's readability, inscribing its "aggressive undercurrent"[8] onto an account that is attentive mainly to the constraints on the subjects' desire.

After a delightful dinner, the second "M.M." undresses and lies down, abandoning herself to Casanova's erotic vigour. The beginning of the story recycles the libertine topos of the "moment":[9] "j'ai compris qu'il ne s'agissait plus de raisonner, et que l'amour exigeait que je saisisse le moment" (2:439) (I understood that it was time to reason no more and that love demanded I should seize the moment [7:6]). Love serves here as a pretext for the satisfaction of one's desires; consent is not evoked, unless a posteriori. The repetition of the verb *to sleep* distinguishes the episode from its previous variations: the kind of sleep it describes is not the "feigned," prelude-to-erotic-playfulness kind, but rather the real kind, subtly transmuting the sexual act into rape.

M.M. dormait: elle ne pouvait pas en faire semblant, elle dormait. Mais quand même elle en aurait fait semblant, pouvais-je lui savoir mauvais gré de cette ruse? Ou vrai, ou feint, le sommeil d'un objet adoré dit à un amant qui raisonne qu'il devient indigne d'en jouir d'abord qu'il doute s'il lui soit permis ou non d'en profiter. S'il est vrai, il ne risque rien; s'il est feint, peut-il lui accorder une satisfaction moins juste, et moins honnête que celle de désavouer son propre consentement? (2:439–40)

M.M. was asleep; she could not be pretending, she was asleep. But even if she had been pretending, could I hold her ruse against her? Be it real or feigned, her sleep tells the intelligent lover of an adored object that he is unworthy to enjoy her the moment he begins to wonder if he may or may not take advantage of it. If it is real, he risks nothing; if it is feigned, can he accord her a more inadequate or more dishonorable return than to doubt of her consent? (7:6)

The convolutions of the passage appear to translate Casanova's difficulty in acknowledging the adverse consequences of pleasure without consent. As Igalens fittingly puts it, the "question of consent only appears once it is presumed obtained."

The absence of risk for the protagonist authorizes all forms of boldness; the text vaguely combines the eighteenth-century fascination with ravishing as an act of abduction and a concern for erotic cooperation between partners, based on a systematic use of "ruses" or stratagems. Shrouding its own potential violence, the episode concludes with an unfailing display of gratitude from the woman, who is henceforth "released from all her anxieties."[10]

"From a Theory of the Moment to the Hypothesis of Rape":[11] The Problem of Consent

In an article on rape in *La Nuit et le moment,* Jean-Christophe Abramovici summarizes the complications of use of the term in contemporary criticism.[12] The same questions retain their pertinence in the case of the *History of My Life.*

Indeed, the text's rape scenes are written at the conjuncture of two discourses: that of public *doxa,* which tends to make commonplace actions that are nonetheless heavily condemned by ancien régime ordinances,[13] and that of libertinage, relayed by a literary corpus from which Casanova borrows both aesthetics and ideology.

On one hand, the eighteenth-century public sphere was relatively tolerant of rape: rare were the trials that resulted in the condemnation of the accused.[14] On the other hand, Casanova, like his contemporaries, was aware of the criminal and judiciary aspects of the act of rape, as well as of the difficulty of demonstrating one's alibi.[15] In the *History of My Life,* he often evokes the "inconvenience" that might arise from an accusation of rape in Venice. He fears the wrath of the courthouse after a collective rape and dreads the disquieting consequences of a charge filed against him by the mother of a young girl whose virginity he had purchased – and whom he had beaten before chasing her away, because she had declined his offers (1:468). The narrator shows no empathy for this "infamous girl, schooled by an even more infamous mother." He limits his pity to bemoaning that the girl had "held on to her dreadful virtue" despite his expense. The social distance and economic domination of the aggressor temper the gravity of the crime: his spending is seen as entailing the right of property. It is equally a fear of justice – British justice, in this case – that leads him to refuse Goudar's offer to sell him a "molesting chair" on which to place la Charpillon:

> L'effet était immanquable, et ce n'est pas l'avarice qui m'empêcha d'acheter la machine, car elle avait dû coûter bien davantage au possesseur; mais l'effroi que j'en eus après une petite réflexion. Ce crime aurait pu me coûter la vie dans la façon de penser des juges anglais. (3:118)

> The action was infallible, and it was not avarice which kept me from buying the contrivance, for it must have cost its owner far more, but the fear which it inspired in me after I reflected a little. The crime could have cost me my life in the view of English judges. (9:295)

Here the use of violence appears to be subjected to an evaluation, generating concern only for the risk taken by the assailant himself, which pushes him toward moderation. As will be shown, it is only later that the protagonist considers the moral and physical costs of the grisly machine to its victim; he rejects a violence whose execution would have antithetically occasioned the withdrawal of pleasure at the very moment of satiation.

Broadly speaking, the *History of My Life* tends to liken any woman ravished to a woman willing. As Georges Vigarello has shown, eighteenth-century discourse is somewhat reluctant to exonerate the victim; she is more often suspected to have voluntarily yielded.[16] The *Encyclopédie* entry for "Viol" (Rape) echoes this point of view. For there to have been rape, the plaintiff had to prove "que la résistance ait été persévérante jusqu'à la fin; car s'il n'y avait eu que de premiers efforts, ce ne serait pas le cas du *viol*, ni de la peine attachée à ce crime"[17] (that there was "a strong and perseverant resistance until the end; had there only been efforts in the beginning, it would not be *rape*, and the prescribed sentence would not apply").

We can find obvious signs of this collective prejudice in the *History of My Life*, for instance in a dialogue between Casanova and the young Mlle de la M – , which follows the narration of Tireta's "impertinence" during Damiens's execution for the failed attempt at Louis XV's life and constitutes its retrospective justification. Tireta, a young and poor Italian who has recently arrived in Paris, is characterized by his sexual vigour and has thus been nicknamed "Count of Six Times" (Comte de Six Coups). During Damiens's execution, he has "strangely taken advantage of his position" to sexually assault Mme XXX, exploiting Casanova's complicity to satisfy his "hearty appetite."

When he answers the young girl's candid questions, Casanova relays a prejudice characteristic of the period, denying the blunt facts of rape:

> Deux choses, me dit-elle, je ne comprends pas. La première, comme [*sic*] Six coups ait pu faire pour commettre avec ma tante un crime, dont je conçois bien la possibilité lorsque la partie attaquée y consent, mais qui doit être impossible si elle n'y consent pas, ce qui me fait juger que puisque le crime fut commis, ma bonne tante doit y avoir consenti. – Certainement, car elle aurait pu changer de posture. – Et même sans cela, car à ce qu'il me semble il ne tenait qu'à elle de lui rendre l'entrée impossible. – En cela, mon ange, vous vous trompez. Un homme comme il faut ne demande que la constance de la position, et il force la barrière assez facilement. Outre cela, je ne crois pas que chez votre tante cette entrée soit comme par exemple elle serait chez vous. (2:43)

> "There are two things," she said, "which I do not understand. The first is how Tireta managed to commit a crime on my aunt which I can see is possible if the party assaulted consents but which must be impossible if she does not – which leads me to conclude that, since the crime was committed, my good aunt must have consented to it."
>
> "Certainly, for she could have changed her position."
>
> "Even without that – for it seems to me she could simply have made it impossible for him to enter."
>
> "In that, my angel, you are mistaken. A well-equipped man asks only for no change of position; granted that, he breaks through the barrier easily enough. Besides, I do not believe that achieving entrance in the case of your aunt is the same as it would be in, let us say, yours." (5:66)

The dialogue, a parody of libertine emancipation, rests upon a supposedly unshakeable logic in which the presumption of the "victim's" passive consent cancels out the "violence variable" and its consequences. Where there is consent, there cannot be crime; however, the crime itself – and here we find an example of classic eighteenth-century circular argumentation – would have been impossible without the consent of the woman in the first place! From there, only a single step is needed to establish passivity in the face of sexual violence as a constitutive artifice of the feminine being, turning it into a ruse to bypass etiquette and satisfy one's pleasure all while maintaining face – and perhaps even avoiding the need for explanations.

While Casanova refutes the anatomical impossibility of rape, and in so doing partially liberates the victim morally, he does not do so to condemn the brutality of the situation or to disapprove of the absence of consent, but rather to glorify the raw phallic power of the "proper man," a power that saturates the entire narrative sequence.[18] The episode therefore suggests a new variation on the question of feminine consent: it considers the female body as naturally disposed to pleasure and treats violence as a necessary ruse to circumvent the weight of social obstacles to open sexuality. Given that during the deed Mme XXX stood still for two hours, Tireta, when confronted by Casanova, explains that he "cannot believe [he's] done anything but make her happy." Exculpating the masculine character, the passage insists on the use of sexual violence as a *pretext*: it can only be "pride" (amour-propre) and an excessive concern with manners that cause women to claim that intercourse is rape or, at the very least, a "lack of respect." Even though the text has for a time been engaged with evaluating the violence enacted against Mme XXX, who was forced to "dissimuler, et souffrir en patience tout ce que le brutal lui avait fait pour ne pas faire rire la Lambertini, et pour ne pas découvrir à sa nièce des mystères qu'elle devait encore ignorer" (2:36) (dissimulate and patiently put up with all that the brute had done to keep La Lambertini from laughing at her and prevent her niece from discovering mysteries of which she should still be ignorant [5:58]), it concludes with the reconciliation of Tireta and Mme XXX. It thus ipso facto suppresses any seriousness and ultimately legitimates the starting hypothesis: that Mme XXX indeed solicited the attention of the "Count of Six Times" to benefit from his extraordinary virility on a daily basis. The entire episode is also based on licentious jokes about anal intercourse. Mme XXX does not complain so much about having been raped as about having endured sodomy, which provokes a series of misunderstandings during her dialogue with Casanova:

Je ne savais que me figurer. Lui aurait-il volé sa bourse? Me disais-je. Après
avoir essuyé ses pleurs, elle poursuivit ainsi:

   – Vous imaginez un crime que par un effort on pourrait encore combiner
avec la raison, et y trouver, j'en conviens, une réparation convenable; mais
ce que le brutal m'a fait est une infamie à laquelle il faut que je m'abstienne
de penser, car elle est faite pour me faire devenir folle." (2:39)

I did not know what to think. "Can he have stolen her purse?" I wondered.
After drying her tears she went on as follows:

   "You imagine a crime which, by an effort, one could reconcile with
reason and hence, I admit, discover some proper reparation for it; but what
the brute did to me is so infamous that I must not even think of it, for it is
of a nature to drive me mad." (5:62)

Mme XXX's euphemisms and her reluctance to clearly name
Tireta's "crime" lead to a pleasant exchange that allows Casanova to
mock her false devotion. When he advises Tireta, acting as a mediator
between him and Mme XXX, the narrator insists heavily on the dubious nature of this sexual intercourse, alluding to a saying by Frederick
II, who was rumoured to have had homosexual experiences: "tâche
de te gagner son amitié non pas tête à nuque mais *de faciem ad faciem*,
comme disait le roi de Prusse" (2:41) (try to gain her friendship – not
front to back but *de faciem ad faciem* [face-to-face], as the King of Prus-
sia said [5:64]). Although, imitating Mme XXX's speech, he pretends
to denounce an "execrable crime," his condemnation is superficial
and mostly ironic. Significantly, the episode ends with Tireta's witty
repartee: "Je n'ai pas su où j'entrais" (2:41) (I didn't know where I
was going in [5:64]), which adds to its comical dimension. Whether
the protagonist is taking advantage of a favourable situation, profiting
from some "welcome happenstance," or seizing a woman by "surprise,"
multiple episodes in the *History of My Life* bring out the libertine topos
of the *moment* and glorify the ability of the masculine subject to com-
mandeer a given circumstance to satisfy his desires. These episodes
evoke the ephemeral character of advantageous conditions and cel-
ebrate the realization of the envisioned act by the hero, thanks to his
"ability" or "courage," with no reflection – except in hindsight – on
consent.

If the account of sexual violence sometimes contributes to the confessional character of the *History of My Life*, the narrator's capacity to
triumph over obstacles is more often a pretext for narcissistic celebration

of his vigour and sexual appetite. Recurring heroic or military meta-phors ("exploits," "prowess"), culturally coded, serve to ratify a triumphalist conception of masculine sexuality, which in turn praises violence as a recourse.

In this respect, the episode of the thunderstorm in Pasiano is exemplary. Situated immediately after the sad narrative of the innocent Lucie's loves, it serves as a makeshift parable, definitively integrating Casanova into the world of grown men. Lucie, "saved" (i.e., spared) by Casanova and abandoned to the violence of her desire, ended up giving herself to an "infamous seducer" who took her away for good. Casanova is eaten up with remorse over the adventure, which is recalled many times in the *History of My Life*. For the narrator, it illustrates the negative effects of a behaviour deemed too virtuous, culminating in sexual frustration with catastrophic consequences. Henceforth, it serves as a defence for the libertine's ethics.

Determined not to cringe from this weakness, Casanova decides to seduce a young bride. She declines his offers, ruining his amorous stratagems. An atypical deus ex machina is then brought in to save the scene: during a voyage in a shared carriage, a violent thunderstorm breaks out, giving the protagonist a perfect occasion to take advantage of the young woman, who is petrified by her fear of thunder. The passage is a variation on the theme of the libertine *moment*, the brevity of which can be read in the galloping rhythm of the narration:

Voulant remettre le manteau sur elle, je me l'approche, et elle tombe positivement sur moi qui rapidement la place à califourchon. Sa position ne pouvant pas être plus heureuse, je ne perds pas de temps, je m'y adapte dans un instant faisant semblant d'arranger dans la ceinture de mes culottes ma montre. Comprenant que si elle ne m'en empêchait pas bien vite, elle ne pouvait plus se défendre, elle fait un effort, mais je lui dis que si elle ne fait pas semblant d'être évanouie, le postillon se tournerait et verrait tout. En disant ces paroles, je laisse qu'elle m'appelle impie tant qu'elle veut, je la serre au croupion, et je remporte la plus complète victoire que jamais habile gladiateur ait remporté. (1:110)

Wanting to put the cloak over her again, I draw her toward me; she literally falls on me, and I quickly put her astride me. Since her position could not be more propitious, I lose no time, I adjust myself to it in an instant by pretending to settle my watch in the belt of my breeches. Realizing that

if she did not stop me at once, she could no longer defend herself, she
makes an effort, but I tell her that if she does not pretend to have fainted,
the postilion will turn and see everything. So saying, I leave her to call me
an impious monster to her heart's content, I clasp her by the buttocks,
and carry off the most complete victory that ever a skillful swordsman won.
(1:153)

The woman appears here to be doubly victimized: first, because she
manifests a personal vulnerability to the thunderstorm that exposes
her to masculine impudence; second, because she is subjected to a
form of the social gaze by the postilion's presence and therefore for-
feits her agency in the face of the protagonist's physical force and
moral blackmail. The remainder of the passage extensively glosses the
likeness between lightning and sexual potency. However, in a departure from classic libertine form, the end of the episode insists on the
necessity of obtaining a posteriori the consent of the desired woman.
Surrendered *in fine* to the laws of pleasure, the young woman will have
to admit, as Mme XXX did, that Casanova "brought her pleasure,"
thus cancelling in the eyes of the reader the potential violence of the
episode.

"Le bon parti d'en rire": Laughter and Sexual Violence in the *History of My Life*

The conclusion of the previous episode seems to illustrate a Casanovian
idiosyncrasy in the narrative treatment of sexual violence: its proximity
to laughter. In fact, every rape scene is systematically transmuted into a
comical or buffoonish scene; mentions of violence are elided, paving the
way for both a *shared laughter* that reconciles the hero with his partners
and/or a *cunning laughter* that unites the masculine protagonist with his
accomplices. These devices and displacements, in allowing one to elude
violence at the very moment of its assertion, must be perceived as an
efficient narrative strategy, favouring the readers' full adherence to the
Casanovian myth.

While moral and religious laws (adultery, blasphemy) have indeed
been shaken, and while violence has indeed taken place, the Pasiano
episode nonetheless ends in "*beaux dialogues*" (charming exchanges) and
a playful atmosphere that entirely neutralizes its scope. In Lucie's case,
Casanova's unwarranted "délicatesse" (tactfulness) has had devastating

consequences. With the bride, carnal pleasure – including the risk of violence – leads to an innocuous outcome: shared laughter.

> – Dites que vous me pardonnez. Convenez que je vous fais plaisir. – Oui. Vous le voyez. Je vous pardonne. Je l'ai alors essuyée; et l'ayant priée d'avoir la même honnêteté avec moi, je lui ai vu la bouche riante.... L'ayant alors remise à sa place, et voyant le beau temps, je l'ai assurée que le postillon ne s'était jamais tourné. En badinant sur l'aventure, et lui baisant les mains, je lui ai dit que j'étais sûr de l'avoir guérie de la peur du tonnerre, mais qu'elle ne révélerait à personne le secret qui avait opéré sa guérison. (1:111)

> "Tell me that you forgive me. Admit that I have given you pleasure."
> "Yes. You can see that for yourself. I forgive you."
> At that I wiped her off, and when I asked her to do as much for me, I saw that she was smiling.... I now put her back in her place and, seeing that the sky had cleared, I assured her that the postilion had never turned around. Joking over our adventure and kissing her hands, I said I was sure I had cured her of her fear of thunder, but that she would never tell anyone the secret of the cure. (1:154)

Once again, the absence of any serious charges lightens the tone and allows it to conclude with the shared laughter of the three characters: Casanova, the young farm-bride, and the postilion, a voyeuristic third-party accomplice who – as it turns out – has enjoyed the spectacle. The very end of the excerpt elaborates on the fantasy of a woman participating *willingly* in an essentially masculine ideology. Far from having rendered his victim "unhappy," Casanova has "cured" her of her fear of thunderstorms.

His relationship to Lucie had forced a cruel dilemma upon Casanova: after twelve days of abstinence, he had to decide between "ending" (finir) or "becoming a villain" (devenir scélérat). Without hesitating, he chose the former. In the case of the thunderstorm, the choice is reversed: better to choose villainy – the word *scélérat* is constantly cited in the episode – than to unduly burden oneself with consent.

The close ties between sexual violence and laughter in the poetics of the *History of My Life* are reaffirmed a few hundred pages later. The young Casanova is part of a small Venetian gang notable for its violence. One evening during the Carnival, they go to have drinks in a certain establishment, where they find "three men peaceably drinking with a reasonably pretty woman." The gang's leader decides to abduct the woman separately from the three men in order to "use her afterward at our good pleasure" (2:187). The woman, presented as the passive object of masculine pleasure, is then yielded to a collective "ravishment" (rapt), explicitly described as such. The passage is characterized by a refusal to take rape seriously, and the "atrocity of the fact," though recognized and named, is once again dissolved in laughter, first among the affair's protagonists, and then with the entire town. The violence in the scene is denied, stylistically speaking, by the use of euphemism, circumlocution, and implicitness, which solicit the complicity of the reader and deny the rawness of the situation. Gallant metaphors cast against type prove to be the pretext for an equivocal game with the reader; their stylistic distancing only contributes to the adventure's comedy:

> Après l'avoir encouragée par des paroles et des verres de vin, il lui arriva ce à quoi elle devait s'attendre. Notre chef, comme de raison, fut le premier à lui rendre ses devoirs amoureux après avoir vaincu avec beaucoup de politesse toute la répugnance qu'elle avait à lui être complaisante en présence de toute la bande. Elle prit le bon parti d'en rire et de se laisser faire.
>
> Mais je l'ai vu surprise, lorsque je me suis présenté pour être le second: elle crut de devoir me marquer de la reconnaissance; et lorsqu'elle vit après moi le troisième elle ne douta plus de son heureuse destinée qui lui promettait tous les membres de la société. Elle ne se trompa pas. Mon frère fut le seul qui fit semblant d'être malade. Il n'avait point d'autre parti à prendre, car la loi qui existait entre nous était irrévocable en ceci que chacun devait faire ce qu'un autre faisait. Après ce bel exploit, nous nous remasquâmes, nous payâmes l'hôte, et nous conduisîmes cette heureuse femme à Saint-Job, où elle demeurait ... Nous dûmes rire tous de ce qu'elle nous remercia de la plus vraie, de la meilleure foi du monde. (1:401)

After we had encouraged her with words and glasses of wine there befell her what she could not but be expecting. Our leader, as was only right, was the first to pay her his amorous duty, after most politely overcoming her reluctance to yield to him in the presence of us all. She chose the sensible course of laughing and letting him do as he pleased.

But I saw that she was surprised when I came forward to be the second; she thought herself obligated to show her gratitude; and when, after my turn, she saw the third, she no longer doubted of her happy fate, which promised her all the members of the band. She was not mistaken. My brother was the only one who pretended to be ill. He had no other choice, for the law among us irrevocably demanded that each of us do what another did.

After this fine exploit, we resumed our masks, paid the innkeeper, and took the happy woman to San Giobbe, where she lived…. None of us could keep from laughing when she thanked us most sincerely and in the most perfect good faith. (2:189)

The legitimation of rape leans here on a dual image of the desirous woman and the prodigal man, complacently theorized throughout the *History of My Life*. Significantly, only François, the younger brother, shies away: in fact, the narrator repeatedly mentions François's sexual impotence and his incapacity to make women happy throughout his memoirs. The protagonist's laughter echoes the woman's gleeful thankfulness; both then join in the hilarity of the entire town when everyone learns she has claimed to have been subjected "to no ill treatment," which prevents a tragic reading of the episode.

A similar evacuation of the serious consequences of sexual violence occurs in Tireta's episode. The narrative progression rests on a double elision of violence. The political violence of the public torture is first avoided by evoking a libertine scene that Casanova deems "pleasant"; the sexual violence is then reabsorbed in collective laughter and a jest about the nature of the crime, which is not rape, but sodomy. Once again – need we state it? – the narrative device entirely obscures the initial violence by shifting its stakes.

Furthermore, whereas Sade expounds upon and exploits the rapport between torture and erotic pleasure, Casanova does not describe Damiens's torture because he positions himself so as not to see anything. Instead, he substitutes a frivolous scene in which the "ruffling sounds of the dress" amusingly suppress Damiens's screams. While he later insists on Tireta's "brutality" – perhaps suggesting a blind spot about his own activity – the sexual violence in question is more than anything subject to "laughter" and is once more a pretext for joking (badinage). The pleasant conversation between Casanova and Mme XXX suggests a justification for the ravishment that relies on a series of arguments excusing, and even exonerating, the culprit.

Violence and Madness: The Case of La Charpillon

Casanova's adventures with La Charpillon are an exception in his career as a libertine, and in the narrative progression: told in the tonality of *rupture*, the episode is a critical experience. It should be read as a flipside to the *History of My Life*, a rare moment when violence threatens to give the story a tragic colour. The temptation of rape is presented as a symptom of the madness that starts to take hold of the narrator: the use of violence brought about a great disjunction and appeared to him as the moment when he "ceased to live" (9:272).

Enamoured with the young lady – who leads him on with her wiles – he tries in vain to obtain her favours. As he does so, La Charpillon dismantles one of Casanova's most firmly entrenched certitudes, one that presides over all his amorous encounters: the certainty that seduction will never fail. This certainty renders any use of force unnecessary, since the partner always eventually consents to pleasure and love. As a result, an absolute refusal from a beloved woman may be the true blind spot of his memoirs. Indeed, this refusal condemns the narrator to fierce madness. This madness, whose template is that of Malipiero's fury against the young Thérèse at the beginning of the *History of My Life*, rests on the image of the destructive female, a genuine "monster" whose victims are inevitably men.

The London episode with La Charpillon differs from other encounters in its treatment of recurring Casanovian images, namely, those of laughter and violence. For a change, from the start of the episode, laughter is the exclusive privilege of the female character. Far from eluding violence, here it constitutes its corollary, a symptom of the war of the sexes. The playful laugh has been converted to a cruel one, tied to a sadistic pleasure totally out of place in Casanova's ethical logic. Isolated in London, Casanova had put up a sign on his house to recruit a young partner. From the start, La Charpillon reminds him of this event:

> J'avais besoin de rire, et envie de punir l'audacieux auteur d'un écriteau de cette espèce. – Comment m'auriez-vous puni? Vous rendant amoureux de moi, et vous faisant après souffrir des peines infernales par mes traitements. Ah, que j'aurais ri! (3:99)

> "I felt the need to laugh and to punish the audacious author of such a notice." – "How would you have punished me?" – "By making you fall in love

with me and then treating you so that you suffered the pains of hell. Oh, how I should have laughed!" (9:272)

Disregarding the warning, Casanova attributes La Charpillon's first reluctance to the customary "resistance" that dictates that a woman should not yield too easily to advances; he even deems it "not at all unpromising" (9:278). However, the initial readability of her behaviour is quickly lost: multiplying contradictory signals, the young woman troubles the habitual logic of his seductions and unsettles his belief about the consensual use of violence. Annoyed by her reiterated refusal, Casanova abandons himself – in vain – to the most ferocious callousness:

> L'amour dans une situation pareille devient facilement rage. Je m'empare d'elle comme si c'eût été un ballot, mais je ne peux venir à bout de rien; il me semble que sa maudite chemise est la cause, et je réussis à la lui déchirer au dos, depuis le haut jusqu'au bas des reins, pour lors mes mains étant devenues griffes je compte sur la plus brutale violence de ma part; mais tous mes efforts furent vains. Je me suis déterminé à finir quand je me suis trouvé destitué de force, et quand l'ayant saisie d'une de mes mains au cou, je me suis senti puissamment tenté de l'étrangler (III, 115).

> In such a situation love easily becomes rage. I lay hold of her as if she were a bolt of goods, but I can accomplish nothing; it seems to me that her accursed shift is the reason for it, and I succeed in tearing it open behind, from the top to her buttocks; thereupon, my hands becoming claws, I count on the most brutal violence on my part, but all my efforts were vain. I made up my mind to stop when I found my strength exhausted and when having grasped her neck in one hand, I felt a strong temptation to strangle her. (9, 291)

This scene of useless violence is repeated several times. In light of its failure to procure the object of Casanova's desire, Goudar offers to sell him a "molesting chair":[19]

> Ce fauteuil que vous voyez a cinq ressorts qui sautent tous les cinq en même temps d'abord qu'une personne s'y assied. Leur jeu est très rapide. Deux saisissent les deux bras de la personne et les tiennent étroitement serrés: deux autres plus bas s'emparent de ses genoux les écartant on ne saurait

davantage, et le cinquième élève le derrière du siège de façon qu'il force la
personne assise au croupion. (3:118)

The chair you see here has five springs, all of which operate at the same
time as soon as a person sits down in it. Their action is very rapid. Two
seize the person's two arms and hold them fast; two more, lower down, take
hold of her legs, spreading them as far apart as possible, and the fifth raises
the back of the seat in such a way that it forces the seated person onto her
coccyx. (9:294)

The incongruous apparition of the molesting chair – an *explicit* sign of
sexual violence – is soon made to disappear; in Casanova's universe, brutality, albeit present, is of an entirely different order. Its use would have,
as mentioned before, antithetically occasioned the withdrawal of pleasure at the very moment of satiation. The fear of British law is doubled
by a refusal to fully abandon oneself to the use of force: "je n'aurais pas
pu me déterminer de sang-froid à m'emparer de la Charpillon par force,
et encore moins par le jeu de cette redoutable machine qui l'aurait faite
mourir de peur" (3:118) (I could not have brought myself deliberately
to obtain possession of La Charpillon by force, still less by the action
of this formidable contrivance, which would have made her die of fear
[9:294]). But the temptation of violence has made the subject falter: it
eventually makes Casanova contemplate suicide.

Nevertheless, at the episode's end, a "mischievous" deed marks in
extremis the symbolic outcome of the crisis, and a return to the original
aesthetic and ideological paradigm that denies violence and triumphs
through laughter. Casanova, following a joint taste for tomfoolery and
a desire for revenge, buys a parrot at the market and teaches him to
repeat, "*Miss Charpillon est plus putain que sa mère*" (3:154) (Miss Charpillon is more of a whore than her mother [9:341]). The story spreads
through the town in no time. Far from being humiliated by this ven-
geance, La Charpillon "la trouvait fort jolie, et en riait toute la journée"
(3:155) (thought it very amusing and laughed at it all day [9:342]).

The *History of My Life* is not a univocal text. While Casanova holds dear-
est the defence of an idyllic, consequence-free vision of sexuality, a vision
that conforms to the poetics defined in his preface and encourages the
reader to laugh alongside the author at his "mischief" (fredaines), the
narrative does not entirely ignore the question of sexual violence. If
there is one Casanova advocating laughter, games, and playful hedo-
nism, there is another who bears the memory of La Charpillon, pushed

from a state of violence to one of fury, horrified by the temptation of rape. Of course, there is also a libertine Casanova who does not hesitate to use force to satisfy his desires and who triumphs over obstacles aided by the imperative of "the moment."

If the rejection of consequences, essential to his ethics of love, rests on the certainty of consent and on the more or less sophistic justification of the hero's insolence, nothing obliges the reader to side with the narrator's point of view. It is important to consider the diversion of rape scenes into pleasant follies as an ambiguous device that is nevertheless essential to the reader's pleasure. The narrative complicity in sexual violence and the equivocal toying with the limits of the speakable, which are associated with Casanova as well as with most of the libertine novelists of the eighteenth century, are wiped out by Sade and his constant apology for violence,[20] thereafter making any "pleasant" form of reading impossible.

NOTES

1 Guillaume Apollinaire, *Casanova, comédie parodique* (Paris: Gallimard, 1952), act 1, scene 5, p. 26.

2 Chantal Thomas, *Casanova, un voyage libertin* (Paris: Denoël, 1985), 17.

3 Françoise Giroud answering Philippe Sollers, *Le Nouvel Observateur*, 5 November 1998.

4 Federico Fellini, "Ce Casanova que je hais…," *L'Express*, international ed., no. 1258, 18–24 August 1975, 9.

5 Georges Vigarello, *Histoire du viol* (Paris: Seuil, 1998), 49.

6 The term is used by Pierre Hartmann in his study on rape in Crébillon's work: P. Hartmann, "Le motif du viol dans la littérature romanesque du XVIIIe siècle," *Travaux de littérature* 7 (1994): 224–30.

7 Vigarello, *Histoire du viol*, 55.

8 For a detailed analysis of this topos and its ambiguities, see Jean-Christophe Igalens, "Fausses endormies: Challe, Godard d'Aucour, Crébillon, Casanova," in *L'Atelier des idées: Pour Michel Delon*, ed. Jacques Berchtold and Pierre Frantz, 363–78 (Paris: PUPS, 2017).

9 On this topic, see Thomas M. Kavanagh, *Enlightened Pleasures: Eighteenth-Century France and the New Epicureanism* (New Haven, CT: Yale University Press, 2010).

10 "Nous nous aimions, et nous avons couronné notre amour. Je me trouve à la fin délivrée de toutes mes inquiétudes. Nous avons suivi notre

destinée, obéissant aux préceptes de l'impérieuse nature" (2:440). (We love each other, and we have crowned our love. I am freed at last from all my anxieties. We have followed our destiny, obeying the commands of imperious nature [7:7]).

11   I borrow this title from Christophe Martin's article about rape in eighteenth-century libertine and sentimental novels: "De la théorie du moment à l'hypothèse du viol: romanciers et romancières face à un topos romanesque jusqu'à *La Nouvelle Héloïse*," in *Féminités et masculinités dans le texte narratif avant 1800. La question du "gender,"* ed. S. Van Dijk and M. Van Strien-Chardonneau, 307–17 (Louvain: Peeters, 2002).

12   J.-C. Abramovici, "Anatomie d'un récit de viol: *La Nuit et le moment* de Crébillon," in *Violences du rococo*, ed. Jacques Berchtold, René Démoris, and Christophe Martin, 285–97 (Bordeaux: Presses Universitaires de Bordeaux, 2012).

13   See Vigarello, *Histoire du viol*, 13.

14   See Vigarello, *Histoire du viol*, 9.

15   Vigarello has demonstrated how discourse contemporary to Casanova was heavily concerned with the question of proof. *Histoire du viol*, 50–6.

16   Vigarello, *Histoire du viol*, 8.

17   Denis Diderot and Jean Le Rond d'Alembert, eds., *Encyclopédie ou dictionnaire raisonné des sciences, des arts et des métiers*, s.v. "Viol." My translation.

18   The whole episode is characterized by the omnipresence of the virile organ and its symbolic manifestations.

19   This notorious machine is present in many contemporary works – for instance, in Sade's work, in Rétif de la Bretonne's *Anti-Justine*, and in Louvet's *Les Aventures du chevalier de Faublas*.

20   See Hartmann, "Le motif du viol," 243.

Chapter Two

The Writer of Dux: Casanova's Dialogue with His Ladies from Autobiography to Correspondence

BRUNO CAPACI

Pour satisfaire une de vos demandes, je vous dirai que j'aime mieux être convaincue que persuadée parce que le premier est le fruit du raisonnement; la raison convainc; le cœur et l'esprit persuadent et trompent…. Je suis contente de votre gaieté au jour de Sainte-Cécile, le cochon au lait que vous avez mangé me rassure sur votre santé, j'en félicite votre estomac, le mien n'en aurait pas souffert autant.

To satisfy one of your demands, I will tell you that I prefer being convinced to being persuaded, because the former is the result of reasoning; reason convinces; the heart and the mind persuade and deceive…. I am delighted about your happiness on Saint-Cecily day, the suckling pig you ate reassures me about your health, I congratulate your stomach, mine would not have agreed with it.
– Cécile de Roggendorff to Casanova, 10 December 1797[1]

While credit for the publication of the complete and definitive text of the *History of My Life* is undeniably owed to the new French editions by Laffont[2] and Gallimard, Casanova's epistolary exchanges with women were first published in Italy in 1912 and immediately received important critical recognition.[3]

A reading of these letters, transcribed by Marc Leeflang from the autograph materials held in the state archives in Prague, provides for interesting marginal notes on the legend of Giacomo Casanova. One could begin with the premise that distinguishes between the narrated women of Casanova's *Histoire* and the living figures found within the correspondence; between the women to whom Casanova grants narrative space and those who make space for themselves, writing first-hand accounts and staying by his side until his death in his refuge at Dux.

These young women write without the aid of a secretary and therefore are free of excessive literary mediation. Their spelling is often imperfect, both in French and in Italian; precisely for this reason, their point of view is all the more interesting, as it sheds light on real aspects of life in the eighteenth century, and in particular their lives with Casanova. Objects of everyday life emerge as if from an archeological dig: through the unpolished but significant testimonies of experience, these letters bring to life a world that exists in the real, dynamic relationship between this group of young women, their world, and a man who, more than anyone, is the living embodiment of the *esprit des lumières* transcribed into an uncommon existence.

We begin with Manon Balletti's letters. A mermaid with a guitar and pen,[4] more singer than actress, Manon was the youngest of a family of actors boasting the title of *officiers du roi*.[5] For this reason, she enjoyed advantages and allowances, but above all she shared the court theatre with Madame de Pompadour and other notable ladies of the period.

Maria Maddalena Balletti, otherwise known as Nena or Manon, was the only woman for whom Casanova bent over backwards, even to the point of a marriage proposal. This very beautiful and completely unaccommodating woman – despite her education as a *jeune fille de qualité* (a young noblewoman) by the Ursuline nuns of Saint Denis – addressed no fewer than forty-one letters to Casanova, which are the subject of my discussion concerning her point of view.

Maria Maddalena Balletti lived a relatively short life – she was born in 1740 and died prematurely in 1776. She was immortalized, however, when Jean-Marc Nattier painted her portrait with a rose, perhaps alluding to her thorny nature. She married the architect Blondel in 1760 and gave birth to two sons, of whom only Jean Battiste survived. Following in his father's footsteps, he became the royal architect. Manon's eyes, "bien fendus, brillants et langoureux,"[6] captured Giacomo Casanova in 1757 when, having escaped from Venice, he took up residence in Rue du Petit Lyon-Saint Sauveur, in the house of the Italian Comedians. Between this young talented woman able to act, sing, and play the harpsichord and guitar and the escapee arose an intense but ill-fated relationship, whose victim – beyond the protagonists themselves – was Manon's harpsichord master and former fiancé, Charles-François Clément, well known for his harpsichord and violin concertos and for his *Essai sur la composition et sur l'accompagnement du clavecin.*

Manon was short-tempered but of firm character and perfectly able to act in her own comedy, and Giacomo Casanova was anything but a cowering escapee, as his portrait was characterized by "good looks and an intelligent and energetic face."[7] These two dissimilar but converging personalities joined together with the resolute determination to square off against one another through their letters and elsewhere. Casanova, after having narrated the story of his incredible escape from the Leads to Cardinal De Bernis, moved on to a series of occupations: secret agent at the Dunkerque naval base, owner of a manufacturing plant, financial emissary to the king of France in Holland – and also an honoured guest in Holland's jails, the lover of Giustiniana Wynne, and a private cabalist for the Marquise d'Urfé. Casanova especially loved being a dinner guest of the Balletti family and passing time in the salon, where the walls were hung with Nattier's portraits of Silvia Benozzi Balletti and her daughter Manon. Casanova met Manon at the apex of his romantic life, and to her he represented the fascinating protagonist of an international intrigue.

According to Charles Samaran, there was an insurmountable distance in the sincerity of the two interlocutors. On the one hand, "a man who carried the story of his escape as an aura around him" and who at the age of thirty-two "had lived several lives"[8] was gambling with the beating heart of a bird; on the other hand, a poor girl listened with admiration to the sweet talker (*le beau parleur*) and was always ready to make a fuss at the slightest delay or epistolary misunderstanding, in order to reiterate her own love constantly and vehemently. Manon Balletti was indeed a child of the stage, and therefore had that free, vivacious, and witty conversation for which comedians are prized and that always amuses. Other commentators see in her writing an example of a natural style, lacking any sort of seductive strategy. In my opinion, this is not exactly the case. Manon wrote her letters in French, with no lack of spelling mistakes, peppering them pleasantly with amusing and ironic quips in Venetian dialect; these letters are not at all the expression of a naive heart, of a pure and transparent character. In these letters, Manon is not the tearful victim of a sly philanderer; she writes in a self-confident tone, she remarks with elegance, she responds in kind to Casanova's jabs and often recounts his epistolary excesses in order to disparage them. In this way we come to understand just how tormented Giacomo was by his insecurities at the beginning of this engagement. A seducer successfully plays offence, but he defends with greater uncertainty what he already possesses, not because of his ability, but because of his affection for the loved one, by whom he is loved in return.

These are the letters of a fiancée, a woman ready to live the rest of her life with Casanova; not only does she want to bind her lover to

herself, but she also tries to establish with him a dialogue nearly marital in its sincerity, quite different from the predictable *badinage* and
instead disposed to an open and mutual revelation of the self. Seduction becomes reciprocal persuasion and brings forth new and unexpected means by which to describe their everyday view of themselves.
These private details and moments of personal openness betoken the
future intimacy of a husband and wife much more than the piquant
temptations of a lover who is simultaneously ingenuous and aware.
Manon postpones the pleasure of erotic revelation with true reticence
and aposiopesis, stated according to the syntax of hypothesis, to hint
at the intimacy that will become real once they are married: "puisque
vous me faites vou dire des choses beaucoup plus tendre que je ne
vous les dirois si j'etois près de vous; ce n'est pas peut être que je ne les
pense bien, mais enfin je ne croirois pas pouvoir vous les dire, mais je
ne puis vous empêcher de les penser" (since you make me say things
that are more tender than what I would say were I next to you; it is not
that I don't think them, really, but I would not dare say them to you, yet
I cannot prevent you from thinking thus).[9] In other cases, the display
of confidence is even more explicit in its reference to an ailment that
immediately unites the fiancés in their profession of a more candid
sincerity, without secrecy or reticence. The model of the English letter appears dominant in the exhibition of details of an almost Galenic
confidence:[10] "Je suis tout a fait laide, mon cher ami, mon échoboulure
est augmentée et je suis toutte rouge, aussi je ne vis pas. Mon sang
s'échauffe et je crains bien de devenir plus sérieusement malade" (I am
quite plain, my dear friend, my rash has increased and I am completely
red, thus I am hardly living. My blood is heating up and I am afraid that
I will get more seriously ill).[11]

This young lady, trained in the art of *marivaudage* in the theatre, where
her own mother was the star performer from 1720 onward, changes the
tone of her epistolary play, knowing that she is addressing someone who
is both refined and irascible, equally inclined to appreciate psychological details and to abuse her with expressions of rage and disgust. After
all, Manon is trying to construct a husband, to educate him in the ways
and means of a relationship – one that will not be passionate and inconstant, but rather reliable and characterized by *tendresse*, which, along with
humeur (constant irritation) is the key word of this epistolary exchange.
Here it is relevant to refer to Marivaux's *Le Jeu de l'amour et du hasard* to
evoke one of the heroine's (and the actress Silvia's) notions about the
nature of a husband versus that of the *aimable homme* (gallant gentleman):

Dans le mariage on a plus souvent affaire à l'homme raisonnable qu'à l'aimable homme; en un mot je ne lui demande que un bon caractère et cela est plus difficile à trouver qu'on ne pense. On loue beaucoup le sien mais qui est ce qui a vécu avec lui?

In a marriage, it's the *reasonable* part of a man which one deals with most of the time – much more than the attractive part. I require of a man only that he have a good nature, and that is more difficult to find than you might think. His character is praised, but who has lived with him?[12]

Perhaps a definition of *humeur* would allow us to reach the heart of the epistolary code. Crébillon states that in a woman, "une nuance d'humeur peut donc seule jeter sur une belle figure la variété necessaire pour prevenir l'ennui de la voir toujours dans la même situation: malheur à la femme trop égale" (a single nuance of moodiness can imprint on a beautiful figure the variety necessary to prevent the boredom of seeing her always in the same situation: woe to the woman who is overly even tempered).[13] Manon's style tends toward the denial of *coquetterie* as well as of the manners of a *petite maîtresse*. She prefers to situate herself within the dialectic between *humeur* as epistolary resource and *humeur* as an element of her nature, which at times renders her writing more uneven than is necessary for her rhetorical-erotic strategy. The *lettre badine*, which Voiture views as a means to circumvent weighty seriousness, falls within the standards of a phlegmatic correspondence, at times melancholic and inconstant in representing the self.

Certainly Manon has a flavour of unevenness, perhaps more than just a nuance, without assuming a morose or irascible character. Perhaps her youthful and thorny nature causes her to be less inclined than other female letter writers to please her epistolary interlocutor. It is not easy, however, to play the game of *humeur* with Casanova, since his writing is often prickly: if not angry, it is certainly prone to getting all worked up over a mere trifle. There are moments in which the epistolary duel requires a display of both force and self-sacrifice, the show of a difficult personality along with professions of devotion. Manon writes:

et qu'est-ce qui vous peut faire croire que je suis prête à changer? Mon humeur ditte [*sic*] vous? Oui, j'en conviens, j'en ai et beaucoup même mais elle ne prouve rien de ce coté là, je vous aime tout de même dans ce moment de ces humeurs et je souffre davantage du chagrin que je vous cause que de celui que je me forme.

and what makes you believe that I am ready to change? My temper, say you?
Yes, I admit, I have one, and a strong one, but this fact proves nothing, I still
love you in those moments of moodiness, and I suffer more from the pain I
inflict on you than from that I create in myself.[14]

Occasionally the epistolary contest presents notes on everyday life;
they sound, however, like a wife's ironic reproaches to her husband: "je
suis fachée de votre mal estomac mai ne fumée donc [sic] pas tant vous
etes bien heureux de pouvoir vous guerir avec des huitres" (I am sorry
about your stomach pain, but do not smoke that much you are quite
lucky to be able to cure it with oysters).[15]

The correspondence is heavily influenced by matrimonial rhetoric, to
enable the oxymoronic coexistence of a bride's self-esteem and her aim
of future devotion. The fiancée cannot allow what the bride will grant. It
is less a matter of sexual favours than of a progressive loss of her freedom,
expressed as a sacrifice of the most unpredictable and inconstant traits
of her character. Just like Giacinta in Goldoni's *Villeggiatura*,[16] Manon
lives her engagement as a sort of test of her and her future husband's
psychological strength. When she finally ends it, she leads us to believe
that she has decided not to sacrifice her liberty to an inconstant and
quarrelsome "Giacometto," who is always attracted by countless other
bagatelles.

What is Casanova's idea of marriage? We could begin with his patri-
otic interpretation of the marriage bond, which praises the foresight of
Venetian husbands. These statements can be found in *Confutazione della
storia del governo veneto di Hamelot della Houssaie*, a text undoubtedly written after the correspondence between the two fiancés.

In this book, Casanova defends the laws, government, and traditions
of Venice; he proclaims the liberality of Venetian husbands and their
farsightedness in establishing a bond of fundamental respect with their
wives:

Io so che il veneziano ha mille riguardi per la propria moglie e che
vuole che sia rispettata come prima persona dopo di lui, che amico della
medesima per bontà di cuore compatisce i suoi capricci e soccombe anche
spesso ai di lei disordini con la borsa, lasciandole godere una onesta libertà
e non potendo soffrire che ella sia gelosa di lui si guarda bene di esserlo di
essa … che vi siano a Venezia uomini curiosi che quantunque ammogliati
si tengano concubina è verissimo, ma non è vero che questa massima sia
in vigore: che il matrimonio sia una cerimonia puramente civile che leghi

l'opinione e non la coscienza. Io non ho mai saputo che questa eteroclita sentenza regni a Venezia.[17]

I know that the Venetian has a thousand regards for his wife and that he wants her to be respected as the first person after him; that out of the kindness of his heart he gives in to her whims, and often to her troubles with the purse, leaving her to enjoy an honest liberty; as he cannot bear her to be jealous, he is careful not to be so.... it is true that in Venice there are some peculiar men who, even though they are married, have their concubines, but it is not true that this maxim is in force: that the marriage is a purely civil ceremony that binds only one's opinion and not one's conscience. I have never seen this disparate decree reign in Venice.

In the *History of My Life*, Casanova curiously overturns this perspective, attributing matrimonial nonchalance to the French of both sexes:

Il semble qu'elles sachent que leurs maris ne sont pas faits pour être leurs amoureux. Le même esprit, à Paris principalement, règne dans les hommes aussi. Les Français sont jaloux de leurs maîtresses, jamais de leurs femmes. (1:47)

[Most girls who are well brought up] seem to know that their husbands are one thing and their lovers another. Men commonly take the same attitude, especially in Paris. Frenchmen are jealous of their mistresses, never of their wives. (5:72)

What sort of husband would Casanova have been? Manon speaks of a man who is at the same time possessive and distant, angry and gentle, at times even jealous. This man, who had a veritable catalogue of conquests at his feet and was the survivor of the most recounted escape of the century, found himself ill at ease with a seventeen-year-old girl. Casanova scholars' critical outlook has always remained faithful to his narrative by celebrating Henriette as the sole woman among its protagonists who was able to keep Casanova in check, at least according to her lasting impression. Perhaps Manon's impression has not yet been completely understood; her forty-one letters narrate a far more romantic liaison than any other, and certainly a more authentic one. It is interesting to observe that Henriette's letters were burned, while those written by Manon were preserved, confirming the unresolved nature of an affair that could not be put to rest with the autobiographical catharsis.

Despite all the efforts to see Casanova as a "man who loved women,"[18] he tended to dominate their impulses through carefully controlled words and measured attentions. Casanova is commonly considered to have been a well-oiled machine, not only of pleasurable sex, but also of intellectual conquest. He varied his key lines of attack on the feminine heart according to its most intimate contradictions, without ever passing judgment; in spite of this, his fiancée, much more than any other woman, wiped clean the slate of his pride, obliging him to confess his defeat in the *History of My Life*. Cases of abandoned Don Giovannis are not common, especially not with the dramatization proposed by Casanova. Manon already belonged to him, but not enough to keep him from losing her. Manon's decision to marry Blondel in 1760 put an end to their neurotic correspondence and astounded Casanova, who could not have imagined this resolution, however much he feared it:

Je me suis mis à écrire à l'infidèle, déchirant toujours ma lettre après l'avoir écrite. A dix heures j'ai mangé une soupe, puis je me suis mis au lit; mais je n'ai jamais pu dormir. Cent projets formés, et rejetés. J'ai décidé d'aller à Paris pour tuer ce Blondel que je ne connaissais pas, et qui avait osé épouser une fille qui m'appartenait, et qu'on croyait ma femme. (2:229)

I began writing to the faithless girl, each time tearing up my letter as soon as I had finished it. At ten o'clock I took a bowl of soup, then I went back to bed; but I could not sleep. Countless plans, no sooner formed than rejected. I decided to go to Paris and kill this Blondel whom I didn't know and who had dared to marry a girl who belonged to me, and whom everyone believed to be my wife. (6:31)

The ritual of abandonment would have assumed melodramatic tones for Casanova had the narrative situation not contradicted the flaunted excess of tragedy, as the whole scene was animated by the presence of the beautiful Esther. A comparison between the text of the *History of My Life* and Manon's letters allows us to highlight any literary omissions or tampering with the details of this liaison, as well as the difference between her truth and Casanova's.

Philippe Lejeune has shown that autobiographical narrative compels us to accept the sincerity of the author's intentions, or more precisely the profession of sincerity, rather than its expository accuracy.[19] Casanova cannot legitimately state that Manon's decision was completely unexpected, as her correspondence contained clear signs of a discontent that was not merely melancholic. Thus we may note that her farewell letter is not one of the forty-one epistles found in Dux. There are other letters with thorny subject matter, but never to the point of ending the liaison. Perhaps the letter existed but was destroyed by Casanova, or perhaps the farewell was so difficult, so cruel in its finality, that it caused Casanova to revise the event in his memoirs, recasting himself as the victim of this capricious young woman. What is certain is that Casanova, in his *History*, downplays the *attachement* he felt for "Silvia's daughter" (note the periphrasis), stating that it was "d'une espèce qui ne me empêchait de devenir amoureux d'une autre" (1:133) (was of a kind which did not prevent me from falling in love with another woman [5:177]). Therefore he maintained a certain mental reservation toward the liaison, or rather refused to acknowledge its importance. Casanova writes of the need for "nourishment" (*nourriture*), without which a libertine cannot live;[20] in this way, he justifies his inconstancy with a moderate affection for his "little wife" (*petite femme*), who was not content to be the object of too temperate a passion. Manon perceived a gap not only in the strength of their affections, but also in their epistolary exchange, and she threatened breakups she was not yet able to carry out, although it seems clear in hindsight that these were preludes to the final letter that Casanova would record so theatrically. In July 1758, Manon writes to Giacomo, now called rather indifferently "Mr.," to affirm that her heart "is so full that it can take no more" (si plain qu'il n'en peut plus), to which she adds with a greater determination:

> Je vous demande Mr pour votre dernière preuve d'amitié que vous me rendiés mes lettres qui doivent avoir très peu de prix pour vous, et qui sont pour moi de la dernière importance. A quoi vous seroit elle bonne si non qu'à vous reprocher un peu de dureté, et à vous faire voir combien peu je la méritte; vous aurés donc la bonté de me les rendre. Il vous sera plus facile alors d'oublier tottalement la pauvre et foible creature qui les a écrittes.[21]

> I ask you, Sir, as a last proof of your friendship that you return my letters which probably are of little value to you and which are of crucial importance to me. What would be its [*sic*] use to you other than to act as a reproach of your harshness and to remind you how little I deserve it; you will be so kind to return them to me. This will make it easier to entirely forget the poor weak creature who wrote them.

The *petite femme* could not be drawn into the emotional vortices of their correspondence without presenting some amount of resistance, due not only to her fierce character, but also to her self-awareness and her social role, which was far from marginal. Manon was less an actress than a young lady performing at the court for the sovereign's celebrations. Silvia had raised her in a very special way, providing her with a complex education suitable to the court where she acted. The young Balletti had a sort of godmother and protector: the Marquise of Monconseil watched over her movements in society and guaranteed her status, choosing – for example – the convent of Belchase, where Manon was sent to await her marriage after her mother's death on 17 April 1758. From then on, Manon became more and more intolerant of the long absences and verbal intemperances of her fiancé. Now destiny had to take its course, and the marriage would take place after quite a lengthy reclusion:

> Je pourrois ètre seure au moins, qu'a pâque; (voyés comme je suis raisonable) je puisse en sortir (de ce bienheureux couvent) pour ètre a vous et que cet union fut la satisfaction de mes chers parans: ha! je serai la plus aise, la plus gaye, la plus heureuse de toutes les créature; je ne m'ennuierai pour ainsi dire point dans mon attente, parce que tout le jour je pensserois que je vous serois bientôt unie, que je retournerois dans peu dans le sein d'une famille jointe avec un mari que j'aimerois a la folie.[22]

> I could at least be certain that at Easter (see how reasonable I am) I will get out (of this blessed convent) in order to be yours and that this union would be the satisfaction of my dear parents: ha! I would be the most pleased, the most joyful, the happiest of all the creatures; I would hardly be bored while waiting for it, as I would think all day long that I will soon be united with you and that I would return in the bosom of a family joined with a husband that I would madly love.

Manon, or Mlle, as Casanova calls her, could not be clearer in the aftermath of her mother's death. The *femme de spectacles* dreams of a family and even accepts the convent, although she will have to pass through a "most narrow gate" (*forte étroite grille*) to meet her "Giacometto." At Easter she is to leave her prison and enter into the bosom of a family, her new family. She will pass from the convent cell to the bridal chamber as a well-groomed lady. Casanova will indeed have the best of wives. But does he really want such a thing? On the one hand, we could say yes, if we verify the request for marriage certificates that the comedy writer Imer made on his behalf to the Venetian curia; on the other hand, his writing in the *History* allows "Nena" very little space. It seems to me that there is a turning point in the letters starting in the middle of September 1758 concerning an event that would be crucial both for Manon and for Giacomo: their planned marriage.

A marriage into the *Comédie Italienne* would not have been unthinkable for Casanova; the nomad would be able to find his resting place in a family[23] and in a company of actors that enjoyed an excellent reputation at the court of France. He could see himself as the son-in-law of Marivaux's actors, who were protected and salaried by Madame Pompadour and Louis XV himself. And indeed, Silvia Balletti had wielded an influence over Giacomo since his first stay in Paris. An apparently insignificant episode reveals Silvia's designs to wed Manon to Giacomo. It is a small gesture that the great actress lets slip when he gives her earrings of tremendous value and exquisite style: Silvia simply passes this sumptuous gift on to Manon (1:130). Manon also tells us that Silvia used to read to her every letter she received from Giacomo. Casanova's writing for theatre may have been the reason for his first contact with the famous actress.[24] That Casanova was a playwright is not at all surprising. The stage, represented by the powerful figures of his mother Zanetta Farussi, to whom Carlo Goldoni's *Pupilla* was dedicated, and of Silvia herself, held for him a kind of ancestral fascination. His autobiography contains moments of theatre, namely plays that use the eighteenth century as its backdrop, creating a sort of performance of the *comédie humaine*. His fascination with the world was the most authentic spark of his narrative flair. But all of this was yet to come. At that time, Casanova limited himself to recounting his escape from the Leads and to leading a lavish lifestyle. Insufferable in real life but pleasant in his writing, opulent in appearance but charming as a storyteller and even as a listener, he also had the traits of a great letter writer. All of these qualities led him to take great gambles in life and to envision himself in theatrical terms.

Manon certainly did not tolerate her fiancé's long absences, nor did she have the stomach for his bouts of melancholy, which appeared in the form of letters filled with furious scenes, brimming with jealousy and accusations. A missive from the beginning of April 1758 records Manon's anguished state of mind; she feels accused and is compelled to justify herself before her private inquisitor:

> Je nai pû repondre ... il ny a qu'un quart d'heure a tout ce que m'avés dit de dure pour un coeur tendre, Mr et je veux aijsaijer de me justifier un peu à présent de toutes les mauvaises qualités que vous m'atribués. Vous m'avez percé le coeur, je n'en puis plus; et il m'a falu bien de la force pour

vous cacher les larmes que vos reproches me font verser. Il m'est bien dur
que l'homme que j'aime le plus dans le monde me traite avec si peu de
ménagemens, connoissant mes sentimens pour lui.

I could not answer … only a quarter of an hour ago you told me such hard
things for a tender heart, Sir, and I want to try justifying myself a little now
of all the bad traits that you attribute to me. You pierced my heart and I
can't bear it anymore; and I needed much strength to hide from you the
tears that your reproaches make me shed. It is very hard for me that he man
I love most in the world treats me with so little care, knowing my feelings
for him.[25]

In September 1758, caught between the obligation to cloister herself in
the convent of Belchase and her duty to consider other marriage propos-
als presented to her by the Marquise of Monconseil, Manon makes fun
of the letters from another suitor with her Casanova. In this passage of
the letter, we can find a moment of *comédie marivaudienne:*

jugés donc mon cher, l'on enveroit votre pauvre petite dans un balot, par la
douane, avec mon claveçin, ma guittarre (car cela entre dans le marché),
j'ariverois ou plutôt je déballerois; et l'on diroit à cet homme, voilà une
femme, que l'on vous envoye. Eh bien, diroit il, qu'elle soit la bien venue;
elle m'apporte une direction: après cela le mariage se feroit etc. etc.

See, then, my dear, your poor little girl would be sent in a bale through
the customs, with my harpsichord, my guitar (for that is part of the deal),
I would arrive, or rather unpack; and this man would be told, here is a
woman they are sending you. Well, he would say, let her be welcome; she
brings me a direction: after that the marriage would be made, etc. etc.[26]

In truth, the *petite femme*'s only desire is for her Casanova to hasten back,
because she does not want to be forgotten in a convent. Writing to Giacomo, she says that her only need is that "vous faites en façon que vous
puissiez revenir en etat de me rendre heureuse, non par la fortune que
vous me pourriez faire, mais pour le plaisir d'etre à vous … un peu de
bien avec vous me rendra plus riche que la plus grand fortune avec un
autre" (you do all that is necessary to be able to come back and make
me happy, not by the fortune that you could lavish on me, but by the
pleasure of being yours … a few possessions with you would make me
wealthier than a great fortune with someone else).[27]

The correspondence between Manon and Giacomo contains not only the history of a failed engagement, but also a character analysis that parallels Casanova's analysis of himself. In these letters we find an impetuous man, often distracted by his own dazzling, extraordinary life. This was a man who dedicated only a very small part of his life to his young fiancée, but who nevertheless could not accept her rejection. In the preface to his autobiography, Casanova asserts that his black moods were due to his old age, while in his youth he was dominated by a sanguine humour, hot and impetuous. Nena's letters instead reveal that melancholy had always been a part of Giacomo's life and writing, causing him to be irascible, suspicious, intemperate, and often depressed. A fiancée must understand the true temperament of her betrothed; therefore, these letters represent not only the *tendresse* of a young woman in love, but also a progressive distancing from a man unable to change his ways. Perhaps the leitmotif in Casanova's correspondents' letters is in fact the perception of a person who, in the blink of an eye, works himself up to become almost hostile toward those who love him, due to his psychological inconstancy, his changeable moods, or perhaps his calculated intent to leave. Manon, like his other female correspondents, reveals mistakes scattered throughout Casanova's narrative; for instance, he was prone to altering his correspondents' personal information (thus, in his narrative, Manon is only fifteen years old). The correspondents also raise voices that have been all but drowned out by his narrative voice. The despised La Charpillon,[28] for instance, demonstrates within her brief missive an implacable and subtle irony concerning the presumed intolerances of her more mature lover:

Monsieur
Comme je pren beaucoup de par a tout çe qui vous regarde je suis très mortifié daprendre la mauvaise nouvelle de votre incommodité, j'esperre que cela sera si peut de chose quaujourd'huy ou demain nous auron le plaisir de vous avoir chez nous bien portant.

et en vérité le presen que vous mavée envoyé est si joli que je ne sai vous faire comprendre combien il me fait plaisir et combien jan fait de cas, et je ne saipas ce qui vous pousse a toujour vouloir me faire anrager de me dire que c'est ma faute que vous êtes remplie de bille pendans que je suis aussi inossante qu'un enfant qui vien de nêtre et que je voudrois vous rendre aussi dou et aussi passien que votre sang deviendroit un vrais sirop clariffiée, cela pourroit vous arriver si vous suiviez mon avi.

Sir

As I take great interest in everything that concerns you, I am very mortified to learn the bad news of your incommodity, I hope that it will be so minor that we shall see you at our place in a day or two in good health.

and truly the present you sent me is so pretty that I don't know how to convey to you how pleased I am and how I like it and I don't know what pushes you to always want to enrage me by telling me that it is my fault that you are full of bile while I am as innocent as a new-born babe and I would like to make you so sweet and so patient that your blood will turn into a clarified syrup if you follow my advice.[29]

Three years after the break-up of the engagement to Manon, this other very young woman severely tested the allure of the seducer, who dedicated ample pages in the account of his stay in London to the "Charpillon effect." In the crisp brevity of her letter, we find the youthful and intemperate satisfaction of one who knows how to bring bile to the soul and liver of this careless libertine. If we compare La Charpillon's own words to those Casanova has her utter in the *History*, we find no hint of deception, but rather sarcasm, as she dares to write, "Your blood will become a true clarified syrup."

Cécile Roggendorff exchanged letters with Casanova from February 1797 until the same month of 1798, finding in her correspondent a sort of educator-philosopher whom she called Longin. The literary egotism of the Dux hermit was intensely stimulated by Cécile's attitude, to the point that he took up his pen once again to begin a *Précis de ma vie*, which was not only an autobiographical abstract, but an account of the period not mentioned in his memoirs.[30] Madame Zenobie, a name the young countess Roggendorff assumed in their correspondence, was certainly a more attractive addressee than the count of Waldstein's mother, to whom Casanova wrote friendly but excessively sycophantic letters.[31] The countess's epistolary impetus was not completely disinterested and cannot be attributed solely to the long friendship between Casanova and her parents; her aim was to be validated at the court of Dux, where she hoped to be introduced to the count of Waldstein in order to propose herself as the chaperone of his daughters Wilhelmine, Paolina, Johanna, and Dorothea. This epistolary exchange with "Zenobie" allowed Casanova a sort of private renaissance on the eve of his death. Cécile was *la dernière amie*,[32] the last voice in his world and the last opportunity to vaunt his conversation. His letters have no harsh reproaches for her, just some friendly gibes. He was all sweetness in his *éloquence éclairée* toward the twenty-three-year-old Cécile, who fully intended to get from her father's old friend any useful recommendation she could for her new role in society. Casanova played the role of mentor with great pleasure, which is the destiny of every libertine *en philosophe*.

Ayez l'esprit libre, cachez vos préjugés, si vous en avez des reconnus; soyez gaie, tollerante, bonne et facile; mais très réservée vis à vis ceux que vous ne connoissez pas à fond. S'ils sont mauvais, vous devez les punir impitoyablement. Rendez vous impénétrable.

Keep a free spirit, hide your prejudices, if you are known to have any; be gay, tolerant, good and easy; but very reserved toward those you don't know very well. If they are bad you must punish them pitilessly. Make yourself impenetrable.[33]

After a year of epistolary conversation, Cécile revealed enthusiasm for their relationship, which would appear to be an infatuation, were it not so evidently the devotion of a disciple and the display of a *pas de deux amoureux*.

Nos amours sont charmantes, mon ami, et ils sont pour mon coeur delicieux; depuis que je vous connais, je suis bien plus aimable, plus bonne, plus solide, plus gaie, plus heureuse et je crois meme avoir un peu plus d'esprit, ce qui me fait plaisir, puisque il me donnerà un mérite de plus à vos yeux.[34]

Our loves are charming, my friend, and they are delicious to my heart; ever since I have known you, I am much more pleasant, better, more solid, more joyful, happier and I even believe that I have become wittier, which pleases me, since it will give me more merit in your eyes.

Among all the correspondents, Cécile de Roggendorff is surely the most malleable, the closest to the feminine protagonists of Casanova's narrative, or at least to those he glorified. In her philosophical gallantry, we find something of Pauline, or of M.M., not to mention Henriette. If Manon did not care to behave in such an intellectually accommodating manner, then it was the young countess of Roggendorff who perfectly executed this elegant dissimulation, this refined curtsy to her *maître* who exulted in the final success of his intellectual charm. Almost at the end of his life and literary career, the bored librarian rediscovered his vigour and eloquence while writing to Cécile:

Ne nous trompons jamais et nous lassons jamais tromper. Pour nous garantir de la tromperie evitons e abhorrons les trompeurs: il est facile de les connaître: il sont tous menteurs et le mensonge a courte vie. Comptez madame, dans le nombre de vos ennemis tout homme qui vous louera en présence: fuyez le: il veut vous séduire.... Soyez sûre que vous ne pourrez jamais devenir heureuse, que vous rendant telle par vos propres soins. Faites-vous respecter.[35]

Let us never deceive and be deceived. In order to protect ourselves from deceit let us avoid and detest cheaters: it is easy to know them: they are all liars and lies have a short life. Count among them, Madam, every man who praises you in your presence: flee him: he wants to seduce you.... Be certain that you will never be happy unless you make yourself such by your own care. Make yourself respected.

In Casanova's letters to the young countess, we find the lucidity of the best moments of his *Soliloque d'un penseur*,[36] where he reflects on the idea and the practice of imposture. He warns the reader about the risk of becoming a victim, not of someone else's deception, but of one's own vanity. This correspondence includes some of the most beautiful pages of eighteenth-century epistolary etiquette, as well as the noble facade of the libertine, who finds himself in the unexpected role of a concerned and efficient mentor. Cécile's *tendresse* toward the old man of Dux is not a manifestation of the "Aurora complex"; it is instead the emotional confirmation of respect for the man who is now the secretary of her heart, the confidant who knows just how to respond to her. We can find this respect in the beautiful *incipit* and the vivacious farewells of the letter dated 30 April 1797:

Si vous avez bien lu dans le livre des destinées et si je suis née pour être heureuse, je crois pouvoir dire de sentir le commencement de cette félicité quand je reçois de vos lettres – oui, mon cher Casanova – mon ami, daignez l'être, puisqu'une voix intérieure me dit que vous êtes l'ami que le Ciel me destine pour m'armer de courage pour supporter toutes mes adversités.... Adieu, mon ami, un de mes plus ardents souhaits, c'est la conservation de votre santé et la prolongation de vos jours; ne me dites plus que vous êtes sur de votre départ, car ce langage m'afflige.[37]

If you have read well in the book of destinies and if I was born to be happy, I believe I can say that I feel the beginning of that happiness when I receive your letters – yes, my dear Casanova – my friend, deign to be it, since an interior voice tells me that you are the friend that Heavens destined me in order to give me courage to bear any adversity.... Adieu, my friend, one of my most ardent wishes is the conservation of your health and the prolongation of your days; do not tell me anymore that you are on the point of departing, for such words afflict me.

These letters by Casanova's correspondents confirm that he was not a ghost in the castle of Dux, nor the irascible old man who bellowed at a military-mannered and rude major-domo, nor yet the melancholic gentleman who walked along the lake with his Finette, a well-bred bitch [*chienne bien élevée*] who trembled at any gruff turn of his voice; instead, he was a writer who loved to reread the thoughts of his women and who knew how to respond to them in ways far beyond the splendours of the boudoir.

NOTES

1   *Lettres de Cécile de Roggendorff à Casanova,* Marco Leeflang and Monique Grenier, eds. (Utrecht, 1996), 25. Both Cécile de Roggendorff's and Manon Balletti's letters to Casanova are from a non-commercial brochure that contains transcriptions of the original letters preserved at the National Archives of the Czech Republic in Prague. Unless otherwise indicated, all translations into English are the editor's.

2   The earlier edition, G. Casanova, *Histoire de ma vie,* published by Francis Lacassin, 3 vols. (Paris: Laffont, 1993), includes letters from Manon Balletti, Francesca Buschini, and Cécile Roggendorff to Giacomo Casanova in vols. 1 and 3.

3   Here I refer to *Lettere di donne a Giacomo Casanova,* ed. Aldo Ravà (Milan: Treves, 1912).

4   I borrow this definition from a passage of the letter that Silvia Balletti sent to Casanova, a day after the celebration in honour of King Stanislas of Poland: "Mi figlia ne a auti (ha avuti) per la sua parte, cioè per il suo canto con la gitarra che è stato accessorio a ciò che ha fatto nella festa che era pochissima cosa, ma dopo il pranso tutta la compagnia che era molto brillante l'ha fatta cantare per più di un'ora con tutto l'applauso possibile" (My daughter had some applause, for her singing accompanying herself on the guitar, a small thing, but after the meal the entire company which was very brilliant made her sing for more than an hour with all the possible

ovations). The complete transcription of the manuscript is quoted from the Dux archives, now kept in the State Archives of Prague, Marr. 8–211. Certain letters, such as this one, have been included in Leeflang and Grenier, *Lettres de Manon Balletti à G. Casanova*, 15.

5   This title is acknowledged in the marriage contract issued in July 1760 between Manon and the *architecte du roi* François Jacques Blondel with a specific reference to the status of the bride's father and brother.

6   Charles Samaran, "Les amours malheureuses de Manon Balletti," in *Casanova Vénitien. Une vie d'aventurier au dix-huitième siè*cle (Paris: Calmann-Levy, 1914), 184.

7   Samaran, "Les amours malheureuses de Manon Balletti," 184.

8   Samaran, "Les amours malheureuses de Manon Balletti," 184.

9   Leeflang and Grenier, *Lettres de Manon Balletti à G .Casanova*, 15; Marr. 8-120-8-261.

10 Bruno Capaci, *Modelli e occasioni epistolari del '700*, in: *Le carte vive. Epistolari e carteggi del Settecento*, 73–89 (Rome: Edizioni di storia e letteratura, 2011).

11 *Lettres de Manon Balletti à G. Casanova*, Marr. 8-138, Paris, September October 1758, 15.

12 P.C. de Chamblain de Marivaux, *Le jeu de l'amour et du hasard*, in *Théâtre complet* (Paris: Seuil, 1965), 275; Marivaux, *The Game of Love and Chance*, in *Three Plays*, trans., adapt. Stephen Wadsworth (Hanover, NH: Smith and Kraus Book, 1999), 85 (translation modified by the editor).

13 Claude Prosper-Jolyot de Crébillon, *Lettres de Ninon de Lenclos au marquis de Sévigné* (Amsterdam: Joly, 1777), 48. These spurious letters, at times attributed to Crébillon, were in fact written by Louis Damours.

14 *Lettres de Manon Balletti à G. Casanova*, Marr. 8-145, 2.

15 *Lettres de Manon Balletti à G. Casanova*, Marr. 8-152, 24.

16 F. Fido, *Nuova guida a Goldoni. Teatro e società nel Settecento* (Turin: Einaudi, 2000).

17 G. Casanova, *Confutazione della storia del governo veneto di Amelot de la Houssaie* (Amsterdam: Pierre Mortier, 1769), 128–9.

18 Lydia Flem, *Casanova: The Man Who Really Loved Women* (New York: Farrar, Straus and Giroux, 1997).

19 Philippe Lejeune, *Le pacte aubiographique* (Paris: Seuil, 1975).

20 Concerning the libertine's lifestyle, see M. Delon, *Le savoir-vivre libertin* (Paris: Hachette, 2015), 165–75.

21 "Quinze lettres de Manon Baletti à Casanova suivies d'une lettre de Silvia Baletti." In Appendix to Casanova, *Histoire de ma vie* (Editions Gallimard), 2:1121.

22 *Lettres de Manon Balletti à G .Casanova*, Marr. 8-148, 16.

23 In this regard, Casanova writes a convincing passage concerning his state of mind while staying with the Balletti family: "It was at supper at Silvia's that my soul reveled in delight. I was made as much of as if I had been a son of the house, and on my side I convinced the whole family that I wanted to be regarded as such" (5, 173) (Ce fut au souper chez Silvia que mon âme nagea dans la volupté. On me fêta comme si j'avais été l'enfant de la maison; et à mon tour j'ai convaincu toute la famille que je voulais être considéré comme tel [2, 130]).

24 *Zoroastro* and *Mollucheide,* both performed in Dresden, where he lived, in 1752 and 1753.

25 *Lettres de Manon Balletti à G. Casanova,* Marr. 8-135, 11–12. (Ravà, *Lettere,* 98, letter from the beginning of April 1758. Ravà partly corrects Manon's original spelling, reproduced here.)

26 Ravà, *Lettere,* 43. Letter of October 1758?

27 Ravà, *Lettere,* 43. Letter of October 1758?

28 Marie Anne Geneviève Augsburger [Auspurger] (1746–77?), known in Paris as Mlle de Boulainvilliers.

29 *Ravà, Lettere,* 112.

30 Leeflang and Grenier, *Lettres de Cécile de Roggendorff à Casanova,* Marr. 21-1, 23–5.

31 Giacomo Casanova, *Epistolario,* ed. Piero Chiara (Milan: Longanesi, 1969), Dux 6 February 1789, 246.

32 Raoul Vèze, *La dernière amie de Casanova,* in "Pages Casanoviennes" (Paris: Jean Fort, 1926).

33 *Lettres de Cécile de Roggendorff à Casanova,* Marr, 40-30, 12 May 1797, 10.

34 *Lettres de Cécile de Roggendorff à Casanova,* Marr, 8-32, 22 September 1797, 18.

35 *Lettres de Cécile de Roggendorff à Casanova,* Marr, 8-32, 22 September 1797, 10.

36 See *Soliloque d'un Penseur* in *Gli onesti e imperterriti piaceri. Satire libertine in Italia,* ed. Bruno Capaci (Rome: Carocci, 2002), 65–88.

37 *Lettres de Cécile de Roggendorff à Casanova,* Marr, 8-28, 30 April 1797, 8.

Chapter Three

Casanova and the Undifferentiated Body

MLADEN KOZUL

The legend of Casanova, the intrepid libertine, in which the figure of the seducer obliterates the texts and the author, implies strict heterosexuality and a conception of seduction according to which a subjective desire imposes its sovereignty by fraudulent schemes. Obviously this particular figure of the seducer, which is the central element of the Casanova legend, does not allow for any instability of identity, sexual or otherwise, nor for a shift of positions in the power game dominated by the libertine's predatory libido.

This legendary image maintains its place in the stock of cultural figures of the West. However, since approximately the 1980s, the scholarly work about Casanova has undermined it in several ways. A particularly interesting one concerns the forms of sexual ambiguity in the *History of My Life*, analysed by François Roustang in *The Quadrille of Gender*.[1] The book shows that, in retrospective, the libertine legend mostly masks contradictions, tensions, and flaws that point to its negation. Casanova's conquering masculinity is in fact constantly wavering. Indeed, what more could we ask to shatter the legend of the male libertine seducer than François Roustang's claim that Casanova's seduction was aimed at conjuring "his fear of women"? According to Roustang, Casanova wards off this fear by "holding women constantly in view while seeing them only though blurred images that make both their identity and their gender uncertain – with the result that Casanova himself becomes uncertain of his own identity and gender" (9). Roustang contends that the "loss of differentiation between the two sexes" in the *History of My Life* is an aspect of "the abyss that constantly threatens to open under [Casanova's] feet," an aspect of the horror – of his fascination with "the shameful, the sordid, and the repugnant" – from which the work originates, and that it constantly strives to reveal and conceal.[2] Roustang writes, "Casanova not only has a fear, he also has a passion for indistinction, a passion for the horror from which he would nevertheless like to turn away."[3]

Readings of the kind Roustang proposes aim to uncover the deep structures that govern the psyche and the composition of Casanova's text. The general rule is that once this deep structure is identified and its operation described, its functioning does not suffer exceptions. Casanova cannot fear women and seduce them by identifying with them, as Roustang claims he does, and at the same time seduce them as if he did not fear them or identify with them. And yet when one reads *The History of My Life*, one finds instances in which Casanova's ways with women do not follow the pattern Roustang describes. This does not mean that Roustang's insight is not pertinent or valuable – quite the contrary. The occurrences of sexual ambiguity and uncertainty about identity and gender are numerous and significant. But if one adopts a historical perspective, these ambiguities show simultaneously how close Casanova is to the doubtful masculinity of our time and how strange and distant to us are the cultural references that nourish these ambiguities in Casanova's writings. From this point of view, the logic of undifferentiation of the body, which pervades his narrative, depends on the imagery generated by the way the human body, and specifically its sexual characteristics, was understood in Casanova's time. To use Thomas Laqueur's terms, in the "one-sex" model, based on the humoral system, differences of sex were seen as differences of degree.[4] Male and female genitals were structurally equivalent. The vagina was imagined as an interior penis, the labia as a foreskin, the uterus as a scrotum, and the ovaries as testicles. The "two-sex" model that stressed anatomical differences and represented male and female bodies as qualitatively different did not become dominant until the mid-nineteenth century. Difference, it came to be believed, resided in nerves, flesh, and bones. According to Thomas Laqueur, in the one-sex world, "Sex, or the body, must be understood as the epiphenomenon, while gender, what we would take to be a cultural category, was primary or 'real.' Sex before the seventeenth century, in other words, was still a sociological and not an ontological category."[5] Casanova's eighteenth century is when modern sex was born. But this shift was neither smooth nor total. Laqueur gathered convincing nineteenth- and twentieth-century evidence for the survival of the "one-sex" model, while elements of the "two-sex" model can already be identified in late eighteenth-century medical treatises. Aspects of both models are blended in the representation of the body in many early modern texts, and Casanova's *History* is one of them.

Casanova was as much an efficient practitioner of medicine as he was ready to use his medical knowledge in his seductions and manipulations and to replace it with lies and fantasies when doing so could serve his purposes. He met a number of physicians, many anonymous, and some medical celebrities of his time, including Albrecht Haller and Théodore Tronchin, with whom he discussed subjects related to their field.[6] He also claimed he had wanted to become a physician himself.[7] *The History of My Life* and a number of Casanova's other texts bear witness to his intense interest in medical theory and practice. Many of their aspects have been well documented.[8] However, none of the scholarship about Casanova and the medicine of his time has been concerned exclusively with the role of medical imagery of the body in his memoirs and fiction.

Of course, in Casanova's time, as today, the interior functioning of the body was accessible only through a composite and historically and culturally specific imagery. Among the representations of varied origins that composed this imagery in Casanova's time, the ones predominantly shaped by medical theories provide the main models for intimate experience of the inner functioning of the body, as well as for medical etiology.[9] The working of the body's medical imagery in Casanova's texts can be seen as an aspect of the general plasticity of the Casanovian body, of its capacity to vary, permutate, and modify the bodies it interacts with. As I hope to show, the undifferentiation of the body in Casanova's texts – the inconsistency, ambiguity, or heterogeneity of its sexual and gendered characteristics – is observable primarily within the framework of the neo-humoral model, which relies on the dialectic of flux and retention of the classical humoral tradition, but broadens this tradition's scope to include bodily humours other than the traditional blood, phlegm, bile, and black bile. Although, within this framework, one certainly finds echoes of other early modern medical theories, and notably of vitalism, humoralism seems to be the dominant model for Casanova's undifferentiation of the body.[10] Thomas Laqueur notes that "in the blood, semen, milk and other fluids of the one-sex body, there is no female and no sharp boundary between the sexes," and that this "physiology of fungible fluids" allows for "endless mutations" where modern physiology would see "distinct and often sexually specific entities."[11]

In what follows, I will first pay attention to scenes whose components echo each other with slight variations in several episodes of the *History of My Life* and *Icosameron* (1787) and discuss their function in the economy of undifferentiation.[12] I will then bring together these scenes and the medical imagery that links them to their cultural background.

Probably the most striking representation of the undifferentiation of the body in Casanova's writing is found in *Icosameron*. The fact that the first fair copy of an early version of *History of My Life* dates from 1790 to 1792 indicates that the two texts were elaborated within the same time. They share the same bodily imagery. It is worth noting that the scenes in which a body appears in the undifferentiation are ambiguous: they all contain similar somatic elements, but at times these elements accentuate a lack of difference and erotic tension, and at other times eroticism and excitement. Of course, the laws of genre apply as well. The degree of undifferentiation that is appropriate for Casanova's utopian narrative would not make sense in a memoir based on the reality effect. But the former, as I will argue, can be read as expressing a general leaning of the latter.

Icosameron is a utopian story about a brother and a sister, Edward and Elizabeth. After a shipwreck, the siblings enter a subterranean world inhabited by Megamicres, perfect creatures whose society gives an example of an ideal world. Utterly exhausted by the events that follow the initial shipwreck, Edward and Elizabeth are on the brink of physical and mental collapse. The Megamicres who surround them defy gender differentiation. The proportions of their bodies equal human bodily proportions. They are androgynous and oviparous, eighteen inches tall, young and beautiful, and although they are neither male nor female, their breasts are especially attractive. To restore Edward and Elizabeth to life, they act in the friendliest manner:

> Ils nous embrassèrent avec la plus vive tendresse; et avec leurs lèvres délicates ils portèrent à nos bouches arides les plus doux baisers, et approchèrent à la fin avec exubérance de joie à notre bouche les bouts de leurs mamelles. (1:233)

> They kissed us most tenderly; their delicate lips brought to our dry mouths the sweetest kisses, and finally, with exuberant joy, they brought the tips of their nipples to our mouths.

The Megamicres lie down beside Edouard and Elisabeth and begin to breastfeed them. This experience is exhilarating:

Nous suçâmes leur lait … quel goût exquis, milords, quel aliment que le lait des mégamicres! Il occupait notre goût, et notre odorat, en éveillant dans tous nos sens toute la volupté dont nous étions capables, tout le plaisir que nous pouvions désirer, et dont aucun mets ne nous avait jamais auparavant fourni la moindre idée. Cette réalité séduisait notre raison par des illusions les plus extraordinaires. Nous pensions … que nous étions dans le vrai séjour des immortels, et que le lait que nous sucions était le nectar, ou l'ambroisie, qui allait nous donner l'immortalité même, dont ces créatures devaient jouir. (Icosameron, 1:234)

We sucked their milk … what an exquisite flavour, my lords, what a food was the Megamicres' milk! It occupied our taste and our smell while awakening in all our senses all the voluptuous pleasure that we were capable of, all the delight that we could desire, of which no food we tasted before could give us the faintest idea. This reality seduced our reason by the most extraordinary illusions. We thought … that we were in the real dwelling of immortal gods, and that the milk we were sucking was the ambrosia which would give us the immortality of those who surrounded us.

Beside themselves with the joy of sucking the milk, Edouard and Elisabeth, ever more euphoric, empty the breasts of several Megamicres, who succeed one another by their side, exchanging kisses with them all the while. But, after a while, their appetite is abruptly cut off:

Ce repas dura une heure, et je crois que nous n'aurions pas fini si lorsque les derniers nous quittèrent nous n'eussions avec effroi observé quelques goutes de lait qui tombèrent de leurs mamelons sur nos poitrines. La couleur nous fit croire que ce fut du sang. Cette vue calma notre insatiable appétit. (1:235)

This meal lasted for an hour, and I think we would have not ended it had we not observed with terror a few drops of milk that fell from their nipples onto our chests. Their color made us think that it was blood. This sight calmed our insatiable appetite.

The Megamicres are free of sickness, aging, and the need to sleep, but most importantly, they feed on the milk of their partners. Since they are androgynous, the milk is not a sign of a specific gendered identity. On the one hand, we the readers may suspect that Edward and Elizabeth's pleasure has an erotic side – after all, they are humans, and gendered.

But on the other hand, in the world of the Megamicres, the two humans, transformed into helpless infants, enter themselves into the process of undifferentiation, affected by their nurses' lack of sexual differentiation. The undifferentiation is related to the exchange of bodily liquids and to the description of the emotions stirred up by this exchange. Both the exchange of bodily liquids and the description of the emotion stirred by this exchange are ambiguous. The nourishing milk provokes voluptuous pleasure as well as terror and is presented as being at the same time milk and blood. The transposition of the elements of this scene into the world of the *History of My Life* further develops this logic of substitution and fusion that affects bodily humours just as it affects those in whose bodies they circulate.

In one of the most explicit and theatrical erotic scenes in the *History of My Life*, Casanova and M.M., a Venetian nun, are making love in the *casin*[13] that belongs to the cardinal de Bernis, the French ambassador to the Venetian Republic. The two lovers choose sex positions that offer the most advantageous points of view to the cardinal, who is observing them through the holes in the wall of a small adjacent room. The last sex position is a standing one, in which Casanova's body is upside down in front of M.M.'s, who grabs his hips and lifts him up:

> Dans cette position, se soutenant sur ses colonnes écartées, elle fut saisie d'horreur voyant ses seins éclaboussés par mon âme détrempée en gouttes de sang. Que vois-je, s'écria-t-elle, me laissant tomber, et tombant elle aussi avec moi…. Elle avait grande peur d'en avoir avalé quelques gouttes; mais je l'ai facilement persuadée que quand même cela serait, il n'y aurait pas de mal. (1:797)

> In this position, steadying herself on her legs spread apart, she was horrified to see her breast splattered with my soul distilled in drops of blood. What do I see? she cried out, letting me fall, and herself falling with me…. She was very much afraid that she had swallowed some drops of it. But I easily persuaded her that even if it were so, it would not have caused her any harm. (4:71–2)

But M.M. still worries about Casanova's health. She asks him not to leave the *casin* before morning and to write her a letter as soon as he wakes up. Indeed, he sends her a letter in the morning to report that he feels fine.

This episode of the *History of My life* superimposes the link between sperm and blood onto the link between milk and blood found in

Icosameron. There, Edward and Elizabeth suck blood-milk from the Mega-micres' breasts. Likewise, in the scene between Casanova and M.M., the blood-sperm is sucked from Casanova's body. Bodily liquids exchange, and thus share, their qualities: milk is bloody red in *Icosameron,* as is sperm in the scene in Bernis's *casin.* Both the bloody milk in *Icosameron* and the bloody sperm in the *casin* are seen by the characters as they spatter their chests. Both liquids are pleasurable, but also provoke shock or fright.

The same exchange of qualities between bodily liquids and the same metonymic relations between them are maintained when, five years later in Aix in Savoie, Casanova meets a double of the Venetian nun M.M. This second M.M. is French, but the lack of elements differentiating her from the first M.M. is highlighted by the use of the same initials to replace her name. Casanova is delighted to find that the two nuns are physically almost identical. This time around, breastfeeding and bloody ejaculation appear together. Casanova is now the one who sucks the milk, as Edward does in *Icosameron.* This second M.M. was seduced and made pregnant and secretly gave birth a short while before meeting Casanova. During an erotic scene, Casanova asks to "suck the sweet relict of her milk." She agrees, but she is "ignorant, ou faisant semblant d'ignorer la grandeur du plaisir que [Casanova] devai[t] ressentir" (2:434) (unaware of, or acting as if she was unaware of, the intensity of pleasure [Casanova] must be feeling [6:282]), which reminds us of the pleasure felt by Edward. M.M. then asks Casanova to reverse roles and allow her to suck the milk from his breast. He agrees, but warns her that he "does not have any." She still sucks his breast "for fun," showing in the process that the anatomical limit to gender undif-ferentiation does not limit the libido invested in it or Casanova's desire to satisfy it. Before parting as friends, they make love for twelve hours, and the last adieu is again "sealed with [his] blood": "si la première M.M. l'avait vu," writes Casanova, "la seconde devait le voir aussi; et elle en fut effrayée, mais je l'ai facilement calmée" (2:448) (if the first M.M. had seen it, the second was entitled to see it too. She was terrified; but I easily calmed her down [7:16]). In *The History of My Life,* the breasts that come closest to those from which the Megamicres dispense the nectar that ravishes Edward and Elizabeth belong to the Countess Ambrosio, whose family hosts Casanova at their castle in Lombardy. Her name, Ambrosio, is a variant of ambrosia, which refers to the source of the gods' immortality and is the metaphor used to describe her milk and Megamicres' milk in *Icosameron.*

In this episode, Casanova travels in a coach with the countess, her infant son, and her sister Clementina, whom Casanova courted. The countess breastfeeds her child. When the child is detached from the breast, Casanova sees "the white liquid still running." He then says to the countess, "Ah! Madame. C'est un meurtre: permettez à mes lèvres de cueillir ce nectar qui me mettra au nombre des dieux" (2:792) (Ah, Signora! It is a crime; allow my lips to gather this nectar which will put me among the gods [8:252]). Here is the scene:

Je me suis nourri à genoux regardant la Comtesse mère, et sa sœur, qui riaient paraissant avoir pitié de moi … insatiable de faire rire, j'ai demandé à Clémentine si elle aurait le courage de m'accorder la même faveur. – Pourquoi non, si j'avais du lait? – Vous n'avez besoin que d'en avoir la source. Je penserai au reste. Mais à ces mots elle rougit si fort que je fus presque fâché de les avoir prononcés. (2:792)

I suckled on my knees, looking at the Countess-mother and her sister, who, both laughing, seemed to pity me…. With my insatiable desire to raise a laugh, I asked Clementina if she had the courage to grant me the same favor.

"Why not, if I had milk?"

"You need only to have the source of it. I will imagine the rest." But at that she blushed so intensely that I was almost sorry I had said it. (8:253)

Casanova's line hints at the fantasized element that he inserts into the scene in which Clementina provides the source of the milk. When the coach arrives at its destination, Casanova takes the infant and has him suck his nipples, which makes the infant "who sucked in vain" cry, but makes the mother laugh.

The erotic aspect of breastfeeding represented by Clementina's blushing at Casanova's line about providing "the source" of the milk is realized in 1771 when, in Rome, Casanova feeds oysters to two young boarders in a convent, Emilie and Armellina. Oysters are frequently referred to in the *History of My Life* as an erotic stimulant. In this scene, he lets an oyster fall between the breasts of one of the young women, goes after it with his hand, and then starts sucking on a breast under the pretext of not losing the water from the oyster that has been spilled on it. He abandons himself to "toute la volupté que m'inspirait le lait imaginaire que j'ai sucé pour deux ou trois minutes de suite" (3:776) (the voluptuous feelings inspired in me by the imaginary milk that I sucked for a good two or three minutes [12:68]), only to hear Armellina ask him if he has had a lot of pleasure imitating a suckling child.

Several other episodes involve similar elements and mechanisms. Together, these occurrences suggest two comments. First, the erotic body is blended with the undifferentiated body in two situations: bloody ejaculation and breastfeeding; second, this blending implies the exchange of qualities between bodily liquids or their substitution for one another. The undifferentiation is also related, as one might expect, to the loss of erotic tension, if one speaks of the narrative; and to the loss of desire, if one bears in mind the protagonist. Indeed, in the *History of My Life*, the breastfeeding remains ambiguous. It provides pleasure and undifferentiates the body at the same time. But the moment when blood is substituted for sperm becomes the point of utter sexual exhaustion, in which the eroticism is wiped out, as the scene in Bernis's *casin* shows. Some years later, in Genoa, stricken by impotence while in bed with a woman he desires, Casanova observes that such state of impotence never befalls him except "à la suite immédiate d'un long travail dont la fin avait été scellée par mon sang" (2:551) (immediately after a long labor whose consummation had been sealed with my blood [7:138]).

How do we interpret the consistency of the mechanisms of exchange, displacement, and substitution in all of these scenes? It may well be that the mechanisms are related to traumas and means of compensation, as noted by Roustang. However, although they arguably rely simultaneously on several models of coherence, they certainly imply physiological mechanisms that are accessible to representation solely through the medical imagery of the body elaborated in humoral theory. How do the exchanges, displacements, and substitutions fuel the leaning toward undifferentiation that these scenes imply?

It is possible to identify at least two points of contact between the breastfeeding scene in *Icosameron* and the physiological and therapeutic imagery shaped by humoral theory. The first concerns the capacity of the androgynous Megamicres to breastfeed. As surprising as this capacity may seem today, this physiological trait is easily imaginable in light of the medical knowledge of Casanova's time, according to which milk was a component of the chyle, and was therefore not specific to women or to females in general. One reads, for example, in James's *Medical Dictionary* (1743–5) that "milk always comes from the chyle, in men as in women, in young girls as in sterile women, in mothers as in wet nurses," and that "every animal subsists, lives and nourishes himself on his own milk."[14] Multiple scenes in the *History of my Life* in which Casanova has his nipples sucked for milk that is not there might be read as a commentary – perhaps ironic – on these medical claims.

The second point concerns the milk-blood coming out of the Mega-micres' breasts. The close relation between milk and blood is attested by the medical theory that views the quality of the milk that emerges from the breast during breastfeeding as dependent on diet. One of Casanova's main medical references is the work of Herman Boerhaave, who claims in *De viribus medicamentorum* (1720) that if a woman tries to breastfeed without having eaten for a long while, since there will be no chyle left in her organism, "the child will suck nothing out but pure blood" (123). Because the Megamicres feed exclusively on the milk of their partners, none of them ever eats food that could provide chyle and, consequently, they cannot produce anything but blood, or rather a liquid that is blood and milk at the same time.[15]

The therapeutic imagery – as opposed to the physiological one – related to milk is at work in this scene as well. The idea that breastfeeding can heal extreme exhaustion is criticized by Gabriel-François Venel in the *Encyclopédie*. In his entry "Lait" (milk), Venel enters into an argument with several authors, among which an unnamed "famous modern writer" (Boerhaave?) who recommends that completely exhausted men lie down with young, beautiful, and fresh wet nurses and be made to suck as much milk as the nurses can provide. If one is to believe Venel's account of the therapeutic suggestion he criticizes, in this position, a very subtle emanation of the young and vigorous body of the nurse would insinuate itself into the body of the seriously ill person and reanimate it. The "ill person" would more than likely be a heterosexual man. Venel agrees that the milk of a woman could cure this very sick person all by itself, which gives medical backing to the scene from *Icosameron*. But he also observes that if this were to happen, the recovery would likely be a result of the sexual appetite, which would act as a cordial because it would be excited by the wet nurse but not appeased by *jouissance* (9:207). Judging by the account of the pleasure that the shipwrecked Edward felt while sucking the Megamicres' milk in *Icosameron*, a similar mechanism is certainly involved in its therapeutical efficiency. For Venel, a representative of vitalist medical theory in l'*Encyclopédie*, this remedy is efficient inasmuch as it functions as a vesicatory or a flogging would, each of them being an "irritant extérieur." The eroticization of breastfeeding, evident in these episodes of *History of My Life* and *Icosameron*, is theorized in the work of the vitalist Théophile de Bordeu.[16] Thus, the vitalist conception of the body is implied in the imagery of undifferentiation, where it completes and complements its prevailing humoralist framework.

There are scarcely any instances in the *History of My Life* in which the appearance of composite humours is explicitly commented upon, apart from the surprise and fear they provoke in those who see Casanova ejaculating blood. The notable exception to this absence of comment is the first scene in Bernis's *casin*. We learn there that before leaving the *casin* the morning after Casanova's bloody ejaculation, while he was still asleep, M.M. spent half an hour with Bernis in the room from which he had witnessed the scene. Later in the morning, in response to his letter to M.M., Casanova receives one in which M.M. reports Bernis's comment: "Il prétend que faisant l'amour ainsi tu défies la mort, car il soutient que le sang que tu as élancé dut partir du cerveau" (1:799) (he insists that, that making love as you do, you are defying death, for he maintains that the blood you spurted out must have come from your brain" [4:73]). Bernis obviously shares the contemporary medical perspective on the dangers of sexual overindulgence. He probably also believes he has witnessed symptoms of a pathology.[17] His view that the blood comes from Casanova's brain relies on the long tradition that holds that sperm is closely related to the brain, if not derived from it.[18] According to Bernis, Casanova, by making love as he does, could die at the moment of ejaculation. Casanova asks why he thinks M.M.'s life is not in danger, although she climaxes more often that he does. M.M. explains that Bernis believes that female secretions cannot come from the brain, "la matrice n'ayant aucune correspondance avec le siège de l'entendement" (1:802) (since the womb has no connection with the seat of understanding [4:76]).

As for the relation between blood and sperm, its starting point is of course the opinion of the ancients, reported in the entry "Spermatique" in the *Encyclopédie*, according to which the entire body is divided into spermatic and sanguine parts. The anatomical imagery related to proximity between the two is reflected in the name of the two arteries called spermatic (testicular, in today's terms), because they were believed to carry the blood to the testicles, where the sperm was "separated" from the blood. After this separation, the role of the spermatic vein was believed to consist in carrying away the blood that remained after this process of "transformation" or "secretion."[19]

Several of the mechanisms of transformation of one liquid into another described by humorism are circular. Milk seemed to have a particular capacity to produce other liquids or facilitate their flow. According to *Dictionnaire Universel de Médecine*, "c'est avec [le lait] seul que se forment toutes les autres parties tant solides que fluides, par le moyen des fonctions vitales"[20] (It's with milk alone that are formed all the other parts of the organism, solids and fluids, by the action of vital functions) including "la sérosité, le sang, la lymphe" (the serosity, the blood, the lymph). But one also reads in *Dictionnaire Universel de Médecine* that "le chyle qui circule avec le sang dans les vaisseaux se sépare de ce dernier dans les mamelles et donne du lait" (5:1284) (the chyle which circulates with blood in the vessels is separated from the latter in the breast where it is transformed into milk), which implies that blood is as essential to the creation of milk as the other way around. Boerhaave's pharmacopeia relates milk intake to the production of semen by asserting that "milk taken in large quantities is a great breeder of seed, and renders persons more salacious than wine or spices." He also holds that "the generation of seed depends upon a good chyle,"[21] just as the generation of milk does in *Dictionnaire Universel de Médecine* we just quoted.

In conclusion, while incorporating elements of the vitalist conception of the body, humoral theory remains the key underlying model behind the processes of undifferentiation that blur the oppositions between male and female physiology, gender roles, and life stages. It establishes communication between bodily liquids and explains the transformations from one liquid to another while confirming at the same time the links between heterogeneous bodies and distant organs. The transformative power of the medical imagery implied in the *History of My Life* pervades various aspects of Casanova's seductive practices and representations of libidinal mechanisms.

NOTES

1 François Roustang, *Le Bal masqué de Giacomo Casanova* (Paris: Minuit, 1984), translated as *The Quadrille of Gender* by Anne C. Vila (Stanford: Stanford University Press, 1988). In his review, James Mill writes that the book offers "the rich potential of unexplored depth in a persona whom many have previously dismissed as a mere lover, and nothing more" (*Rocky Mountain Review of Language and Literature* 43, 1/2 (1989): 125.

2 Roustang, *Quadrille of Gender*, xiii–xiv.

3 Roustang, *Quadrille of Gender*, xv.

4 Thomas Laqueur, *Making Sex: Body and Gender from the Greeks to Freud* (Cambridge, MA: Harvard University Press, 1990).

5 Laqueur, *Making Sex*, 8.

6 A complete record of these episodes in *The History of My Life* is reviewed and commented upon by Didier Kihli-Sagols, *La Comédie médicale de Giacomo*

    Casanova: Les Mémoires de Casanova: un voyage littéraire dans la vie médicale du temps des Lumières (Paris: Thélès, 2005).

7 Kihli-Sagols, *La Comédie médicale de Giacomo Casanova*, 151.

8 See primarily Sabine Herrmann, *Giacomo Casanova und die Medizin des 18. Jahrhunderds* (Stuttgart: Steiner, 2012); and Vito Cagli, *Giacomo Casanova et la medicina del suo tempo* (Rome: Armando, 2012). Casanova's medical treatises were also recently published, most notably the ones on obstetrics, in Romano Forleo and Federico Di Trocchio, *Giacomo Casanova e le ostetriche: un capitolo di storia della medicina del XVIII secolo* (Turin: Centro scientifico, 2000). Many other references are listed in the bibliographical sections of *Histoire de ma vie*, in the Gallimard and Laffont editions.

9 As demonstrated by Severine Pilloud and Micheline Louis-Courvoisier, who analysed the prevalence of medical models of the body in patients' letters to the famous physician Samuel-Auguste André David Tissot in "The Intimate Experience of the Body in the Eighteenth Century: Between Interiority and Exteriority," *Medical History* 47 (2003): 451–72.

10 Casanova's medical concepts and his interpretations of healing practices are also marked by Paracelse. See Vito Cagli, *Giacomo Casanova et la medicina del suo tempo* (Rome: Armando Editore, 2012), 36–7. For a general discussion of early modern medical theories, see Laurence Brockliss and Colin Jones, *The Medical World of Early Modern France* (Oxford: Clarendon, 1997).

11 Laqueur, *Making Sex*, 35.

12 Giacomo Casanova, *Icosaméron, ou Histoire d'Edouard et d'Elisabeth, qui passèrent quatre-vingt et un an ches les Mégamicres habitants aborigènes du Protocosme dans l'intérieur de notre globe, traduite de l'anglais par Jacques Casanova de Seingalt Vénitien* (Prague: L'Imprimerie de l'école normale, 1787), vol. 1–5, trans. Abr. R. Zurer as *Casanova's Icosameron, Or the Story of Edward and Elizabeth Who Spent Eighty-One Years in the Land of the Megamicres, Original Inhabitants of Protocosmos in the Interior of Our Globe* (New York: Jenna, 1986). References are indicated in the body of the text, translated by M. Kozul, since the English edition provides only an abbreviated version.

13 Casanova frenchifies *un casino*, Italian diminutive of *una casa*, a house. Like its French equivalvent, *une petite maison*, it refers to a private house, rather small, consecrated to entertainment or pleasure, including games of chance, social gatherings, and amorous encounters. Both terms, Italian and French, are now archaic.

14 Robert James, *Dictionnaire universel de médecine* (Paris: Briasson, David l'aîné, Durand, 1746), 4:731. The quote is from Diderot, Eidous, and Toussaint's

translation/adaptation of James's *Medical Dictionary*, translated into English by Mladen Kozul.

15 Casanova's iatromechanical conception of the circulation of humours is clearly demonstrated in the episode in which he explains the efficiency of a blood draw for a woman deprived of her period by the equivalence between the quantity of the blood drawn and the quantity of blood she would have lost in her periods. Casanova heals her by sleeping with her for three weeks straight (1:889–92).

16 See Théophile de Bordeu, *Recherches anatomiques sur la position des glandes et sur leur action* (Paris: G.F. Quillau père, 1751), 254.

17 Tissot reports the case of a boy, not yet sixteen, who overindulged in masturbation "with such fury, that instead of sperm, he brought about blood" (Un jeune garçon qui n'avait pas encore seize ans s'était livré à la masturbation avec tant de fureur, qu'enfin, au lieu de sperme, il n'avait amené que du sang), Samuel Auguste André David Tissot, *Onanisme, ou Dissertation physique sur les maladies produites par la masturbation* (Lausanne: Antoine Chapuis, 1760; Paris: Garnier, 1905), 45.

18 Tissot reviews the opinions of ancients and moderns about sperm to prove its importance for the humoural economy and to explain why its loss in masturbation is so detrimental. The idea of proximity between brain and sperm perdures from Hippocrates and Galen to Friedrich Hofmann, Tissot's contemporary. See *Onanisme* (Paris: Garnier, 1905), 55–63. On Tissot's works and theories, see Antoinette Emch-Deriaz, *Tissot: Physician of the Enlightenment* (New York: P. Lang, 1992).

19 *Encyclopédie, ou Dictionnaire des sciences. des arts et des métiers*, par une société de gens de lettres (Paris: Briasson, David, Le Breton, Durand / Neufchâtel, Samuel Faulche et Cie, 1751–65), 15:450.

20 James, *Dictionnaire universel de médecine*, 4:731.

21 Herman Boerhaave, *De Viribus Medicamentorum, or A Treatise of the Virtue and Energy of Medecines* (London: J. Vilcox, 1720),126–7.

PART II

EMERGING SOCIABILITIES

Negotiating Sociabilities in Casanova's *History of My Life*

CLORINDA DONATO

In the century of encyclopedism, in which encyclopedias of every stripe dominated print culture (and here I include not only the canonical works carrying the word *encyclopedia* in their title, but also compilations such as the Jesuit accounts of the New World, Prévost's fifteen-volume *Mémoires et Aventures d'un homme de qualité,* and Raynal's six folio volumes of the *Histoire des deux Indes*), let us count Casanova's *History of My Life* as an encyclopedia of European sociability.[1] While scholarship has focused primarily on Casanova's sexual exploits in Paris or London, his experiences in sociability in other cities and towns across Europe are also important, for they provide not only indices to the social practices and customs of any number of small and/or peripheral social venues, but also, with regard to the topic of this volume, indices to those aspects of Casanova's intellectual and social life that enable us to see him as more than a libertine legend – as the erudite, socially flexible, and highly informed member of Europe's itinerant republic of letters that he was.

To this end, this study focuses on his experiences in a number of less-noted "Casanova places," such as Berne, Rimini, and Siena, from which we may cull several examples of his adaptation to emerging local centres of sociability. Through this adaptation, he renegotiated social activity in ways that furthered his agenda and reputation, and ultimately the contents of the *History of My Life.* Indeed, the more than one thousand pages that fill the three-volume La Pléiade collection constitute a study of sociability in a variety of settings, both worldly and regional, with Casanova negotiating multiple sociabilities and acquiring immediate access within them. This adaptability is surely one of the hallmarks of his life as he has written it, and, as we are learning, it was one of the most salient features in the construction and performance of an eighteenth-century life. Indeed, research in eighteenth-century studies increasingly highlights the role of circulation on every level, as the International Society for Eighteenth-Century Studies 2015 conference emphasized in its conference description: "Opening Markets invites historians of all kinds to address a wide variety of related subjects, including cross-cultural encounters and the evolution of the relationship between town and country and between the sexes." Two of the conference's themes, "Movement and Change" and "Meeting Places and the Exchange of Knowledge and Ideas," could easily be affixed as subtitles to Casanova's *History of My Life*.

Drawing upon the critical framework offered by Antoine Lilti's rewriting of French sociability in the eighteenth century, Pierre-Yves Beaurepaire's extensive reflections on cosmopolitan networks and European Freemasonry, Kenneth Loiselle's study of eighteenth-century fraternalism, and the work of Charles Withers on the geographies of enlightenment, including the notion of sexual geographies, this chapter considers the ways Casanova cultivated his social quotient and cachet, as well as his unique ability to quickly establish relations with both men and women from a variety of stations in life through a relaxed yet determined project to conquer them as friends, social partners, and of course lovers. Some of the particular aspects of Italian culture that helped him achieve these goals with little trouble will also be explored, such as the very open structure of the Italian *conversazione*, often likened to the French salon, which welcomed a wide variety of social classes to discuss the broadest range of conversation topics.

Casanova and Freemasonry

While Casanova's telling of his life stands out as perhaps the most exciting and interesting autobiography of the eighteenth century, its ability to grab and hold our attention has to do with its uniquely conversational mode of relaying personal information, one that blends a number of genres into one: the anecdotal, the novelistic, and the epistolary. The sense that Casanova is talking directly to his reader is due in no small measure to his ability to reproduce and retell what he had heard from others as part of the conversations in which he engaged. Such conversations were the stuff of the erudite, cosmopolitan traveller, who repeatedly found himself in new social settings where he was expected to explain himself. Thus, travel and conversation went hand in hand. As John V. Fleming has noted, business and cultural travel increased exponentially during the eighteenth century, with "bankers, diplomats, lawyers, and whole army regiments moving about with a new vigor."[2]

The Masonic lodge played an important role in the lives of Casanova and others like him as they moved through Europe. As our understanding of Masonic networks grows, scholars have increasingly commented on the role played by Casanova's initiation into Freemasonry and the access it provided him. Fleming describes the Masonic lodge as "an intellectual safehouse," entrusted with the transmission and spread of ideas, as religious institutions had been in previous centuries. And academies, particularly those in Italy, functioned in ways that paralleled and often overlapped with the roles of the Masonic lodges. The Italian academies, in particular, combined serious conversation with playful erudition, as expressed in the names chosen for their associations: the Academy of Fisticuffs (Accademia dei Pugni), the Academy of the Defective (Accademia de' Diffetuosi), the Academy of the Restless (Accademia degli Inquieti), and the Academy of the Comfortable (Accademia degli Agiati). This same playful tone permeates much of Casanova's *History of My Life*, certainly a function of his experience with Italian academic sociability (a topic that deserves more in-depth treatment that we can give it here, but that others have been addressing in recent years).[3] It also behooves us to remember that several others led lives similar to Casanova's, such as the Milanese Joseph Gorani, a Freemason and the author of a volume of secret accounts and scandalous anecdotes about Italian courts, the *Mémoires secrets et critiques des cours, des gouvernemens et des mœurs des principaux états d'Italie* (1793). Gorani, in his *Mémoires pour servir à l'histoire de ma vie*, like Casanova, recounts the intimate sexual details of multiple encounters during his youth, education, and military and political service at various courts throughout Europe.[4] Indeed, examples abound of social opportunities, often Masonic, that allowed the likes of Casanova and Gorani to acquire the socially viable knowledge that would later enrich their writings.

The printed word and the spoken word in the service of humanity constituted the fundamental precept of Masonic activity. Masons, in fact, produced both kinds of words prolifically, engaging in writing and conversation so as to spread knowledge, as directed by one of the most influential early Freemasons on the continent, Andrew Michael Ramsay (1686–1743). Ramsey was a Scottish ex-pat in France and a Catholic convert who travelled from lodge to lodge. He laid out the practices of a good Mason in his famous oration of 1737 to the Grand Lodge of

France. The fourth quality of the good Mason as outlined by Ramsay
bears repeating:

> The fourth quality required in our Order is the taste for useful sciences and
> the liberal arts. Thus the Order exacts of each of you to contribute, by his
> protection, liberality, or labour, to a vast work for which no academy can
> suffice, because all these societies being composed of a very small number
> of men, their work cannot embrace an object so extended. All the Grand
> Masters in Germany, England, Italy, and elsewhere exhort all the learned
> men and all the artisans of the Fraternity to unite to furnish the materials
> for a Universal Dictionary of the liberal arts and useful sciences, excepting
> only theology and politics.[5]

The geographer Charles Withers has asked, "Where was the Enlightenment?"[6] The answer can be found in the transmission of print culture
throughout Europe, but also in the conversations that took place in any
number of lodges, academies, and *conversazioni*.[7] The filiated network
of Masonic lodges, whose reach we are only now beginning to understand, offered sites where groups large and small, depending on the
place, met in varying degrees of contact. There were also several gatherings whose meetings closely paralleled Masonic encounters, offering a
club-like atmosphere of sociability in which both entertaining and serious conversation concerning science, philosophy, economics, and the
liberal arts could transpire. Such meetings were certainly active when
Casanova visited Berne in 1760, in our first example from the *History
of My Life*. Let us first remind ourselves, though, of Casanova's initiation into Freemasonry some ten years prior in Lyon. He documents this
event in the *History of My Life* when he exhorts all "well-bred young men
who intend to travel" to join lodges, because doing so will allow them
to freely negotiate their cosmopolitan sociability. As Casanova has made
explicit, Freemasonry gave him opportunities to be recognized for his
erudition, providing him with a venue for testing his ideas, and for
developing a reputation as an erudite cosmopolitan who could hold
forth on the most current issues of the day. The lodge was a place where
he could perform his learning, empowered by the quality of his virtue,
intellect, and social skills. He describes how he became a Freemason in
Lyon in 1750:

> Un respectable personnage que j'ai connu chez M. de Rochebaron, me
> procura la grâce d'être admis parmi ceux qui voient la lumière. Je suis
> devenu *franc-maçon* apprentif. Deux mois après j'ai reçu à Paris le second

grade, et quelques mois après le troisième, qui est la maîtrise. C'est le suprême. Tous les autres titres que dans la suite du temps on m'a fait prendre sont des inventions agréables, qui quoique symboliques n'ajoutent rien à la dignité de maître.

Il n'y a point d'homme au monde qui parvienne à savoir tout; mais tout homme doit aspirer à tout savoir. Tout jeune homme qui voyage, qui veut connaître le grand monde, qui ne veut pas se trouver inferieur à un autre, et exclu de la compagnie de ses égaux dans le temps où nous sommes, doit se faire initier dans ce qu'on appelle la maçonnerie, quand ce ne serait pour savoir au moins superficiellement ce que c'est. Il doit cependant faire attention à bien choisir la loge dans laquelle il veut être installé, car malgré que la mauvaise compagnie ne puisse agir en loge, elle peut cependant s'y trouver, et le candidat doit se garder des liaisons dangereuses. Ceux qui ne se déterminant à se faire recevoir maçons que pour parvenir à savoir le secret peuvent se tromper, car il leur peut arriver de vivre cinquante ans maître maçon sans jamais parvenir à pénétrer le secret de cette confrérie. (1:1026, Appendices)

A respectable personage whom I met at the house of Monsieur de la Rochebaron procured me the privilege of being admitted into the company of those who see the light. I became an apprentice *Freemason*. Two months later at Paris I received the second degree, and some months later the third, which is the mastership. It is the highest. All the other titles which were conferred on me in the course of time are pleasing fictions which, though symbolic, add nothing to the dignity of Master.

There is not a man on earth who succeeds in knowing everything; but every man should aspire to know everything. Every young man who travels, who wishes to know society, who does not wish to be inferior to another and excluded from the company of his equals in the age in which we live, should be initiated into what is called Freemasonry, if only to acquire a superficial knowledge of what it is. However, he must be careful to make the right choice of the lodge of which he wishes to become a member, for though evil company cannot act in the lodge, it may be present in it, and the candidate must beware of dangerous connections. Those who decide to become Masons only to learn the secret may well be deceiving themselves, for a man can be a Master Mason for fifty years and never learn the secret of the brotherhood. (3:116)

It should be noted that this text was heavily revised by Casanova, and much of the detail about the importance, for a young man, of becoming a Freemason was cut in a subsequent version, also published in the Pléiade edition.[8] It may be that when he rewrote it he wanted to appear less dependent on Freemasonry. Nonetheless, the first draft gives us insight into the meaning and role of Freemasonry in his life. Though it presents a somewhat disparaging view of the formal aspects of Freemasonry, it is adamant about the importance of the right lodge in providing the cultural traveller with a social entrée. Masonic lodges, and other gatherings that he describes, allowed him to feel his "moral strength" and uncover the "greatest possible amount of knowledge." The lodge encouraged the proper cultivation of the self through sociability in "good society." Indeed, the lodges, along with academies and economic societies, cultivated a cosmopolitan outlook: foreign visitors were welcome to consult their libraries and attend their cafés, which is exactly what Casanova did while in Berne. His recounting of his Bernese sojourn indicates his status as an erudite, cosmopolitan gentleman who could quickly adapt to the social layout of the emerging Swiss capital that was attempting to establish itself in the European network of sociability.

The status he had acquired in his ten years of Masonic belonging is best understood through the reflections of Pierre-Yves Beaurepaire, who has devoted important pages to the codes of sociability acquired by Casanova. Beaurepaire discusses the fine line between the acceptance and rejection of itinerant masons who travelled throughout Europe. He has culled a set of impressions about the role of foreigners who visited lodges, but he uses the case of Casanova to make his most salient points. Beaurepaire cites Casanova's telling in the *History of My Life* of the warning he received from the playwright and poet Crébillon the Elder: his very "Italianate" French would be charming for a while, but others would tire of it quickly should he fail to master the French language. Crébillon agreed to teach Casanova proper French, which he did, purportedly, three times a week for a year. Casanova derived some very important lessons from his mentor, especially about how to speak and behave, as Freemasons were concerned with respectability and with affirming their adhesion to a community of the elected. Beaurepaire has explained the task of the Casanova type in *L'autre et le frère.* "The foreign adventurer must stage his difference, 'his exoticism' without raising in the mind of his host the fear of the 'alien.'"[9] While they were somewhat suspicious of "adventurers," the more "elite" masons were also fascinated by them. This means that the foreign Masons had to negotiate the fine line between their "exotic" difference and acceptable behaviour, without appearing too odd. In Berne, Casanova managed to achieve recognition as an erudite foreigner whose presence lent cachet to Berne's nascent sociability, while revealing at the same time his ability to fully negotiate the Bernese brand of sociability. We should also notice that in Berne he was on equal footing with the locals when it came to French, and in some ways he was closer, as an Italian, than they were to the Latinate world of erudition, as became apparent in his dealings with the Bernese.

Berne's Sombre and Scientific Sociability

Although Freemasonry had been banned by Leurs Excellences de Berne, as the ruling patrician class was called, in 1745, a Masonic under-current of contacts, interests, and meetings appears to have persisted despite the ban, and it may well have provided the network of contacts that enabled Casanova to meet with the most important representa-tives of Bernese life and erudition in 1760. Indeed, Masonic activity re-emerged in Berne to such an extent that renewed legal measures were taken against it in 1764.[10]

In order to fully understand the society into which he entered, a few words about Berne's attempts to enter the European marketplace of enlightenment are in order. Eighteenth-century Berne had begun to expand its sphere of European relations, thanks in large part to its longstanding cultivation of the French language, together with Ger-man. French was an important political tool, as well as an emerging cultural and economic instrument in maintaining order in the Pays de Vaud, which had been ruled by Leurs Excellences de Berne since the sixteenth century. Any number of the young scions of the two hundred ruling families could work throughout the Pays de Vaud as "bailli," or administrative representatives of Berne, in the French-speaking areas under its jurisdiction. The increasing influence of French through-out Europe and the strong ties between France and francophone Switzerland meant that Berne had an opportunity to make economic and cultural strides, and its success depended upon becoming a cen-tre of sociability that could draw the attention of foreign notables. Building a good reputation was essential, as was affording the visitor a minimal level of social amenities, such as cafés, bookstores, libraries, and meeting places under the aegis of erudite societies of some sort. At the latter, the visitor might associate with local notables and with those who had acquired European reputations. A publishing house was another necessary feature of a city that aspired to be important,

not to mention a periodical or two that would appear with the imprint
of the city.

Casanova went to Berne in 1760. It might seem odd that he should
have gone to a city that had had virtually no influence on the European cultural scene in the first half of the eighteenth century, with the
exception of Albrecht von Haller's poem *Die Alpen.* Yet over the course
of three short years, 1757 to 1760, Berne had seen a sudden fervour
of cultural and literary activity, thanks to two of its favourite sons, the
brilliant and dashing young patrician Vincenz Bernhard von Tscharner
and the eminent anatomist and poet Albrecht von Haller. Haller had
returned to Berne following an illustrious career in Göttingen, where
over a seventeen-year period he had become a powerful figure in scientific circles throughout Europe. His network consisted of some 1,500 correspondents (of whom Casanova was one) with whom he exchanged tens
of thousands of letters.[11] He had been the Dutch anatomist Boerhaave's
most brilliant student, but had also dedicated himself to the literary
arts, composing the poem *Die Alpen* in 1729, which evoked the pristine
beauty of the Alps as a representation of the Swiss character and values. In 1736 he was recruited as the chair in medicine, anatomy, botany,
and surgery at the newly founded University of Göttingen. In 1739, he
launched the most illustrious German periodical of the eighteenth century, *Die Göttingische Gelehernte Anzeigen,* known as the *Göttingische Anzeigen
von gelehrten Sachen* after 1753, the year Haller, homesick, resigned from
his position and returned to Berne, just in time to collaborate with his
erudite compatriots who wanted to attract talent to Berne. Haller had
acquired a great deal of experience in publishing and setting up a periodical in Göttingen, and he put that experience to full use in Berne. He
also identified a person in Naples who could manage the journals, knew
French well enough for translation purposes, and excelled in classical
languages. That person was Fortunato Bartolomeo De Felice, a physicist,
cultural mediator, and future publisher for the Typographical Society of
Berne, who had renounced his Franciscan orders and embraced Protes-
tantism. He had made a name for himself through his translation into
Latin of the Scottish physicist John Arbuthnot's 1733 *Essay Concerning
the Effect of Air on Human Bodies.*[12] The contact with De Felice, believed
to have been a Mason himself, was made through Tscharner's correspondence with De Felice's mentor, the grand master of the Neapolitan
Masonic Lodge, Raimondo di Sangro, the prince of San Severo, documented in a letter of 1756. Haller had cited De Felice's translation and
notes extensively in his magnum opus, *Elements of Physiology,* published in

Latin. An erudite figure in his own right, though wrongly characterized as an abbé gallant by Voltaire, De Felice was obliged to leave for Switzerland undercover, as the result of a scandal involving a passionate affair with Countess Agnese Arcuato Panzutti. De Felice helped her escape from the convent where her husband had locked her away because of ongoing marital strife, travelling with her in Germany and Switzerland until their limited means forced them to return to Italy. She had no choice but to return to the convent, while he was mildly reprimanded by the ecclesiastical authorities "over a cup of hot chocolate," according to Giuseppe Gorani.[13] Unhappy with the strictures of the Catholic Church regarding celibacy, the increasingly repressive environment following the death of the enlightened Pope Benedict XIV, and the unequal treatment of women, De Felice, prompted by his mentor, Raimondo di Sangro, the prince of San Severo and grand master of the masonic lodges of Naples, decided to leave Italy for Switzerland, where he would be able to undertake the encyclopedic project he had conceived with Di Sangro, the *Encyclopédie* d'Yverdon (1770–80). He arrived in Switzerland in 1757 and immediately set to work, opening a literary café and establishing two periodicals under the guidance of Haller and Tscharner. Both of these periodicals, the Italian-language *Estratto della letteratura europea* and the Latin *Excerptum totius Italicae nec non Helveticae literaturae*, were first published in 1758.[14] The periodicals received high praise, and with their imprint of Berne gave the city some of the cachet it was seeking. However, they were not published in Berne, but rather by Giuseppe Galeazzi in Milan, with the direct collaboration of Pietro Verri and Cesare Beccaria, for whom they became an important precursor to *Il Caffè*, the most important eighteenth-century Italian-language periodical.

There is every reason to believe that Casanova was familiar with these journals, especially considering the languages of their publication and the fact that they were closely tied to the most important members of the Milanese Enlightenment. He mentions being "in the shop of a book-dealer where [he] went to read the gazette" (dans la boutique d'un libraire où j'allais lire la gazette) when he saw a young man, who relayed a message to him. He reports on his meeting with De Felice at the library, which has been determined to be the Burgerbibliothek, as well as with a Bernese man of letters who was making a name for himself:

Je suis sorti avec [Monsieur de Chavigny], et nous allâmes à la bibliothèque, où j'ai connu M. Félix moine défroqué plus littérateur que lettré, et un jeune homme nommé Schmith lettré, qui promettait, et qui était déjà bien

connu dans la république littéraire. Un docte en histoire naturelle, qui
savait par cœur dix mille noms des différentes coquilles m'ennuya parce
que sa science m'était tout à fait étrangère. (2:356)

I left with [M. de Chavigni] and we went to the library where I met M.
Felix, an unfrocked monk, who was rather more facile than erudite, and
a promising young scholar named Schmid, already well known in the
republic of letters. A man learned in natural history who had the names of
ten thousand different shells by heart bored me because I knew nothing of
his science. (6:184)

Casanova demonstrates here that he had absorbed the prejudice of
many of the Bernese against Fortunato Bartolomeo De Felice, whom he
calls M. Felix. He describes him as facile rather than erudite, reserving
the term *erudite* for Friedrich Samuel Schmidt zu Rossan, an archeolo-
gist, who had published a few books but was a far lesser scholar than De
Felice. Yet as a native son, he was praised and admired, and Casanova
pays him due homage. Casanova has no patience, however, for the weari-
some learned man talking about shells, the pastor Daniel Sprüngli, who
bored him to tears, as did his science, which, Casanova implies, consisted
of no more than memorization. However, Casanova proves his mettle as
he brilliantly negotiates some of the more austere forms of sociability
that he encountered among the Bernese in his meeting with the "Grand
Haller," in which he had the opportunity to discuss the anatomical and
occult sciences that so interested him. To meet with Haller, who was
performing his government function as a "bailli," he travelled to Roche,
on Lake Geneva. He paints a Plutarchian portrait of the scholar in the
most sombre and respectful of terms, quoting Haller's declaration that
the only way to uphold the law is to prove its value by example. They discussed literature and science and in particular Boerhaave, who in Haller's
eyes had been, after Hippocrates, "le plus grand de tous les médecins; et
plus grand chimiste du premier, et de tous ceux qui avaient existé après
lui" (2:373) (the greatest of all physicians; and a greater chemist than
Hippocrates and all those who had existed after him [6:205]). Anatomy,
chemistry, and the physiology of the bodily fluids as investigated by Boerhaave were of interest to the Freemasons in their pursuit of preserving
life and discovering the life force through, for example, the ability to
make artificial blood or to find the philosopher's stone, a chemical substance that would turn mercury, copper, or other substances into gold.
Though referred to as a stone, it was not really a stone at all, but rather a

powder or tincture known as the "materia prima," said to act as an elixir of life, capable of healing, prolonging life, and even granting immortality. The quest for the philosopher's stone/elixir of life had begun in the Middle Ages and was still being sought after by any number of alchemists, who were also chemists, pharmacologists, and metallurgists in what appears to our eyes as a mixing of pseudo-science and serious scientific pursuits. It is not surprising, then, that Casanova asked Haller about this aspect of Boerhaave's work and inquired whether he himself believed in the possibility of the stone's existence. Haller answered, "Je travaille depuis trente ans pour la trouver impossible, et je ne peux pas parvenir à cette certitude" (2:373) (I have been working for thirty years to show that it is impossible, and I cannot convince myself of it [6:206]). In bringing up the philosopher's stone, Casanova was picking up the thread of a conversation he had been having with an eighty-five-year-old woman whose erudition he found thoroughly engaging. She was a friend of Boerhaave's and possessed a gold plate that he had transformed for her from copper. She assured Casanova that Haller possessed the philosopher's stone but had not succeeded in expanding his lifespan to several centuries. Once again, the search for the stone was pursued by Masons throughout Europe, with the prince of San Severo being among the most involved in this research, especially in relation to blood, as Casanova mentions elsewhere in the *Histoire.* The prince had succeeded in producing a blood-like substance, which he showed off to grand tourists who came to Naples to experience the liquefaction of this blood in the vials he had prepared. The prince believed he was close to discovering the philosopher's stone once he had created this substance that had the properties of blood and, he believed, would be capable of sustaining life.[15]

Casanova's desire to draw our attention to his erudition is woven throughout these pages, as is his intellectual solidarity with the Swiss in his expressed preference for Latin (with a moment of backlash against French) in his discussion with Haller about the power of Latin. These pages also contain a remarkable sexual-scientific performance that Casanova witnessed and elucidated in clinical terms and gestures for his housekeeper-mistress, Dubois, shortly after he arrived in Berne.[16] Having spent an afternoon at a Bernese bathhouse where a Swiss girl washed him, served him coffee, and took care of all his needs, he piqued Dubois's interest by his telling of the experience. She expressed a desire to go there, and they embarked on a visit. When they arrived at the bathhouse, two girls were assigned to them. As Casanova and his mistress undressed and entered their respective bathtubs, followed by the girls who had been assigned to wash them, Dubois had second thoughts and refused to be touched. So as to accommodate the couple, the two Swiss girls, "qui s'étaient déjà trouvées plusieurs fois dans des parties pareilles, se mirent en position de nous divertir avec un spectacle qui m'était très bien connu; mais que ma bonne trouva tout à fait nouveau" (2:355) (who had no doubt often taken part in similar diversions, prepared to entertain us with a spectacle which I knew very well but which was completely new to my helpmate [6:183]). Surprised at the fury with which one of them performed in the role of the man and at his own loss of libido, Casanova turned from the woman he loved, "whose charms were sufficient to captivate all of the senses," commenting that "the strange strife of the two young Maenads" (the Greek term *Maenad* or "raving ones" was used for the female followers of Dionysus) occupied Dubois's attention as well as his own. Because Dubois thought Casanova's spa attendant "must be a boy, not a girl," Casanova called attention to her breasts, which proved her physiological status as a woman, to which Dubois responded that "she may be a boy all the same":

Je me tourne, et la fille même, me voyant curieux, met devant mes yeux un clitoris; mais monstrueux, et raide. Je dis ce que c'était à ma bonne toute ébahie, elle me répond que ce ne pouvait pas être cela, je le lui fais toucher, et examiner, et elle doit en convenir. Cela avait l'air d'un gros doigt sans ongle, mais il était pliant: la garce qui convoitait ma belle gouvernante lui dit qu'il était assez tendu pour le lui introduire, si elle voulait bien le lui permettre mais elle n'a pas voulu, et cela ne m'aurait pas amusé. (2:355)

I turn, and the girl herself, seeing my interest, displays a clitoris, but enormous and stiff. I tell my amazed helpmate what it is, she replies that it cannot be that, I make her touch and examine it, and she has to give in. It looked like a thick, nailless finger, but it was flexible; the wench who coveted my beautiful housekeeper, told her that it was stiff enough for her to put it into her if she would permit, but she refused, and it would not have amused me. (6:183)

Once again, we can point to Casanova, the scientifically up-to-date man of the world in all things sexual. Indeed, his narrative reflects his knowledge of sexual science and the emerging discourse on lesbians, lesbian sex, and hermaphrodites. As he was drawn in by the clinical aspect of what he was watching, titillation was subverted by erudite curiosity.

Casanova describes the organ in terms used by anatomists, inviting his mistress to touch and examine the clitoris as if it were a lab specimen. He also reports that it was firm enough to be functional, a fact corroborated by what they saw and, most certainly, by what Casanova had read, possibly in the writings of the University of Padua anatomist Antonio Vallisneri (1661–1730), who had reported on a similarly described clitoris that functioned like a penetrating penis. Casanova's scientific acumen takes precedence here over passion and transport, and his language is reminiscent of Vallisneri's definition of the clitoris, including those of the monstrous variety described in the latter's *Saggio alfabetico d'Istoria medica e natural* (written in 1726 and published by his son in 1733, after Vallisneri's death in 1730). Here are some excerpts from Vallisneri's article "Clitoris":

CLITORIDI. Clitoris, seu mentula, muliebri. Questa è una delle sedi principali de' Venerei femminili diletti, che dolcemente solleticata *oestrum excitat, & furorem auget*. E' posta sopra la parte superiore di quel luogo, che le savie donne tanto tengono celato. La sua figura, e grandezza ordinaria è come l'ugola, ma alle volte così mostruosamente cresce, che emula il membro dell'uomo, di cui si veggano le storie appresso questo vizio naturale troppo famigliar nell'Egitto, facendo l'uffizio da uomo colle Vergini anche le donne, fu ordinato per legge, che a tutte le fanciulle appena nate lì dalle sopra la Clitoride un botton di fuoco, per impedirne l'accrescimento;… Da quella pendola soverchia carne nasce alle volte l'equivoco appresso chi non è pratico di simile Anatomia, essendo prese per uomini mostruosi, e per Ermafroditi coloro, che hanno un tal vizio , quando veramente son donne.[17]

Clitoris, seu mentula, muliebri. This is one of the principal seats of female pleasure, that when lightly rubbed, *oestrum excitat, & furorem auget*. It is found above the highest part of that place that wise women keep covered. Its shape and normal size are similar to the uvula, but sometimes, it grows so monstrously, that it emulates a man's organ, a natural vice that we see all too often in Egypt. There, by law, a burning coal is placed on Virgins' clitorises to prevent them from growing…. That pendulum of extra flesh creates confusion for those who do not understand anatomy. They are believed to be monstrous men, or Hermaphrodites, instead of the women that they are.

Vallisneri imparts clinical information together with anthropological and legal information. In the second half of the article, however, he adds a narrative dimension, telling the story of a woman whose parents thought she was a man and dressed her as one. She had a beard and appeared to be male. However, one day, her belly was found to be growing. In front of the priest, she confessed to sleeping with a young man, after which the parents asked Vallisneri to determine her physiological gender. Vallisneri responded,

> Risposi che ... a me mandasse [il Parroco] l'infantata paziente, per osservare, se quella parte che credevano il corno, con cui cozzano gli uomini colle donne, fosse forata, e se per quella orinasse, o il seme spandesse; che se tale era, poteva chiamarsi Ermafrodito, se imperforata, era la Clitoride allungata, ed esser vera Donna. Si trovò senza foro, laonde donna la dichiarai, e fù dal suo Drudo, ridente il popolo, sposata, e con nera barba sul volto vestita da Donna, e vive ancora, mutato avendo genio, e mestiere.[18]

> I answered that ... the parish priest should send the pregnant patient to me so that I could determine whether that part that they believed to be the horn with which men butt against women had an orifice in it, and if he/she urinated or ejaculated through it, for if that were the case, he/she could be called a hermaphrodite; if there were no orifice, and it were instead an elongated clitoris, she can be considered a true woman. It was found to be without an orifice, so I declared her a woman and she was married to her paramour, and in front of the bemused public, with a black beard on her face, dressed like a woman, and she is still alive today, having changed both her gender and her trade.

Bellino/Teresa, Giovanni Bianchi, and Rimini

Casanova's work shows other intertextualities with the research on sexuality in the eighteenth century, such as the link between the spa attendant's erect clitoris and Haller's theory of irritability, which explains bodily movement in reaction to touch. Even more importantly, Casanova's writing brings together a fascination with monstrous bodies, the origin of sexual desire, and the relationship between physiology and sexuality that was proposed by Rimini anatomist Giovanni Bianchi's 1744 medical novella titled *Breve storia della vita di Catterina Vizzani, Romana, Che per ott'anni vestì abito da uomo in qualità di Servidore la quale dopo vari Casi essendo in fine stata uccisa fu trovata Pulcella nella sezzione del suo Cadavero*

(Brief history of the life of Catterina Vizzani, Roman woman, who for eight years wore a male servant's clothing, who after various vicissitudes, was in the end killed and found to be a virgin during the autopsy of her cadaver).[19] As Paula Findlen has noted, Casanova's relationship with the purported young actor Bellino (in reality Teresa), who appeared on the stage to be a man, with a visible penis that was lifelike to the touch, took place in Rimini in 1744.[20] Findlen hypothesizes that Casanova had read Bianchi's medical novella and had used it as grist for his description of Bellino/Teresa's gender doing and undoing, which closely resembled those of the transgendered Catterina Vizzani/Giovani Bordoni, replete with dildos and various instances of gender fluidity. Casanova, in his dealings with Bellino/Teresa, poses many of the same questions that Giovanni Bianchi does about the fluid boundaries of desire, the construction of gender, and the origins of desire and pleasure in men and women alike. Once again, Casanova demonstrates an awareness of the most fascinating anatomical topics of the day and their controversial corollaries, which he provocatively stages in his memoirs, thereby not only telling the story of his life, but also educating his readers about current scientific and social topics. He does so by presenting information in the format of the autobiography, which, as stated earlier, can be compared to any other kind of compiled work. As a point of comparison, let us consider Casanova's visit to Siena, and the experiences in sociability that he acquired under the guidance of the highly cosmopolitan Abate Ciaccheri.

Giuseppe Ciaccheri, Casanova, and Siena as a Site of Sociability

The Abate Giuseppe Ciaccheri (1725–1804) was Casanova's guide for the week he passed in Siena during the April 1770. Casanova describes his Sienese sojourn over multiple pages in the *History of My Life*, paying particular attention to the Italian form of sociability known as the *conversazione*, a salon-like gathering. Casanova's rendition of his experiences at the *conversazione* to which the Abate Ciaccheri brought him one evening is particularly relevant to our discussion about the regional sites of sociability where Casanova thrived. These pages describe in great detail how men and women mingled in small yet culturally vibrant eighteenth-century cities such as Siena and Rimini, and how women were assigned well-defined roles, either as entertainers through song, improvisation, and recitation or as authors of less noble pursuits:

Il me fit voir dans ces huit jours tout ce qu'il y avait de digne d'être vu dans
la ville, et tous les gens de lettres, qui ne manquèrent pas de me rendre la
visite. Vers le soir il me conduisit dans une maison, où il m'a dit qu'il n'y avait
pas de façon à faire; point de noblesse, point de présentations: on parlait
pour rire, on y chantait, on faisait de la musique instrumentale, on lisait des
belles pièces des vers, une jeune fille en faisait pour suppléer à sa laideur, sa
sœur cadette fort jolie en goûtait la beauté, et se contentait de donner de
la matière pour en faire à ceux qu'elle enflammait d'amour avec toute sa
charmante personne. Ces deux sœurs avaient deux frères, dont un jouait du
clavecin, l'autre était peintre. Telle fut la maison où Ciaccheri me fit passer
la soirée avec un autre abbé jeune professeur qu'on appelait Pistoi. (3:624)

In the course of the week he [Ciaccheri] showed me everything worth
seeing in the city, and made me acquainted with all the men of letters, who
did not fail to call on me. Toward evening he took me to a house, where, he
said, everything was free and easy – no formality, no introductions. People
talked to be amused; there was singing, there was instrumental music,
beautiful verses were read aloud; one girl composed them to make up for
her ugliness, her very pretty younger sister enjoyed their beauty and was
content to afford a subject for them to those whom all of her charming
person fired with love. The two sisters had two brothers, one of whom
played the harpsichord, the other was a painter. Such was the house to
which Ciaccheri took me to spend the evening, with another Abate, a young
professor, whose name was Pistoi. (11:211)

The *conversazione* was a modern gathering that often cut across class to
include government functionaries who mingled with nobles and clerics,
thus extending the boundaries of the closed courtly setting of noblemen
and ladies, such as the one described by Castiglione in *Il Libro del Cortegiano*. Indeed, performing women were a staple of the *conversazione*, as were
men who became their protectors and created opportunities for them to
mix with other men, an activity that contributed to male status. Such was
the relationship between Maria Fortunata, the ugly woman with whom
"you fell in love" if you listened to her poetry, according to Casanova,
and the Abate Ciaccheri, who told of his passion for the young poetess
whose career he now directed. Casanova inquired whether Maria Fortunata improvised like Corilla, but the abate responded no, that he did not
want to spoil her, despite her stated interest in performing as an *improvi-
satrice*. A discussion ensued between Casanova and Ciaccheri about how
improvisation ruins a real poet's virtues, forcing the poet to focus more

on form than on content. The juxtaposition of this particular description of women poets with the visit shortly beforehand to Pisa, where he participated in social gatherings of a similar nature accompanied by a monk named Stratico, sheds light on yet another local context for sociability:

> Il avait choisi deux ou trois filles de condition qui unissaient à la beauté le génie pour leur apprendre à chanter des impromptus en les accompagnant sur la guitare. Il leur avait communiqué le talent de Corilla qui était alors célèbre, et qu'on a couronnée *Poetessa.* (3:619).

> He had chosen two or three well-born girls who combined beauty with talent, so that he could teach them to sing improvisations accompanying themselves on the guitar. He had taught them the art of Corilla, who was then famous and who ... was crowned *Poetessa.* (11:205)

At the same time, however, this entire discussion was also to be read through the prism of the reputation of Corilla Olimpica (Maria Maddalena Morelli, 1727–1800), the great Arcadian improviser who was received at the Capitoline and the first woman to join the ranks of Italy's greatest poets. Casanova offers a critical analysis of this moment when a woman broke the "glass ceiling" of the arts, immortalized by Mme de Staël in the novel *Corinne, ou l'Italie* (1807).

The discussion about women who perform (and the "spoiling" of their art) threatened to spoil their reputations as well. This threat reveals the common perception of women who performed publicly and the obstacles they faced in their desire to be evaluated based on the quality of their art instead of on the lascivious lifestyle they were believed to lead. But it also reveals the conflicted position of a male public that had to ostensibly protect the common moral good, while at the same time desiring nothing more than to attend the public spectacle of performing women to experience the transport it produced. The thrill of this transport and the condemnation alike are documented in the many poetic compositions written about female performance by men of letters of every stripe. However, just as many poems were written to condemn the women, as if, in a fit of guilt, the male gaze turned from transported and sensual to condemning and punitive. The *conversazione* in Siena gives us the opportunity to see yet another site of sociability in European social interaction in the eighteenth century.

Casanova's *History of My Life* thus constitutes a nexus in which numerous forms of eighteenth-century life – exchange, travel, scientific pursuits, musical appreciation, journalistic awareness, correspondence networks, sexual networks, Masonic networks, and conversation – come together in a rich, encyclopedic cross-section of sociability. His multifaceted talents and observations deserve far better than the limiting label of libertine legend. Casanova is rather an *Enlightenment* legend, one who shared with many the trappings of the erudite, cultured traveller and an itinerant lifestyle. Like many others, he performed the Enlightenment by transferring and exchanging ideas through networks and their numerous nodes of activity.[21]

NOTES

1 Antoine-François Prévost, *Mémoires et aventures d'un homme de qualité qui s'est retiré du monde* (Paris, 1728–31), 15 vols.; Guillaume-Thomas Raynal, *Histoire philosophique et politique des établissemens & du commerce des Européens dans les deux Indes* ([Amsterdam], 1770), 6 vols. For a discussion of the many volumes comprising the Jesuit accounts, see *Jesuit Accounts of the Colonial Americas: Textualities, Intellectual Disputes, Intercultural Transfers*, ed. Marc André Bernier, Clorinda Donato, and Hans-Juergen Luesebrink (Toronto: University of Toronto Press, 2014).

2 John V. Fleming, *The Dark Side of the Enlightenment: Wizards, Alchemists, and Spiritual Seekers in the Age of Reason* (New York: W.W. Norton, 2013), 156.

3 See Luciano Boschiero, "The Young and the Restless: Scientific Institutions in Late 17th and Early 18th Century," Columbia University Academic Commons, https://academiccommons.columbia.edu /search?utf8=%E2%9C%93&search_field=all_fields&q=luciano+boschiero; and Paula Findlen, "Founding a Scientific Academy: Gender, Patronage and Knowledge in Early Eighteenth-Century Milan," *Republics of Letters: A Journal for the Study of Knowledge, Politics, and the Arts* 1, no. 1 (1 May 2009), https://portal.research.lu.se/portal/en/journals /republic-of-letters-a-journal-for-the-study-of-knowledge-politics-and-the-arts.

4 The parallels between Gorani and Casanova deserve more in-depth treatment than we can offer here. Interest in Gorani and similar figures has been growing. Gorani also wrote a *Histoire de ma vie* that was first published at the beginning of the twentieth century. On Gorani, see Maria G. Vitali-Volant, "Aventure, histoire, écriture de soi à la fin du XVIIIe siècle. Giuseppe Gorani (1740–1819) Lettres et mémoires," PhD diss., Université Paris VIII- Saint Denis, 2004; and Vitali-Volant, "Le hasard et la nécessité: figures du hasard dans les *Mémoires pour servir à l'histoire de ma vie de* Giuseppe Gorani," *Italies*, http://journals.openedition.org/italies/220. On the sexual exploits detailed in his autobiography, see Giovanni dall'Orto,

"Gorani, Count Giuseppe," in *Who's Who in Gay and Lesbian History: From Antiquity to World War II*, ed. Robert Aldrich and Garry Wotherspoon, 220–1 (London: Routledge, 2002).

5   See Ramsay's Oration, http://ecossais.net/html/ramsay-s_oration.html.

6   Charles Withers, *Placing the Enlightenment, Thinking Geographically about the Age of Reason* (Chicago: University of Chicago Press, 2017), 6.

7   I emphasize French here, for, as we know, Italians corresponding and conversing among themselves in the eighteenth century often did so in French. And French was so prevalent in the Venetian Republic that one of the most important publishing houses of the republic, the Seminario di Padova, routinely published in French, seeking to become Europe's French-language publisher and the point of distribution of French-language texts, an endeavour that was crowned by its revised edition of the Encyclopédie méthodique, the *Encyclopédie méthodique de Padoue*, with all revisions and new articles composed in French by the likes of Girolamo Tiraboschi, historian and librarian for the Estes in Modena.

8   The revised text reads:

Un respectable personnage que j'ai connu chez M. de Rochebaron me crut digne, comme il me dit, de voir la lumière. Cela veut dire qu'il me présenta à la loge, d'où je suis sorti frammaçcon. Deux mois après je suis devenu à Paris dans la loge du duc de Clermont compagnon, puis maître. Il n'y a point de plus haut grade dans la framaçonnerie: ceux qui s'imaginent d'être d'avantage à cause des nouveaux titres qu'on a inventés se trompent, ou veulent tromper.

Il n'y a point d'homme au monde qui puisse parvenir à savoir ce que c'est que la framaçonnerie sans y être initié, mais ceux qui se déterminent a s'y faire recevoir pour apprendre ce qu'on appelle le secret peuvent se tromper, car s'ils n'ont pas le talent de le pénétrer, il pourra leur arriver de vivre cinquante ans maîtres sans jamais le savoir. Le secret des maçons est tel qu'il ne peut être communiqué à qui que ce soit par personne, car personne ne peut être sûr de le savoir. Il est donc inviolable par sa propre nature (1:590–1).

9   "L'aventurier étranger doit mettre en scène sa différence, 'son exotisme,' sans éveiller dans l'imaginaire de l'hôte la peur du 'forain.'" Pierre-Yves Beaurepaire, *L'autre et le frère* (Paris: H. Champion, 1998), 146.

10   See "Loge zur Hoffnung," http://www.logezurhoffnung.ch/index.php /freimaurerei/geschichte.

11   These letters have been indexed in a database created by Martin Stuber's team through the ongoing project "Albrecht von Haller and the Eighteenth-Century Republic of Letters."

12   (An Essay concerning the Effects of Air on Human Bodies.) Clarissimi viri Johannis Arbuthnot ... Specimen edfectuum aëris in humano

corpore. Quod primum ex anglico idiomate interpretatus est gallico Clar. Boyerus … Mox vero latine reddidit, atque additionibus, auctariisque illustravit, ornavit, auxit P.F. Fortunatus de Felici (Naples, 1753), 335.

13   For a thorough discussion of De Felice's affair and his views on celibacy as contrary to natural law and human rights, see Alessandra Doria, "'Un oggetto considerabile di mondana politica.' Celibato del clero e critica illuminista in Europa nel XVIII secolo," PhD diss., Università degli Studi, 2013, 93–100.

14   *Estratto della letteratura europea*, ed. Fortunato Bartolomeo De Felice (Berne, 1758–62); (Yverdon, 1762–66). A Latin journal, *Excerptum totius Italicae nec non Helveticae lieteraturae*, was also published in Berne at the beginning of his stay there.

15   See Francesco Paolo De Ceglio, "Playing God: Testing, Modeling, and Imitating Blood Miracles in Eighteenth-Century Europe," *Bulletin of the History of Medicine* 91, no. 2 (2017): 411.

16   According to Judith Summers, *Casanova's Women: The Great Seducer and the Women He Loved* (London: Bloomsbury Publishing, 2011), 230, Madame Dubois was a respectable French widow whom Casanova met in Holland. She had lost her means of support following her husband's death and subsequently became Casanova's housekeeper and mistress.

17   Antonio Vallisneri, *Saggio d'istoria medica e naturale colla spiegazione de' Nomi, alla medesima spettanti, posti per Alfabeto*. In *Opere fisico-mediche stampate e manoscritte del cavalier Antonio Vallisneri, raccolte da Antonio suo figliuolo*. 3 vols. (Venice: Sebastiano Coleti, 1733), 3:389.

18   Vallisneri, 389–90 (my translation).

19   The translation of the volume is mine and reflects the original Italian. The Italian original was written in 1744 by Giovanni Bianchi, an anatomist from Rimini. In 1751 John Cleland published a bowdlerized "translation," heavily rewritten and adapted to a British audience *[An] His[toric]al and Phy[s]ic[al] Dissertation on the Case of Catherine Vizzani, Containing the Adventures of a Young Woman, Born at Rome, Who for Eight Years Passed in the Habit of a Man, Was Killed for an Amour with a Young Lady; and Being Found on Dissection, a True Virgin*. A second edition of this translation was published in 1756, with a slightly altered title.

20   See Paula Findlen, "Medicine, Pornography, and Culture in Eighteenth-Century Italy," in *Italy's Eighteenth Century: Gender and Culture in the Age of the Grand Tour*, ed. Paula Findlen, Wendy Wassyng Roworth, and Catherine M. Sama (Stanford: Stanford University Press, 2009), 240.

21   I am indebted to Charles Withers, "Above and Beyond the Nation: Cosmopolitan Networks," chap. 3 of *Placing the Enlightenment*, for the formulation of my conclusion.

Chapter Five

Casanova, Mercury, Mercurio

MALINA STEFANOVSKA

Literary critics have compared Casanova to Don Juan, a myth in whose elaboration he may have participated personally, as he spent the last few days before the premiere of Mozart's *Don Giovanni* holed up with the composer and his librettist Da Ponte, writing the opera. A variant of its second act, moreover, was found in his papers. While *Don Giovanni* was modelled on Molière's *Don Juan*, which in its turn was a reworking of Tirso de Molina's, another mythical figure may be an even more appropriate symbol for understanding Casanova: Mercury, Jupiter's valet and messenger in Molière's *Amphitryon*.[1] In this comedy of seduction and scheming, the cleverest character is not Jupiter, who seduces Amphitryon's young wife by impersonating the absent general, but Mercury, a rascal god who takes out his mercurial mood on the hapless Sosie – a common noun for "a double" in French – by becoming his "sosie." Casanova knew the comedy well; he alludes to it as he comments on an unfaithful mistress who used his valet as an informant to a rival: "j'ai su après que Mercure avait averti Jupiter qu'Amphtryon avait changé de chambre" (3:361) (I learned afterward that Mercury had informed Jupiter that Amphitryon had moved to another room [10:218]).

But his relationship to mercury is even more compelling, for Mercury/Hermès inhabits the *History of My Life* under many guises: as a planet; a metal that eludes capture; a god of boundaries and transitions; the protector of thieves, merchants, travellers, and pimps; a messenger of the gods; and a shady love go-between, "a Mercurio," who can stand for Casanova.

The first meaning is the metal, with which Casanova had an elaborate coexistence. This unrepentant sinner availed himself at least eight times in his life of this traditional medicine for curing syphilis, abundantly and – according to what he wrote in the *History of My Life* – always success-fully. His bouts with *la vérole* remain among the direst in the ledgers of his existence as a libertine, mercury regimens providing a sort of regular rhythm, a pause in his active life. By the time he wrote about mercury, his body was most likely thoroughly infused with the toxic metal and – judging by the absence of long-term effects, other than perhaps the loss of teeth – they cohabitated relatively well. At any rate, mercury poisoning did not prevent him from spending thirteen hours a day writing his auto-biography, after finishing the equally voluminous novel *Icosameron*. The only negative effect that he attributed to its cure was that at one point in his life it had brought him religious fervour, or bigotry, a malady, he writes, "beaucoup plus mauvaise que la v…, et dont je ne me croyais pas susceptible" (1:559) (far worse than the pox, and one to which I thought I was immune [3:82]). Casanova had no doubts that such a transforma-tion came from: "this impure and always very dangerous metal": "L'esprit suit le corps. L'estomac vide je suis devenu fanatique: le mercure dut avoir fait un creux dans la région de mon cerveau où l'enthousiasme s'était logé" (1:561) (The mind obeys the body. With my stomach empty, I became a fanatic; the mercury must have made a hollow in the region of my brain, in which enthusiasm had taken its seat [3:85]).

Witticisms aside, Casanova was not ignorant of the metal's properties and effects, for he had early knowledge of chemistry, and had even taken some classes in it. It was mercury that he used to make one of his first "coups" as a con man. Early on in his travels, penniless, he stopped in Portici, and, over a meal that he ordered without having the slightest idea how he would pay for it, he met a Greek merchant who had a quantity of various chemical substances for sale, among them mercury. Casanova then remembered "an amalgam of mercury made of lead and bismuth" that increased the substance's quantity by one fourth, yet looked so similar to the pure metal that it could be sold to unsuspecting customers. He seized the opportunity and staged an elaborate deceit that brought him not only enough money to continue his travel to Naples, but also generous presents from the merchant, who, although he realized that he had been duped, resigned himself to it, as he certainly counted on tricking others.

But, no less than through Casanova's chemical manipulations and their monetization, the production and trade of mercury around him were promoted by the other "commerce" – the sexual one – he indulged in. Their conflation throughout his life provided him with one of the funniest anecdotes in his memoirs. On his first trip to Rome, then a young abbot, he spent some time in the small Istrian town of Orsara, ill from an interaction with a prostitute. There he was provided with the usual mercury regimen by the local surgeon and nursed by the young governess of the priest who took him in. He recounts that he could not resist her inviting willingness, figuring that he was cured enough that with some precautions, he would not have to turn her down and humiliate both of them. Several months later, now in military garb and on his way to the Orient, he stopped again at Orsara. As soon as he disembarked, a man accosted him, expressing his utmost gratitude and hoping that he would stay in town for a while: it was the surgeon, who had barely been able to make a living in the small and healthy town. He saw his fortunes rise after Casanova's stay, as the governess, who had caught Casanova's "galanterie" – an eighteenth-century euphemism for sexually transmitted disease – had passed it on to the priest, who in turn infected a friend, who shared it with his wife, who then infected a libertine who did so well that the surgeon soon saw the number of his clients top fifty. Indeed, Casanova's use of mercury is telling, as an increase in the mercury trade was concomitant with the general context of increasing travels and intercourse in the eighteenth century, a context in which he and a host of other travellers and adventurers participated.[2]

As a chemical element, mercury also plays a substantial role in another project of his times, his utopian novel *Icosameron*. It is a basic element of the underground world into which Edouard and Elisabeth, the two siblings who are its principal protagonists, fall after a shipwreck. They are first saved from the hermetically closed box by the Megamicres, small human-like creatures, who dissolve the lead by using a "red liquor." Edouard later learns that it is "their mercury, much more active than ours" and that "in a smaller or larger quantity, this fluid metal dissolves all others." Mercury is the basis of the Megamicres' ovoparian reproduction, as it remains at the constant temperature of human blood or milk and allows the newly laid eggs placed in it to grow and mature. Its red colour is the same as their air, their water, and the milk with which they feed each other.[3] Clearly, mercury saturates Casanova's fictional universe as much as it did his body, or the alchemical experiments with which he duped the Marquise d'Urfé. In his letter to the prince de Courlande, he even claimed that it enabled him to produce in Mme d'Urfé's laboratory the famous "arbre de projection" (3:391) (tree of projection [10:253]) sought by alchemists intent on creating gold.

The symbiotic relation that emerges between Giacomo and mercury goes beyond the physical usage, though, to cross into the literary realm. For a start, it consists in similitude: quicksilver, the metal's familiar name, denotes a swift reaction and a capacity to elude capture, a crucial trait of all adventurers and conmen. Casanova demonstrated this capacity early on in an encounter with Signore Bragadin, a rich patrician whose cerebral attack he witnessed and whose life he managed to save, capturing by the same token the man's blind trust in his magical capabilities. Additionally, the encounter involved a mercury unction placed on his chest by a doctor, which, as Casanova rightly intuited, was nefarious for such cases. He swiftly washed it off and had the presence of mind to back it up with a quickly invented knowledge of Kabbalah, thus ensuring for himself the status of Bragadin's adoptive son and a decent monthly allowance for as long as the rich bachelor lived. The ability to elude capture, found in quicksilver, was also regularly displayed by Giacomo, most strikingly in his flight from the notorious Leads prison. Its masterful retelling guaranteed him entry into European salons and, in the form of his earliest published piece, into literary history. The same quick wit fuelled his feats of seduction, his entry into high finance, and the lively dialogues and tight narrative of his autobiography.

On a symbolic level, however, it was not the metal but the eponymous deity with whom Casanova formed the closest relationship. Both as a protagonist and as an author, he is the very figure of the wily, swift, and temperamental go-between. A parallel with the "god of highways and crossroads, of messages and merchants" was inspired by the French philosopher Michel Serres. Hermès, after whom Serres named his groundbreaking series on the mutual interference of science and literature, stands as the figure of the transversal, elusive, indirect, and often impure communication between science and literature:

> Communiquer c'est voyager, traduire, échanger: passer au site de l'Autre, assumer sa parole comme version, moins subversive que transverse, faire commerce réciproque d'objets gagés. Voici Hermès, dieu des chemins et carrefours, des messages et des marchands.

> To communicate is to travel, to translate, to exchange: to cross to the Other's site, to adopt and adapt his speech as one's own, in a transversal more than a subversive gesture, to engage in mutual commerce of found objects. Here comes Hermès, god of highways and crossroads, of messages, and of merchants.[4]

This communication, interference, translation, trading, and borrowing between disciplines and narratives is central to Casanova's writing, establishing his life narrative as an appropriate reflection of and mediation between the disparate trends of his century as reflected in a singular human consciousness. His relationship to Mercury is just one example of such "mutual commerce" between chemistry, magic, alchemy, medicine, and the other alchemy – that of the verb, as Mallarmé called poetry.

As a matter of fact, mercury was not the only merchandise whose circulation and trade Casanova facilitated. The rest included coaches and carriages bought in one country and sold in another; painted silk fabrics produced in his manufacture or bought for personal consumption; gold watches, rings, or tobacco boxes that he regularly acquired, lost at gambling, or gave as presents; currencies, credit instruments, and bills of exchange transferred across borders; ideas and rituals disseminated through Masonic lodges; letters of recommendation regularly obtained and given to others; news and anecdotes spread in salons; and last but not least, disease and genetic material generously strewn along his route. Casanova bought and sold, gave and received, trafficked and mediated. The adventures recounted in the *History of My Life* provide a remarkably precise account of the circulation of innumerable commodities and persons in his times. As such a chronicler of exchanges, and as an indefatigable traveller and adventurer, he was under Mercury's protection. But one could also claim that he fashioned his life after what the deity stood for, if we explore more closely his role in facilitating exchanges and in mediating between circles, networks, disciplines, countries, and people.

Money, the fundamental medium of exchange, is a good place to start. Casanova's life was structured around financial exchanges, transactions, and manipulations. Endowed with a swift mathematical mind and superior calculating capacities honed through ample practice, he carefully recorded the currencies of every small duchy or state he crossed and their exchange rates with other currencies. Among the many long-vanished coins he mentions, a few still haunt our collective memory and our fairy tales: sequins, grosh, maravedi, dinar, ducats, louis, pounds, liards, thalers, écus, piasters, kopecks. He knew them all and took such detailed notes that he was able to quote the sums disbursed and their comparative worth thirty years after the fact, a feat perhaps even more impressive than his memory of his many amorous conquests. This systematic accounting woven into his life narrative has even spurred comparative analyses by economists interested in eighteenth-century currencies. A couple of examples illustrate his proficiency in rates and methods of exchange. Fired by his protector in Rome, desperate and uncertain of what to do next, Casanova does not omit the recap of his finances:

Lorsque j'ai pris congé du cardinal Acquaviva, il me donna une bourse dans laquelle j'ai trouvé cent médailles que les Castillans appellent doblones da ocho. C'était la valeur de sept cents cequins, et j'en avais trois cents. J'en ai gardé deux cents, et j'ai pris une lettre de change de seize cents écus romains sur un Raguséen qui avait maison à Ancône et s'appelait Giovanni Buchetti. (1:247)

When I took leave of the cardinal Acquaviva, he gave me a purse in which I found one hundred coins of the sort the Castilians call *doblones de a ocho*. They were worth seven hundred zecchini and I had three hundred. I kept two hundred and procured a bill of exchange for sixteen hundred Roman scudi on a Ragusan who had an office in Ancona and was named Giovanni Bucchetti. (1:320–1)

Many years later in London, racked with pain upon learning on the same day that he has lost Mme d'Urfé's financial support and that he must part with his beloved Pauline, he cannot help observing that the surprising "lettre de crédit à vue de vingt millions" (letter of credit at sight for twenty million) that the young woman had received from Portugal "ne faisait cependant que deux mille livres sterling a peu près, car les Portugais comptent par *res* qui est une monnaie indivisible comme le maravédis en Espagne" (3:78) (came to only about two thousand pounds sterling, for the Portuguese reckon in *reis*, which is an indivisible coin, like the *maravedi* in Spain [9:245]). Among his observations on English customs and politics, one oddity that he deemed worth recording at some length is the preference for banknotes over gold guineas, even though using them entails a monetary loss of 1 per cent. Such examples abound in the *History of My Life*.

The question of exchanges and the bizarre currency in which they were carried on is also given a prominent place in *Icosameron*. Such precise details demonstrate a keen preoccupation with all aspects of finance and exchange. Casanova, who treated money as something to swiftly throw back into circulation rather than capital to accumulate takes on the role of a currency translator if not an actual broker, in his obsessive narrative recording of all entries and expenses. This perspective was all the more reflective of an increasingly global economy in which the general exchangeability of goods was being theorized at this time, and in which the circulation of gold was starting to be replaced by that of paper money, which, as Casanova noted in England, was based on confidence.

But the pecuniary motif that runs through Casanova's narrative touches only one aspect of his mediating role, which extended to other areas of social commerce. During his constant adventures, Casanova was an active participant in extensive networks of travellers, diplomats, spies, gamblers, opera divas, actresses and dancers, Freemasons, and adventurers of all kinds. Some of them were as peripatetic as he was, and he systematically records his encounters with the same people in each place he visited. Thus he first frequented the abbé de Bernis, with whom he shared a lover, the nun M.M. in Venice, then again in Paris, and many years later in Rome. After meeting the notorious count of Saint-Germain in Paris, he saw him again in Brussels and in Amsterdam; in Saint Petersburg, sixteen years after he seduced her, he ran into the Parisian shopkeeper La Baret, who had eloped and become an actress under the stage name of l'Anglade (3:260). The gambling cheat and pimp Pochini seemed to chase him all over the globe: from the Greek island of Cerigo (Cythère) to Amsterdam seventeen years later; then to Stuttgart, where Pochini pimped his two alleged nieces and cheated Casanova at gambling; to London, where Pochini was prostituting his alleged daughters, and finally to Vienna, where he robbed Casanova after enticing him with yet another girl. The text is full of similar examples. In this constant circulation, some individuals, as Casanova did, changed names and created successive identities, the better to thrive under Mercury's protection. Take, for instance, Teresa Imer, a comedian's daughter whom Casanova knew in his Venetian youth, and with whom he allegedly had a daughter. When he ran into her in Hague and met her again in London, Casanova records her successive name changes, which mystified her contemporaries and even some historians: Tranti or Trenti, then Pompeati after a husband who committed suicide, and finally Mrs. Cornelys, after a Dutch lover who helped her financially. Casanova's many contacts formed elaborate networks that he helped substantiate by leaving written traces of them: the Freemasons he visited in every major European capital introduced him to other brothers in their cities and wrote introductory letters on his behalf for his travels elsewhere.[5] Likewise the broad network of bankers was no doubt tightened by the "bills of exchange" that Casanova transferred from one city to another upon arriving. In an initial visit, he and the banker would exchange information and other services: the banker would tell him of a good inn, inform him about theatre life and actresses of interest, help him rent a place or find a servant, recommend a wine merchant, etc. In Saint Petersburg, for instance, he immediately visited the Greek merchant Demetrio Papanelopoulo, to whom he was recommended by a violinist he knew from his youth in Padua and whom he had met anew in Berlin after many years. Papanelopoulo, who had already honoured a bill of exchange signed by Casanova in Dresden, received him very well, credited him with 100 roubles per month on account of his allowance from Signore Bragadin, and helped him find a servant and rent an inexpensive carriage. Invited to his home, Casanova there met another merchant who, in turn, told him of Italian visitors of interest, such as a Paduan count and his mistress, a dancer, and others. These, among many similar examples, show that information circulated in parallel with credit, enhancing commerce simultaneously in the fields of sociability, finance, and sex, and that in these overlapping and crucial networks of the eighteenth century, Casanova represented an important node – mobile, active, and with many contacts, which are well recorded in his memoirs.

He played this brokering role equally well in the literary exchanges and academies of his time. There, without being a major figure, he was a welcome member and participant, no less than in the theatre circles of any city he visited – circles that brought together sex (often venal), gambling, and high nobility. At times all of these networks were intertwined in a chain of transmission and communication in which participants swapped bills of exchange, sex, contagious diseases, money, information, and even reputed surgeons. In each of them, Casanova had his entries, allies, and recommenders who directed him to others. To each he undoubtedly brought something of value in return: his own contacts, his wit, his charm, his craft of faro, or his storytelling art.

When Michel Serres, in the text quoted earlier, attributes to Hermès the capacity to "cross to the Other's site,"[6] he has in mind the cross-pollination of otherwise distinct areas of inquiry, from physics to science fiction, from mathematics to the novel, and so on. As a mediator, Casanova was an outstanding agent in such a circulation between different realms of knowledge, types of discourse, and even languages. Before he recreated himself as an author in a language he learned late – a feat of self-translation in its own right – he continually worked on all sorts of translations, transpositions, and appropriations. Engaging in what Serres calls a "commerce of found objects" meant in Casanova's case gleaning Kabbalah skills in manuals such as *Salomon's clavicula*; peppering his personal travel impressions with those lifted from books such as Ange Goudar's *Chinese Spy*, to which he contributed; constructing detailed descriptions of risk and gains based on an extensive practice of faro playing; and combining his interest in medicine and women in the pamphlet *Lana Caprina*.

So it was with translation proper. As a budding contender in the republic of letters, Casanova translated Homer from ancient Greek to Italian. The same strategy may have motivated his translation of Cahusac's tragedy *Zoroastre*, produced in the theatre; his "rewriting" in Italian of popular novels by Mme de Riccoboni; his parodic rendition of Racine's *La Thébaïde ou les frères ennemis* for a theatre in Dresden, where he combined linguistic translation and transposition from the genre of tragedy into comedy; and his translation of Voltaire's play *L'Ecossaise*. Other transposition endeavours were even more unusual: anticipating the French twentieth-century Oulipian writers, in Dresden he wrote an entire play without the sound "r," which the leading actress (whom he was courting) could not pronounce. It is evident that in this case the granting of favours was expected to be mutual. The interpenetration between different types of knowledge was even more apparent in his less-known elucubrations, such as the lengthy explanations of the Megamicres' language in *Icosameron*, a linguistic system that translates speech into tones and letters into colours. Casanova set up an entire euphonic system in which language consists solely of vowels, but to be understood, its value has to be set by an initial musical tone. The Megamicres' writing is carried out in several colours. What is more, their sociability is transmuted into a strange eroticism, since the androgynous creatures feel euphony not only through their hearing but also through "the entire skin that covers their body." An apex of the fantasy of mediation is found in yet another project Casanova described, consisting of a lottery that used letters rather than numbers.

He also practised that same art of "crossing to the Other's site" when he represented himself in Paris and London as a candid and naive traveller, a "Persian" of sorts inspired by Montesquieu, or when he nimbly took on the role of financial expert or hydraulic engineer, both equally foreign to him, to please the Prussian king. At times Casanova thus brokered non-existent know-how, predicting shipping risks to the banker and ship owner M.D.O., trading in foreign currencies for Mme d'Urfé, or explaining to French financiers the profit mechanism of the Genoese lottery. Whether as a *truchement* – the old French word for interpreter – or as a trickster, Casanova systematically assumed the role of the mediator in exchanges, for his profit.

Here we are reaching the more questionable features of Mercury, a protector god of thieves, pimps, and frauds. Casanova carefully trod and at times crossed the fine line between cheating and make-believe. One could say in his defence that his creative imagination was involved in his outright hoaxes no more than in his writing of *Icosameron*.[7] The same transposition was at play when he channelled his phenomenal libido, when it was no longer capable of bringing him real conquests, into the memorable erotic narrative of the *History of My Life*. Seduction by narration, as efficient as when he was entertaining real-life audiences, is at work there.

Seduction was also the prime domain in which Casanova admitted to taking on the role of Mercurio, a love messenger and go-between. He was well aware of this meaning, current in the eighteenth century: during his budding church career in Rome, he passed on love letters between his French tutor's daughter Barbaruccia and her secret lover, acknowledging that he should not have "constituted himself a Mercurio in that affair." He did it anyway, moved by her tears. When they eloped, he was fired by his protector and had to abandon the eternal city and all prospects of an ecclesiastical career. In the meantime, he had taken on the same role between the cardinal S.C. and the beautiful marquise de G., with a more venal intent. The cardinal, who had received a love sonnet from the poetically inclined marquise, did not feel capable of responding to it in verse and hired the young abbé as his ghostwriter. Casanova, soon attracted to the poetess, had to solve the difficult problem of how to seduce her: how to write the sonnet so that the marquise would know he did it, and that he knew she understood it, yet so that the cardinal would not be in the know. The project of inserting himself into the relationship and of ejecting one of its rightful participants – in other words, of reconfiguring the exchange to his benefit, a problem that Casanova repeatedly solved – was compounded here by the need to leave written traces of his intentions that would be visible to one interlocutor and invisible to the other. This effort can be viewed as a feat of mediation between two systems of interpretation, a sort of translation problem whose apex was acted out in a hilarious scène à trois in which the cardinal asked Casanova to read aloud for all three the marquise's poem and his (the cardinal's) alleged response, composed in fact by Casanova. Needless to say, the young man acquitted himself so perfectly that he was on the verge of reaping the benefits with the marquise when his stint as Barbaruccia's Mercurio cut short his stay in Rome.

It is noteworthy that Casanova owed the greatest love of his life, Henriette, precisely to translation, which – together with his mediating skills both as a *truchement* (interpreter) and a trickster – is skilfully thematized in his narrative. He first saw the young woman in the inn where he was staying; she was in bed with an army captain who spoke only Hungarian,

German, and Latin. Casanova heard him curse in Latin at the guards of the moral police, who barged into their room and threatened to arrest the couple if they could not produce a marriage certificate. After he intervened on their behalf, all three were invited to dinner by the general who had helped them get rid of the guards. Henriette, dressed as an officer, was treated as a man by the ladies, and as a woman in disguise by the men, a fact that enhanced her liberty and encouraged the erotic innuendos that pervaded the evening. Casanova recounts the following dialogue between her and an overly inquisitive lady:

Il est singulier, dit Mme Querini au masque, que vous puissiez vivre ensemble sans jamais parler. – Pourquoi singulier ? madame. Nous ne nous entendons pas à cause de cela moins bien, car la parole n'est pas nécessaire aux affaires que nous avons ensemble.

Cette réponse que le général traduisit en bon italien a toute la compagnie qui était à table, fit éclater de rire; mais Mme Querini fit la bégueule: elle la trouva trop démasquante. Je ne connais pas, dit-elle au faux officier, des affaires auxquelles la parole, ou du moins l'écriture ne soit nécessaire. – Vous m'excuserez madame. Est-ce que le jeu n'est pas une affaire? – Vous ne faites donc que jouer? – Pas autre chose. Nous jouons au pharaon; et je tiens la banque.

On rit alors à perte d'haleine; et Mme Querini dut en rire aussi. Mais la banque, dit le général, gagne-t-elle beaucoup? – Oh ! Pour cela. Le jeu est si petit qu'il ne vaut pas la peine de compter.

Personne ne se donna la peine de traduire cette réponse à l'honnête officier. (1:509)

"It is strange," said Signora Querini to the masquerader, "that you can live together and never speak to each other."

"Why strange, Signora? We understand each other none the worse, for speech is not necessary in the business we do together."

This answer, which the general translated into good Italian for the whole company at the table, provoked a burst of laughter; but Signora Querini affected the prude: she thought it too revealing.

"I do not know," she said to the pretended officer, "of any business in which speech, or at least writing, is not necessary."

"I beg your pardon, Signora. Is not gaming a business?"

"Then you do nothing but play cards?"

"Nothing else. We play faro, and I keep the bank." This time the laughter lasted until everyone was out of breath; and Signora Querini could not help laughing too.

"But does the bank," asked the general, "win a great deal?"

"Hardly. The stakes are so small that it's not worth counting up."

No one took the trouble to translate this answer for the worthy officer. (3:20–1)

After this exchange, Casanova, confident that he could establish a privileged understanding with the free-spirited adventuress, decided to accompany them to Parma and serve "as an interpreter between these two officers who could not understand each other," hoping to come to an "amicable arrangement." During the trip, he admits having some trouble with translation. When Henriette uttered "pleasantries" that made him laugh, Casanova, seeing the Hungarian officer frustrated because he did not understand, would try to translate her *mots d'esprit* into Latin, but he explained them so badly that the officer did not laugh. He was mortified by what he knew must be Henriette's poor opinion of his Latin, but admits that this opinion was justified. He had not yet realized then, as he did later, that "dans toutes les langues du monde ce qu'on apprend le dernier est leur esprit; et c'est très souvent le jargon qui fait la plaisanterie" (1:514) (In all the languages in the world what one learns last is their wit; and it is very often idiom which makes the joke [3:26]).

And yet, even though the intricacies of translation escaped him, Casanova understood perfectly the nature of his role as an interpreter: while facilitating the linguistic exchange, he needed to weave a bond between Henriette and himself, and at the same time exclude the third party, the "worthy officer." His bungled translations contributed to this strategy of insertion and ejection, one he had already perfected in the Roman love triangle mentioned earlier. Their *dialogue de sourds* continued through the ride to Parma: curious about their encounter, Casanova was told by Henriette that he should hear the story from the Hungarian captain, who proceeded to tell it in Latin after being reassured that such was indeed her will. Then, at her demand, Casanova reinterpreted the captain's story to her, laying out to each in turn the mutual terms of their initial arrangement and of their pending separation (the thirty sequins that the captain had promised her she absolutely refused, accepting only the ride to Parma and making the cruel request that the captain not recognize her if they ever met again). Acting simultaneously as the interpreter who registered their agreement and the notary who guaranteed the accuracy of its translation, Casanova thus interceded in their separation while negotiating in

French, a language he shared only with Henriette, his own intrusion into the couple. This episode amply illustrates his skill as a trickster adept at substituting himself for a rival, as does Mercury in Molière's *Amphitryon*.

But Casanova did not always derive a benefit from his brokering. The same lack of proprietary impulse governed his attitude to women and to material objects, which he often threw back into circulation under a logic that anthropologists have theorized as fundamental for creating the social bond. It is worth revisiting in this respect the anecdote cited early in this chapter, in which the Greek merchant to whom Casanova had sold his recipe for augmenting gold gave him as a parting present "a note good for a cask of muscat wine" and a "magnificent case containing twelve silver-handled razors." These objects were soon regifted: the razors were given to the bishop of Martorano, who was to be his superior but whom Casanova quickly abandoned, foregoing an ecclesiastical career; the wine, divided into two portions, was given to his host in Naples, where he headed after Martorano, and to a distant cousin whom he discovered there. In exchange, the latter presented him immediately with a cane "worth at least twenty once" and "a traveling suit and a blue redingote with gold buttonholes, all of the finest cloth" (1:247). From the verve with which Casanova carried out these gift exchanges and described them later, it is clear that though they were born of financial necessity, they and the bonds they created were ultimately in the service of Casanova's indomitable joie de vivre. Mercury, as we know from Molière's comedy, after all sought mostly pleasure and amusement. And perhaps the effect of their mediation – registering and weaving the social bond – is more important than the messages they delivered.

NOTES

1 Jean Baptiste Poquelin, Molière, *Œuvres complètes*, 2 vols. (Paris: Gallimard, 2010). The best English translation is by Richard Wilbur.

2 See Kevin Siena, ed., *Sins of the Flesh: Responding to Sexual Disease in Early Modern Europe* (Toronto: Center for Reformation and Renaissance Studies, Victoria University, 2005); and Claude Quétel, *The History of Syphilis*, trans. Judith Braddock and Brian Pike (Baltimore, MD: Johns Hopkins University Press, 1990).

3 See chap. 3.

4 Michel Serres, *Hermès I, Communication* (Paris: Minuit, 1969), 10. (My translation).

5 Their status, however, he mostly kept secret, and mapping their network was a daunting task for the Pléiade editors.

6 See 113.

7 As the gods' messenger, Mercury is privy to magic, since he transmits their messages of miracles and wonders to humans. Casanova as Mercury is playing with magic, going between its universe of belief, wonder, childhood, witchcraft, lightning, and Kabbalah, and the world of reason, calculation, Enlightenment, and disbelief. Part of his narrative charm lies in this capacity for recreating the magical quality of his life.

Chapter Six

Casanova, the Love of Paris

PIERRE SAINT-AMAND

This chapter examines Giacomo Casanova's account of his first trip to Paris, a sojourn he describes as his "first apprenticeship" in the title of the chapter (mon premier apprentissage) about the first version of this voyage.[1] This narrative can be read as the plot of a veritable Bildungsroman contained within the *History of My Life,* drawing on all the tropes that typify the genre. Casanova's apprenticeship can be tracked on multiple levels: he is schooled in French as he is inculcated with the forms of libertinage peculiar to the locale. As Chantal Thomas writes in her fine book on the memoirist, "At first glance, Paris struck him as the city par excellence, the city of fashion and speed, of imposture and quackery, elegance and wit…. It is thus the very hub of libertinage."[2]

Casanova's very arrival in Paris occurs under particularly novel-like conditions that introduce the traveller to French difference. As soon as the stagecoach leaves Lyons for Paris, he feels unwell from the unaccustomed movement of this strange vehicle: he describes an uncomfortable "oval" vessel that "ondoyait" (1:593) (rocked [3:118]). But this rocking motion is thoroughly unlike that of a Venetian gondola, and Casanova succumbs to nausea. His upset stomach exposes the young Italian to the scrutiny of his French fellow passengers and to new rules of politeness (he is subjected to a proper scolding). Casanova quickly overcomes his foreignness with his clever wit. His "bad company" is forgotten and he makes an ally of his former critic. Lessons in French and etiquette are traded. Casanova is told he must forsake his Italian candour in exchange for French guile. One does not say, he learns, that others are "wrong" but that they are "not right"; "no" must be forgotten, in favour of "pardon" (1:594; 3:119).

At first welcomed into the theatre milieu, Casanova rapidly penetrates elite Parisian society. One of his first encounters in the Balletti household is with the elder Crébillon. The young Italian impresses the playwright by reciting a scene from his *Rhadamiste et Zénobie*. Charming the venerable writer, Casanova wastes no time in landing none other than the renowned man of letters as his personal French tutor. Casanova winningly narrates his apprenticeship as if luck belonged on his side. In the scene where he meets Crébillon, the French lessons are preceded by the writer's predictions of a glorious future for the young man. Crébillon recognizes Casanova's originality and reveals to him the secrets of French society. For his part, Casanova manages to turn his poor mastery of French to his advantage. Here is how the scene unfolds:

Pour un premier jour je trouve, Monsieur, que vous promettez beaucoup. Vous ferez des progrès rapides. Je trouve que vous narrez bien. Vous parlez français à vous faire parfaitement comprendre; mais tout ce que vous avez dit, vous l'avez prononcé par des phrases italiennes. Vous vous faites écouter, vous intéressez, et vous attirez pour cette nouveauté une double attention de la part de ceux qui vous écoutent: je vous dirai même que votre jargon est fait pour vous captiver le suffrage de ceux qui vous écoutent car il est singulier, et nouveau, et vous êtes dans le pays où l'on court après tout ce qui est singulier; mais malgré tout cela vous devez commencer demain, pas plus tard à vous donner toutes les peines pour apprendre à bien parler notre langue, car dans deux, ou trois mois les mêmes qui vous applaudissent aujourd'hui commenceront à se moquer de vous. (1:604–5)

For a first day, Monsieur, I think you promise very well. You will make rapid progress. You tell your story excellently. You speak French in a way which is perfectly comprehensible; but all that you said, you put in Italian constructions. You make people listen to you, you arouse interest, and the novelty of your language renders your listeners doubly attentive; I will even say that your idiom is just the thing to gain their approval, for it is odd and new, and you are in the country where everything odd and new is sought after; nevertheless, you must begin tomorrow, and no later, to make every effort to learn to speak our language well, for in two or three months the same people who now applaud you will begin laughing at you. (3:133)

The meeting with Monsieur de Beauchamp, the tax collector, bears the same seal of good fortune. Again, we see the misplaced humour, the candour coloured with rudeness that Casanova knows how to put right, earning him the great man's friendship. At the Italian theatre, the Venetian traveller is dazzled by "les dames toutes chargées de diamants qui entraient dans les premières loges" (1:1040) (the ladies covered with diamonds who were entering the first-tier boxes [3:136]). He sizes up an "immensely stout" woman "covered with jewels" and escorted by "a richly dressed man." Exchanging civilities with this man, Casanova commits a faux pas by calling his interlocutor's wife a "grosse cochonne" (1:1040) (a fat sow [3:136]). But the misstep is quickly repaired by shared laughter, which forms a bond between the two men. Casanova ends up as a guest of this corpulent couple, who extend to him a true lesson in nobility and grace. As for his entry into the world of "excellent acquaintances," he writes, "J'ai trouvé dans cette maison la profusion qu'on trouvait à Paris chez toutes les personnes de cette espèce. Grande compagnie, gros jeu de commerce, et grande gaieté à table" (1:1041) (In their house I found the lavishness which was the rule among all people of their sort in Paris: a great crowd of guests, a great many parties at cards, and great gaiety at table [3:137]). This penetration into the dazzling universe of the elites is experienced by Casanova as a personal triumph of genius, an extraordinary and exceptional acceleration, a victory over commonplace time: "pour se faufiler [à Paris] il faut le temps. Pour ce qui me regarde je sais qu'en vingt-quatre heures je me suis vu déjà occupé, et sûr de m'y plaire" (1:1041) (It takes time to make one's way in [to Parisian society]. For my part, I know that in twenty-four hours I was already kept occupied and was sure that I would enjoy myself there [3:137]).

No doubt Parisian euphoria awaits him in the new connections he makes through his friendship with the famous Claude-Pierre Patu, the lawyer and poet who escorts him around Paris. The encounter with Mademoiselle Le Fel reveals to Casanova the reality of liaisons between actresses and noblemen. With humour and consternation, he discovers the strange hybrid offspring produced by these liaisons. At first he sees the actresses' libertinage in a naive and innocent light. Here, for example, is the incongruous little band living under Mademoiselle Le Fel's roof and the amused exchange between the Venetian and the opera actress:

Elle avait trois enfants en bas âge charmants, qui voltigeaient par la maison. Je les adore, dit-elle. La beauté de leur physionomie, lui répondis-je, a dans tous les trois un différent caractère. – Je le crois bien. L'aîné est fils du duc d'Aneci; celui-là est du comte d'Éguemont, et le cadet est fils de

Maisonrouge qui vient d'épouser la Romainville. – Ah ah! Excusez de grâce. J'ai cru que vous étiez la mère de tous les trois. – Je le suis aussi. (1:1041)

She had three small and charming children, who fluttered about the house.
  "I adore them," she said.
  "The beauty of their faces," I said, "is of a different sort in each of the three."
  "And well it may be. The eldest is the son of the Duke of Aneci, that one is by Count Egmont, and the youngest is the son of Maisonrouge, who has just married La Romainville."
  "Oh, oh. Excuse me, I beg you. I thought you were the mother of all three of them."
  "And so I am." (3:138)

As Casanova discovers these arrangements that defy convention, these genealogies muddled by the theatre of life, what causes him to smile is the scandal of the same and the deceit of difference. Such libertine arrangements can be related to Michel Foucault's distinction in *La Volonté de savoir* between the deployment of sexuality (dispositif de sexualité) and the deployment of alliance (dispositif d'alliance). The latter entails forms of control: "a system of marriage, of fixation and development of kinship ties, of transmission of names and possessions"; in contrast, the deployment of sexuality "has its reason for being, not in reproducing itself, but in proliferating, innovating, annexing, creating, and penetrating bodies in an increasingly detailed way." The deployment of alliance is buttressed by systems of law; that of sexuality operates on a footing of mobility and contingency.[3]

Mademoiselle Le Fel raises these "petits bâtards (1:1041) (little bastards [3:138]) in exchange for a pension, a life of comfort. Casanova's misunderstanding opens his eyes to the distinctive form of deployment that characterizes Parisian libertinage: the deployment of the *arrangement,* which is also endorsed by the libertine novel and easily accommodates official marriage bonds. A particularly rich example is found in Andréa de Nerciat's novel *Félicia ou mes fredaines,* which illustrates the gamut of arrangements while elaborating a theory of the practice. It all begins with the marriage of Sylvino and Sylvina, who adopt the eponymous Félicia. The young heroine is the first to be affected by the couple's infidelities. But the rest of the novel evolves through an accumulation of arrangements among the characters who parade successively through the narrative. "S'arranger" (coming to an agreement) becomes the catchphrase of this extensive libertine community, which is constantly in the process of recomposition. "Laissons tout ceci s'arranger" (Everything can be arranged), Monseigneur tells Félicia.[4] The couples that form are notable for operating alongside existing family relationships: daughter (Félicia) and adoptive father (Sylvino), uncle (Monseigneur) and nephew (d'Aiglemont). This logic of transient arrangement dictates the outlines of future relations, such as between Milord Sidney and Monrose. The foursomes continue to play out in keeping with the novel's moral touchstone: "We found no one who would object to this arrangement" (nous n'avions personne qui pût trouver à redire à cet arrangement).[5] Nerciat's arrangements must be understood within the larger framework of hospitality and friendship.

A similar situation is revealed to Casanova through the case of his friend Carlino Bertinazzi. Invited to dine at the home of the actor's landlady, Casanova discovers another anomalous familial arrangement revolving around uncertain paternity: "Il m'a donné un beau dîner chez Madame de la Caillerie, où il logeait. Cette femme était amoureuse de lui. Elle avait quatre enfants qui voltigeaient par la maison; j'ai fait mon compliment à son mari sur les grâces de ces petits, et le mari me répondit qu'ils appartenaient à Carlin" (1:1046) (He gave me a fine dinner in the house of Madame de La Caillerie, where he was lodging. The lady was in love with him. She had four children, who fluttered about the house; I complimented her husband on their childish charm, and her husband replied that they were Carlino's [3:146]). Casanova is impressed with the wisdom and decency of this arrangement. Madame de La Caillerie's husband, he concludes, is an "honnête homme" (a decent man), and he comes up with an apt assessment of this affair: "Il aimait Carlin autant que sa femme l'aimait avec la seule différence que les conséquences de sa tendresse n'était pas celles qui font naître des enfants" (1:1047) (He loved Carlino as much as his wife loved him, with only the difference that the consequences of his fondness were not those which result in children being born [3:147]). Here we witness an original staging of paternity, with attribution that is shared, alternating, and liberated from parental functions. The lover is matter-of-factly the natural father. Turning again to the children, Casanova makes a show of concern:

[– M]ais en attendant c'est vous qui en avez soin, et c'est vous qu'ils doivent reconnaître pour père, et dont ils porteront le nom. – Oui: cela serait en droit; mais Carlin est trop honnête homme pour ne pas s'en charger,

quand il me viendra dans l'esprit de m'en défaire. Il sait bien qu'ils sont à
lui, et ma femme serait la première à s'en plaindre s'il n'en convenait pas.
(1:1046–7)

But in the meanwhile it is you who take care of them, and it is you whom
they should recognize as their father, whose name they will bear.
    Yes, that would be so in law; but Carlino is too decent a man not to look
after them when I take it into my head to get rid of them. He knows very
well that they are his, and my wife would be the first to complain if he did
not admit it. (3:146)

Casanova considers the traffic in names, the swapping of women
between Parisian marriages, the slippage of symbolic paternity, as an
ordinary matter, an amusing slub in the fabric of lineage. Such recom-
bined couplings are ultimately fodder for merriment:

Deux des plus grands seigneurs de la France troquèrent de femme très
paisiblement, et eurent des enfants qui portèrent le nom non pas de leur
vrai père, mais du mari de leur mère; il n'y a pas un siècle que cela est arrivé
(Bouflers et Luxembourg), et les descendants de ces enfants sont connus
aujourd'hui sous le même nom. (1:1047)

Two of the greatest noblemen of France changed wives quite calmly and had
children who bore the names not of their real fathers but of their mothers'
husbands; this happened not a century ago (Boufflers and Luxembourg),
and the descendants of their children go under the same names today.
(3:147)

In the *History of My Life*, Casanova plays the role not only of judge but
of party to these frivolous combinatorics, as revealed by the episode with
Corallina, daughter of the actor Pantalon (Carlo Veronese) and mistress to the prince of Monaco. The Venetian is embraced by the couple
(he notes that he shares the same "illicit hours" (heures indues) as the
official lover, producing an amusing trio: "Dans les premières rencon-
tres je tirais la révérence et je m'en allais, mais dans la suite on me disait
de rester, car les princes tête à tête de leurs maîtresses ordinairement ne
savent que faire. Nous soupions en trois" (1:1047) (On the first few of
these occasions I bowed and left, but later I was asked to stay, for princes
alone with their mistresses usually do not know what to do. The three
of us would sup together [3:147]). Once, thinking he might negotiate

Corallina's favours in the absence of the prince of Monaco, Casanova finds the tables turned on him as, supplanted by another lover, he must forfeit the promised tête-à-tête. In Casanova's words, "Le prince de Monaco, me dit-elle, ne reviendra de Versailles qu'après-demain. Nous irons demain à la Garenne, nous dînerons tête à tête, nous chasserons au furet, et nous reviendrons à Paris contents" (1:1048) ("The prince of Monaco," she said, "will not return from Versailles until the day after tomorrow. Tomorrow we will go to the warren, we will dine together in private, have a hunt with a ferret, and come back to Paris satisfied" [3:149]). The journey is, however, suddenly interrupted when Coraline is whisked away from Casanova at a crossroads in a lightning-fast swap of carriages:

> Le lendemain à dix heures nous montons dans un cabriolet, et nous voilà à la barrière de Vaux-Girard. Au moment de la passer voilà un vis-à-vis à livrée étrangère qui nous rencontre: Arrête, arrête.
>
> C'était le chevalier de Wirtemberg qui sans même me daigner d'un regard, commence à dire des douceurs à Coraline … puis elle me dit, en me prenant la main et toute riante: J'ai une grande affaire avec ce prince: allez à la Garenne, mon cher ami, dînez-y, chassez et venez me voir demain. En me disant cela, elle descend, elle monte dans le vis-à-vis, et elle me plante. (1:1048–9)

> The next morning at ten o'clock we get into a cabriolet and are soon at the Vaugirard barrier. Just as we are going through, along comes a vis-à-vis with a foreign livery: "Stop, stop!"
>
> It was the Chevalier de Württemberg, who, not condescending to give me even a look, begins flattering Corallina … she … then, taking my hand and with her face all smiles, says:
>
> "I have important business with the Prince: go to the warren, my dear friend, dine there, hunt, and come to see me tomorrow."
>
> So saying, she steps out, gets into the *vis-à-vis*, and abandons me. (3:149)

Casanova's ire of course propels him directly to the bordello of the Hôtel du Roule. While his visit to this place is intended to "cool him off" in his pursuit of Corallina – even though he does find a lookalike – he nevertheless returns to her story to relate a series of interlocking affairs, a concatenation of baroque genealogies. Corallina's restored relation with the prince of Monaco even provides the narrator with the opportunity to emphasize these arrangements, these families born of transitory liaisons. Casanova rattles off the substitutions of lovers and husbands:

> Mais Coraline sut tant faire qu'elle se raccommoda un mois après avec le prince et de si bonne foi qu'elle lui donna au bout de neuf mois un poupon. Ce fut une fille qu'elle appela Adélaïde et que le prince dota. Puis le prince la quitta après la mort du duc de Valentinois pour aller épouser Mademoiselle Brignole génoise, et Coraline devint maîtresse du comte de la Marche, qui est aujourd'hui le prince de Conti. (1:1051–2)

> Corallina managed to patch it up with the Prince a month later, and to such effect that nine months later she gave him a child. It was a girl, whom she named Adélaïde and whom the Prince dowered. Then the Prince left her after the death of the Duke of Valentinois to marry Signorina Brignole, of Genoa, and Corallina became the mistress of Count de La Marche, who is now Prince of Conti. (3:153)

But of all the arrangements on the Parisian landscape, the spectacle that without a doubt dazzles the young traveller most of all is that of the adulterous couple formed by Louis XV and his mistress, Madame de Pompadour. They are the resplendent model for all the extramarital intrigues that abound in the court and the city alike. The narrator tries to get as close as possible to the libertine couple. When he visits Fontainebleau with Mario Balletti to attend an opera, Casanova is seated beneath Madame de Pompadour's box and ends up conversing with the king's mistress, playing as he so often does on his foreign nationality. A single (and still famous) quip suffices to impress her:

> Ma réponse un peu verte fit rire Madame de Pompadour, qui me demande si j'étais vraiment de là-bas. – D'où donc? – De Venise. – Venise, Madame, n'est pas là-bas; elle est là-haut. (1:1053)

> My rather sharp answer brought a laugh from Madame de Pompadour, who asked me if I really came from "down there."
> "From where?"
> "From Venice."
> "Venice, Madame, is not down; it is up." (3:155)

Later, when Casanova appears at the court of Fontainebleau, he is dazzled by the person of Louis XV, in particular by the king's head, and it is through Madame de Pompadour's desire that he manages to contemplate the royal majesty and perceive the indescribable grace of the monarch's gaze upon his subjects:

[Je] vois le Roi qui passe se tenant appuyé avec un bras à travers les épaules de M. d'Argenson. La tête de Louis XV était belle à ravir, et plantée sur son cou l'on ne pouvait pas mieux. Jamais peintre très habile ne put dessiner le coup de tête de ce monarque lorsqu'il le tournait pour regarder quelqu'un.... Je me suis trouvé certain que Madame de Pompadour était devenue amoureuse de cette physionomie, lorsqu'elle parvint à se procurer sa connaissance. (1:1054)

I see the King pass supporting himself with one arm around Monsieur d'Argenson's shoulders. Louis XV's head was ravishingly beautiful and set on his neck to perfection. Not even a most skillful painter could draw the attitude the monarch gave it when he turned to look at someone.... I felt certain that Madame de Pompadour had already fallen in love with that countenance when she contrived to make his acquaintance. (3:156–7)

Casanova's relation with the licentious king is also exalted in his account of the O'Morphy sisters. The memoirist becomes a strange mediator, a go-between in the younger sister Louison's liaison with the king, accomplishing a handoff that affords the Venetian a royal thrill. Indeed, the commodification that will deliver the young woman directly into the monarch's bed begins with a portrait of her commissioned by Casanova (with the complicity of her elder sister, an Irish actress at the Opéra-Comique who had worked in Flanders):

J'ai dépensé six louis pour la faire peindre toute nue d'après nature par un peintre allemand qui la fit vivante. Elle était couchée sur son ventre, s'appuyant de ses bras, et de sa gorge sur son oreiller, et tenant sa tête comme si elle était couchée sur son dos.... J'y ai fait écrire dessous *O-Morphi*. Mot qui n'est pas homérique, mais qui n'est pas moins grec. Il signifie *Belle*. (1:1084)

I paid six louis to have her painted naked by a German painter, who produced a living likeness. She was lying on her stomach, resting her arms and her bosom on a pillow and holding her head as if she were lying on her back.... I had him write under it *O-Morphi*. The word is not Homeric, but it is Greek none the less. It means "beautiful." (3:200)

A copy of this portrait ends up making the rounds at Versailles, burning itself into the king's eyes and making him demand to see the original, the incarnation of "beauty"; Casanova calls her "Helen," after the Greek model: "La Morphi tressaillit de joie quand je lui ai dit qu'il s'agissait d'aller à la cour avec sa sœur et avec le peintre conducteur.... J'ai su le surlendemain de la Morphi même qu'une demi-heure après le roi vint seul ... tira de sa poche le portrait, regarda bien la petite, et dit: *Je n'ai jamais vu rien de plus ressemblant*" (1:1085) (La Morphy jumped for joy when I told her that she was to go to court with her sister under conduct of the painter.... I learned the next morning from La Morphy herself that a half hour later the King came, alone ... drew the portrait from his pocket, looked carefully at her younger sister, and said: "*I have never seen a better likeness*" [3:200–1]).

The end of this adventure is no surprise: O-Morphi ends up installed in an apartment in the legendary Parc aux Cerfs, Louis XV's famous "seraglio." The elder sister receives no less than "a thousand louis" in exchange for Helen's captivity. The actress thanks Casanova for making her rich: "Mon grand plaisir fut celui de voir la joie de cette bonne Flamande qui, contemplant cinq cents doubles louis, se croyait devenue riche, et qui me regardait comme l'auteur de sa fortune" (1:1085–6) (What gave me the most pleasure was seeing the joy of the worthy Flemish girl, who, gazing at five hundred double louis, thought she was rich, and who considered me the first cause of her good fortune [3:200–1]).

As in his previous Parisian adventures, Casanova is particularly fascinated by the offspring born of these liaisons, the "other" family of transgression. In fact, the fruit of the king's relation with Helen O-Morphi is a bastard son, tactfully hidden from the queen: "La petite au bout de l'an accoucha d'un fils qui est allé on ne sait pas où, car Louis XV ne voulant rien savoir des bâtards qu'il eut tant que la reine Marie vécut" (1:1086) (At the end of a year the girl bore a son, who became no one knows what, for Louis XV would never hear anything about his bastards as long as Queen Marie was alive [3:202]). This does not prevent Casanova from constructing a destiny for the son that brings him together with another child of Louison, born of her marriage to an officer. In the *History of My Life*, Casanova adroitly crosses the paths of these two children, the bastard and the legitimate son, the royal and the low-born.[6] And the text interweaves the two portraits, uniting the image of commodification and the image of legitimate birth: "O-Morphi fut disgraciée au bout de trois ans. Le roi lui donna quatre cent mille francs qu'elle porta en dot à un officier de l'état-major en Bretagne. J'ai vu un fils de ce mariage

François Boucher, *Girl Reclining*, 1751

l'année 1783 à Fontainebleau. Il avait vingt-cinq ans, et il ne savait rien de l'histoire de sa mère, dont il était le vrai portrait" (1:1086) (O-Morphi fell into disgrace after three years. The King gave her four thousand francs, which she brought as a dowry to a staff officer in Brittany. I saw a son from this marriage at Fontainebleau in the year 1783. He was twenty-five years of age, and he did not know the story of his mother, whose living image he was [3:202]).

We encounter a very different impression with another celebrated visitor to Paris: Saint-Preux in Rousseau's *Julie ou La Nouvelle Héloïse*.[7] His visit to the city provides an interesting intertext for Casanova's memoirs. As with Casanova, Saint-Preux's experience of libertinage begins early in his sojourn. Certain episodes of the "Lettres parisiennes" form a strange parallel to the *History of My Life*: for example, Saint-Preux visits a brothel, as does Casanova, who ends up at the Hôtel du Roule. If Casanova makes his way there in good cheer and of his own volition, Saint-Preux in contrast places the onus for his visit on blindness or the trickery of the senses. Practically pushed there by Swiss officers who want him to "changer de ton" (212) (change my tone [241]), he arrives at a woman's house, where he immediately feels alienated: "je vis à des bras de cheminées de vieilles bougies ... et partout un certain

air d'apprêt qui ne me plût point" (Upon entering I saw in chimney
sconces old candles that had just been lit, and overall a certain affected
air that pleased me not at all). As for "this order of women" (cet ordre
de femmes) that he encounters in the house, they strike Saint-Preux
as "société dégoütante" (213) (disgusting company [242]). In contrast,
Casanova finds Madame Pâris's women at the Hôtel du Roule to be
pleasant, refined company. But in the end, Julie's lover succumbs to
the "agaceries" (214) (provocations [242]) of these same women and
to the haze of white wine (which Saint-Preux mistakes for water) and
finds himself in "un cabinet reculé, entre les bras d'une de ces créatures" (214) (a distant chamber, in the arms of one of those creatures
[244]). Rousseau's traveller, who writes under Julie's critical eye, dis-
tances himself from this Parisian experience with nothing short of
disgust. Saint-Preux pronounces a severe judgment upon Parisian marriages. Though both foreign visitors are to some extent overwhelmed,
Saint-Preux feels none of Casanova's euphoria. For him, Paris remains
above all the city of "liaisons secrètes (193) (secret affairs [221]); it
runs wild with "la galanterie (193) (amorous adventures) that cor-
rupt the union of the two sexes. Saint-Preux pursues his denunciation
of what he terms "ces étranges usages" (194) (these strange customs
[223]) of the city:

> L'adultère n'y révolte point, on n'y trouve rien de contraire à la bienséance ...
> et le désordre n'est plus blâmable sitôt qu'il est joint à l'infidélité.... On
> dirait que le mariage n'est pas à Paris de la même nature que partout
> ailleurs. C'est un sacrement, à ce qu'ils prétendent, et ce sacrement n'a
> pas la force des moindres contrats civils; il semble n'être que l'accord de
> deux personnes libres qui conviennent de demeurer ensemble, de porter le
> même nom, de reconnaître les mêmes enfants, mais qui n'ont, au surplus,
> aucune sorte de droit l'une sur l'autre. (193–4)

> Adultery causes no revulsion, nothing about it goes against propriety ...
> and license is no longer blameworthy, the minute it is combined with
> infidelity.... One would say that marriage in Paris is not of the same nature
> as everywhere else. It is a sacrament, at least that is what they pretend, and
> this sacrament lacks the force of the most minor civil contracts: it seems to
> be no more than the consent of two free persons who agree to live together,
> to bear the same name, to recognize the same children; but who have, other
> than that, no sort of claim to each other. (222)

If Casanova chooses to dismantle the symbolic power of marriage, to expose the transfer of names as a game, Saint-Preux, for his part, upholds not only the sacred status of the marriage union, but also the force of law that is threatened by Parisian marriages (they are from start to finish all-embracing parodies of the legal system). These marriages do not even achieve the status of a contract; they are legal unions that imitate free unions, by a simple "consent" whereby "les époux sont ici des garçons et des filles qui demeurent ensemble pour vivre avec plus de liberté" (194) (spouses here are bachelors and maidens who live together in order to enjoy greater freedom [222]). Marriage in Paris has sold out to mere "commodité" (convenience), an informal "vivre ensemble" (194) (being together [222]) with no loftier aim than "s'arranger" (194) (making arrangements [222]). Casanova's mirth is thus drowned out by the grinding of Rousseau's teeth.

In fact, we find the Parisian model of unions in Casanova's own stories. The *History of My Life* stages many instances of paternal ambiguity, the great gesture of uncertain progeny. The play of resemblance, hesitation, and secrecy in the theatre of filiation, the sublimation of blood into the virtuality of alliances, and the joyful dissemination of Casanova's portrait along the genealogical line of transmission from parent to child never cease to delight the memoirist.[8]

Another area of contrast between Casanova and Rousseau is the Parisian public scene. It provides Saint-Preux the experience of a strange performance of sexual identity, a dangerous crossing where the sexes lose their respective essences in favour of reciprocal imitation and specular seduction. The promiscuity of men and women in the city of Paris becomes the stage for a transposition of one gender to another. There are, he mentions, women who simulate masculinity to the shock of the foreign observer. They lose "la grâce de leur sexe") (something of their sex's grace), Saint-Preux writes, in favour of "manière intrépide" (192) (an intrepid … manner [220]), "maintien soldatesque" (191) (a soldier-like demeanor [219]); natural modesty plays out instead as masculine "hardiesse" (brazen approach [220]). (They are very different in that regard from Swiss women, who confirm their identity by bonding with one another, imitating one another, keeping among themselves.) This is not the case in Paris, where "les femmes n'aiment à vivre qu'avec les hommes; elles ne sont à leur aise qu'avec eux" (192) (women like spending their time with men, only in their presence are they at ease [220–1]) forming a sort of "gynécocratie" (192) (gynecocracy [220]). The same of course goes for men: "Paris est plein d'aventuriers et de célibataires qui passent leur vie à courir de maison en maison, et les hommes semblent comme les espèces se multiplier par la circulation. C'est donc là qu'une femme apprend à parler et penser comme eux, et eux comme elle" (192) (Paris is full of adventurers and bachelors who spend their lives running from house to house, and men like money seem to multiply by circulating. So that is where a woman learns to speak, act, and think like them, and they like her [221]). We know the power of attraction that such women exercise on Casanova. We may remember especially an unforgettable conquest in an inn between Bologna and Rimini: Henriette, dressed in an officer's uniform, which Casanova calls a costume of "caprice" 1:508), and spoken of in the masculine: "Cette fille n'avait que l'habit d'homme qui la couvrait, pas la moindre nippe de femme; pas seulement une chemise. Elle en changeait avec celles qui appartenaient à son ami. Cela me semblait nouveau et énigmatique" (1:514) (The girl had nothing but the male attire she was wearing, not a scrap of woman's clothing, not even a shirt. When she changed hers, she put on one of her lover's. This was something as new to me as it was puzzling [3:26]). Her seduction blossoms in the way feminine beauty becomes augmented by a man's outfit and coiffure.[9] In the end, it is no accident that she happened to be ... a French woman.

The chronicle of Paris shows us a Casanova enjoying exactly this status of adventurer and bachelor, opening up his spirit and body to the joyful circulation so maligned by Jean-Jacques Rousseau.[10]

NOTES

1　*Histoire de ma vie* (Paris: Gallimard, 2013–16), appendix, 1, 1030. (I quote principally from this first redaction of vol. 3, 1019–1109).

2　Chantal Thomas, *Casanova, Un voyage libertin* (Paris: Denoël, 1986), 91. Where no English edition is cited, quotations are translated by Jennifer Curtiss Gage.

3　See Michel Foucault, *La Volonté de savoir* (Paris: Gallimard, 1976), 140–1; Foucault, *The Will to Knowledge*, vol. 1 of *The History of Sexuality*, trans. Robert Hurley (New York: Random House, 1978), 106–7.

4　Andréa de Nerciat, *Félicia ou mes fredaines*, in *Romans libertins du XVIIIe siècle* (Paris: Laffont, 1993), 1107.

5　de Nerciat, *Félicia*, 1183.

6　On the fiction of Casanova's own illegitimate birth, see François Roustang,

The Quadrille of Gender: Casanova's Memoirs (Stanford: Stanford University Press, 1988), 31–2.

7 *Julie ou La Nouvelle Héloïse* (Paris: Garnier-Flammarion, 1967); *Julie, or, The New Heloise*, trans. Philip Stewart and Jean Vaché, in *The Collected Writings of Rousseau*, ed. Roger D. Masters and Christopher Kelly (Lebanon, NH: Hanover University Press of New England for Dartmouth, 1997). All references to *Julie* are made in the body of the text, indicated by the page number.

8 Indeed, Casanova gloats over what François Roustang calls "the salad of generations," referring to the trouble about paternity that he exploits, especially the confusion that comes from children born of unions on which he throws a veil of doubt and secrecy. I refer again to *Le Bal masqué de Giacomo Casanova*, 163. But the entire chapter 12 about the transgression of difference is useful.

9 Later, seeking an "arrangement" with Henriette's companion, a Hungarian officer, Casanova is thrilled about dressing her up as a woman. He searches for a panoply of feminine accoutrements for her, shopping for new adornments: "Il me faut de la fine toile pour faire vingt-quatre chemises à une femme, du basin pour faire des jupons, et des corsets, de la mousseline, des mouchoirs, et d'autres articles ... robes, bonnets, mantelets, tout enfin" (1:527) (I need fine linen to make twenty-four chemises for a woman, dimity to make petticoats and corsets, muslin, handkerchiefs, and other things.... Dresses, hats, mantles, in short everything [3:41–2]).

10 Translated from the French by Jennifer Curtiss Gage.

Chapter Seven

Paris in Three Movements

CHANTAL THOMAS

Casanova travelled to Paris four times, between 1750 and 1767, following his changing ambitions. I will not speak here of the short visit of July 1761, since it produced nothing of consequence for Casanova's evolution. This is not the case with the other three visits.

His first stay, between 1750 and 1752, was a time of discovery: "I was new," he writes in his memoirs. He is twenty-five years old. He is "new," and the world he discovers appears new to his eyes. He trembles with astonishment and admiration. He can hardly get his fill of the spectacle that is Paris. The other side of this, or rather what coats such a state of excitement before the unknown, is a feeling of ignorance, of fragility: the fear of harming somebody, of talking nonsense: "Dans le commencement de mon séjour à Paris il me semblait d'être devenu le plus coupable des hommes car je ne faisais que demander pardon" (1:594) (At the beginning of my stay in Paris, it seemed to me that I had become the guiltiest of men, for I did nothing but beg pardon [3:120]). And he indeed often has good reason to ask for forgiveness. For example, the time when at the Comédie Italienne he points out to his neighbour, a very fat man, an enormous woman covered in diamonds, and asks, "Qui est donc cette grosse cochonne? – Monsieur; c'est la femme de ce gros cochon. – Ah! Monsieur! Je suis un étourdi, et je vous en demande mille pardons" (1:608) ("Who on earth is that fat sow?" and the man answers, "She is the wife of this fat pig," to which Casanova replies, "Ah! Monsieur, I am a fool and I ask for a thousand pardons" [3:136, modified]). Usually when Casanova acts in a ridiculous manner, he becomes furious and is totally set apart from those who laugh, but in Paris he justifies those who make fun of him, for he has only two desires: to acquire their knowledge, and to possess the same assurance in the use of the French language, the forms of sociability, and sartorial elegance.

The fact that Casanova is a foreigner is immediately revealed to the Parisian public by his outmoded clothes. That he is Italian is apparent as soon as he opens his mouth. With humility, the young man accepts the warning of the great Crébillon: in the beginning his mistakes in French may cause laughter (a laughter without malevolence), but they will quickly become a handicap. The man speaking is Crébillon the Elder, the playwright with a noble tongue, the author of tragedies, and a royal censor. Casanova never mentions Crébillon *fils*, his son, the libertine writer whose books such as *Le sopha* and *La nuit et le moment* were well crafted to provoke the father's censorship.

This silence indicates Casanova's extreme care to avoid expressing a libertine philosophy. This is doubtless in part a choice, and in part the expression of a singular temperament. In fact, all the while multiplying his seductions, Casanova never sees in himself "the cold gaze of the libertine" (to use Roger Vailland's title.) He loves to love and to be loved. He adores falling in love and relishes it when his sexual adventures unfold in a sentimental atmosphere: tender moments and tears are welcome. Endowed with compassion, he is always happy to revel and to spend his money, and more generally to offer pleasure, whether by organizing parties or by arranging marriages, not without having had – in passing and in all innocence – his pleasure with the bride. (This according to the formula: "Love, Madame, is a blank check.") Casanova is fond of effusive scenes, of gratitude. He is thus situated at the very opposite of those principles defended, developed, theorized, and embodied by the Sadian libertines, or by the couple Merteuil-Valmont in Laclos's *Les Liaisons dangereuses* (Dangerous liaisons]), principles according to which one can do anything and everything, transgress all prohibitions (this is even recommended), *except* fall in love, become dependent on another person. To love is the supreme error.

"Do you love, Juliette?" asks Saint-Fond in Sade's *L'Histoire de Juliette, ou les Prospérités du vice*. Answer: "I love nothing, Saint-Fond, I have only caprices." In reality she is in love, as Valmont is in love with la Présidente. But confronted with the laws of libertinage, they dare not admit this, and thus sacrifice the beloved object. In contrast, Casanova does not hesitate to answer the question, "Are you in love?" He proclaims, feverish and exalted, "Yes, I'm in love!" He succeeds in that strange alchemy of immediately transforming his innumerable whims – born from the purely libertine impulse of curiosity – into love stories, or at least into amorous moments. He certainly seduces, but only to better taste the euphoria of love. Thus he does not see himself on the side of Crébillon *fils* but rather of Crébillon the Elder, and in painting – if he had to state his preference – not on the side of Fragonard, creator of the famed painting *Le Verrou*, but on that of Greuze, the painter of fluttering rosy-cheeked girls, of scenes of return and forgiveness where tears flow endlessly.

Discreet concerning his libertine acquaintances – he behaves like them, but with the added exigence of feeling in love – Casanova does not linger before beginning another apprenticeship in the French language, this time not with a virtuous author, but in bad company: "Mais j'ai appris de toi des mots que je n'ai jamais entendu sortir de sa bouche: *à gogo, frustratoire, dorloter.* Qui te les a appris? La bonne compagnie de Paris, Mme de Boufflers, par exemple" (1:795) ("I have learned words from you which I never heard pass his lips: *à gogo* (galore), *frustratoire* (frivolous), *dorloter* (to coddle): Who taught them to you?" "Good society in Paris, Mme Boufflers, for example" [4:67]). Thus, he maintains total silence concerning the bad company of gamblers, libertines, and all those marginal types whom he frequents in Paris and elsewhere, characters for whom acting and speaking correctly were hardly the major goals.

During his first stay in Paris, Casanova immediately understands the prestige of appearance. He obeys the rule of fashion, of a city where it is not being but appearance that decides your fate. Casanova is ready for adventure: "Encore une duchesse! Mon âme nageait dans la joie" (1:616) (Another Duchess! I asked nothing better" [3:148]). Where Rousseau denounces the horrors of alienation, Casanova chants the pleasures of inventing oneself, of creating one's own character. From this point of view, while in writing the *History of My Life* he is nourished and occasionally directly influenced by Rousseau's *Confessions,* in his most private convictions and in his existential philosophy he never ceases to oppose them. Appearance, that abyss of vanity, that deceptive mirror that for Rousseau constitutes absolute evil, to the contrary opens up, for Casanova, an entire field of possibilities, the domains of play and freedom. These two passions are at the heart of his personality and are effectively displayed in the *History of My Life.* Casanova's autobiographical tale may be read as the staging of a tireless desire to play, in the double sense of amusement and gambling. The intellectual opposition between the two cannot be better illustrated than by Casanova's visit to Rousseau in the company of the marquise d'Urfé, in 1759. Rousseau's austere lifestyle depresses Casanova, as does the vision of a man of genius living with Thérèse, an illiterate servant woman. The picture that Casanova paints lets us imagine the daily existence of the philosopher, with his violent critique of Parisian women, those *mondaines* who, instead of remaining discreetly at home, endlessly go out into the world. Rousseau condemns their frivolity, their desire to shine, their unbridled taste for conversation (see *La Nouvelle Héloïse*). The woman who hosts a salon is evidently an abomination. It is interesting to note that for the misogynists – and here I am thinking of Schopenhauer and Nietzsche – women are detestable insofar as they are natural beings, creatures of physiological reproduction. Or, conversely, when they have spiritual intentions. Everything that Rousseau denounces is precisely what pleases Casanova. If for himself he values love and freedom above all else, he also appreciates these qualities in a woman (see his tale of Henriette).

During this visit in his youth, placed under the sign of astonishment and rapture, Casanova's ambition is only literary, as he states to his teacher Crébillon: "Mon principal projet venant ici fut celui de me donner de toute ma force à l'étude de votre langue, et de votre littérature" (1:603) (My principal purpose in coming here was to apply myself entirely to the French language and French literature [3:134]). Even if he has dreamt of spending his entire life in Paris, he in no way attempts to do so. In "good society" and confronted with money and power, Casanova distinguishes between three types of behaviour: *se faufiler* (to slip into the superior caste of society without notice), *figurer* (to take the stage and succeed in one's performance), and *en imposer* (to be simultaneously actor and director; to create one's own spectacle; to manipulate the credulous). At the age of twenty-five, still "new," Casanova is thrilled to be accepted so easily. He is happy just "*se faufiler*" (slipping in)

On his second stay, from 5 January 1757, to 1 December 1759, Casanova is already thirty-two years old. He has just escaped from the Leads prison in Venice. He is determined to move to Paris and show off his talents: "Que voudriez-vous faire à Paris? –Qu'y ferez-vous vous-même? – Je mettrai à profit mes talents" (1:1012) (What do you expect to do in Paris? – What would you do there yourself? – I will turn my talents to account [5:14]). He uses the tale of his escape from prison as a letter of recommendation. And it works! He proposes a royal lottery and obtains it; he is consulted on several secret missions, including that of writing a report on the French naval forces. It seems that he succeeds in everything; and when he fails, as with his fabric manufacturing project, he finds the endeavour nevertheless entertaining. He pretends to have occult powers and captivates the rich marquise d'Urfé, herself moonstruck with alchemy. In an irresolvable ambiguity between credulousness and cynicism, he promises her the very extravagances that she desires, inventing surreal episodes. Paris shines with all its lights, and pleasure follows him everywhere.

Casanova is at the peak of his powers, in full enjoyment of his sexual resources and of his talent for transforming life into a theatre of a thousand unexpected developments. Thanks to the allowance granted him by his Venetian protector, to the lottery, and to the encounter with the marquise d'Urfé, he finds himself with a small fortune. In the *History of My Life,* the word *fortune* means both "luck" and "wealth."

One thing he was told during his first stay in Paris has lost none of its timeliness: "Vous êtes en France, monsieur, où l'on connaît le prix de la vie, et où l'on tâche d'en tirer parti" (1:614) (You are in France, Monsieur, where people know what life is worth and try to make the most of it [3:144]). Paris is always the "charming Paris" of the young man for whom everything is new. The world stage seems completely open to him. He takes the stage and, concerning Mme d'Urfé, he manipulates.

During his last stay in Paris in autumn 1767, the flower of youth has faded. Casanova is now forty-two years old, which in those times and in his case is a weighty number. In fact, all notations of Casanova's age are important. First because of the extreme attention he attaches to his physical capacities: his health, his sexual prowess, and his appetite, in the broad sense of the word, that is to say, his eagerness for nourishment and his enthusiasm for taking advantage of life. (It is not by chance that medicine was his first choice of career.) Second, because – and this is related – far from privileging strategizing, Casanova counts on the brilliance of his presence. One would say, in the language of the stage, that he counts on his *entrances.* In his portraits of libertines, Sade always includes two numbers: their age and the amount of money at their disposal. Casanova does so as well. But in contrast to what occurs in Sade's universe, where money always comes from crime (such that the older the libertine, the richer he is), Casanova becomes poorer and poorer with age. Unfortunately for him, the numbers indicating his age and his fortune are in inverse proportion. The goddess Fortune loves only the young. She is ready to abandon Casanova. Nothing remains the same. His protector, M. de Bragadin, has died. The marquise d'Urfé becomes inaccessible (in his memoirs, Casanova declares her dead); the city is unrecognizable: "J'ai trouvé non seulement des nouveaux bâtiments qui ne me laissaient plus connaître les rues, mais des rues neuves toutes entières, et si singulièrement composées dans leur architecture, que je m'y perdais. Paris me paraissait devenu un labyrinthe" (3:422) (I found not only new buildings which kept me from recognizing the streets, but whole new streets, and so strange in their architecture that I lost my way in them. Paris seemed to me to have become a labyrinth [10:290]). This is a "new world," and this newness – unlike the exciting novelties of his previous stays – repels him. To add to his distress, Charlotte – the young pregnant woman whose protector he has become and whom he has begun to love – dies in childbirth. (The destiny of Charlotte, dead at seventeen years of age, is in itself material for a novel. And this is true for a great number of secondary characters in the Casanovian text.) Casanova is in despair. Fearful of feeling the flame of happiness extinguished in him, he makes a resolution: "j'ai vu que si je n'oubliais pas Charlotte, j'étais un homme perdu" (3:432) (I saw that if I did not forget Charlotte, I was lost [10:302]). This decision on the side of voluntary forgetfulness is to be read as an echo of the words left on the surface of a mirror by Henriette many years before: "Tu oublieras aussi Henriette" (You will also forget Henriette). From one woman to the other, Casanova has passed from a free and easy forgetfulness – nourished by an excess of vitality and an overabundance of desire – to a forgetting by necessity, forgetting as the only weapon against pain. Casanova's experience of Paris is caught between these two modes of forgetting. More concretely, it is also caught between two different manners of sensing exclusion. He is now obliged to leave Paris because of a *lettre de cachet* written at the demand of a relative of the marquise d'Urfé. (In the course of this altercation, Casanova, oblivious of Crébillon's lessons, declares to the young aristocrat that he will teach him to talk "à coups de pieds au cul" (by kicking him in the behind). But in fact, each of his visits ends with an order of expulsion from Paris or the threat of imprisonment). Still, only the *lettre de cachet* of November 1767 strikes him with a definitive prohibition. Nothing remains of the "charming Paris" of bygone years. This is true for the narrative time, and even more so for the time in which Casanova is writing, that is to say the time of the Revolution, around 1790. Casanova flees from a Paris that itself – through its architectural and social metamorphoses – has excluded him. But isn't there already another and even craftier principle of exclusion, one that has operated from the very beginning?

In light of this final episode, we can ask ourselves about the theme of *Paris, open city,* or *Paris, stage for all success.* The *lettre de cachet* in fact touches on all that is rebellious and unacceptable in Casanova, all that in Venice, as well as in Paris, makes of him a stranger, a dangerous element, somebody who is accepted for the amusements he offers, and nothing

more. In his portrait titled *Avanturos*, the prince de Ligne – a great aristocrat and the very essence of eighteenth-century elegance – writes of Casanova, "Il n'y a que les choses qu'il prétend savoir, qu'il ne sait pas: les
règles de la danse, de la langue française, du goût, de l'usage du monde
et du savoir vivre" (There are only things that he pretends to know, but
really doesn't: the rules of dance, of the French language, of taste, of the
customs of the world and the art of living).[1] Is this to say that Casanova
failed in his frantic desire to be received by high society and to share in
its refinements? Without a doubt. Yet it was within this indomitable part
of himself that he was able to find the right distance to decipher the theatre of appearances. In it, he also found the reserves of energy and talent
necessary for the creation of that extraordinary novel of apprenticeship
that is the *History of My Life*.

Casanova was able to make the prince de Ligne, the marquise d'Urfé,
and the maréchal de Richelieu laugh at him in the same way that Marcel
Proust was always treated as an outsider by those very same characters
who, today, exist thanks only to his genius.

NOTE

1 Prince de Ligne, *Mémoires, Lettres et pensées*, preface by Chantal Thomas
   (Paris: Editions François Bourin, 1990), 776 (translation by the author).

PART III

REPRESENTATIONAL SHIFTS AND LEGACIES

Rewriting, Revolution, Melancholy: Two Versions of the First Stay in Paris

JEAN-CHRISTOPHE IGALENS

Both new editions of *Histoire de ma vie* (History of my life),[1] which were published in France at the beginning of 2013,[2] are based upon the manuscript organization left by Casanova and not that of the revisions made by the nineteenth-century editors, which were kept until then. This organization is not a stabilized state of the text, which was continuously taken up and revised by its author. However, it invites readings along new lines: it is now possible to reflect *a minima* on the meaning produced by such an organization. One emerging question concerns the nature, function, or effects of Casanova's heterogeneous division into "chapters" and "fragments": the latter, functioning as titles and organizational modes, was erased by the publishers until the recent new editions.

In the second and third volumes of the manuscript, three long "fragments" follow one another. The first fragment constitutes the end of the second volume of the manuscript, from the magical operation of Cesena until the departure for Paris – and includes the amorous episode with Henriette; the second one is the "final" version of the first stay in Paris. As a matter of fact, the manuscript includes two versions of Casanova's first stay in Paris. The first, retained by the old editions, was probably written between the end of 1789 and 1790. It is divided into chapters 9 to 14, which conclude a "fourth" volume corresponding to an abandoned, intermediary volume numbering. The second, written around 1795–6, corresponds to the final state of the volume numbering chosen by Casanova. This "Fragment et commencement du 3e tome de mes mémoires" (Fragment and beginning of the third volume of my memoirs), as Casanova names it, gives up divisions into chapters and presents the whole of the first Parisian stay as well as the voyages to and from Paris. Finally, the third fragment includes all of the Venetian section situated between the return from Paris and the imprisonment under the Leads, where the liaisons with C.C. and M.M. unfold. This succession, in the third volume, of two long "fragments" – one on the subject of Parisian life, the other on Venetian life – manifests a work of composition, organization, and rhythm that must be taken into consideration.

This chapter has interest in the differences between the two versions and constitutes, from that point of view, a preliminary study and a change of perspective; a preliminary study because, in this case, one can confront two modes of organization for a single, narrated period; a change of perspective because the two passages present the same sequence of events and the same overall composition: they differ more in the treatment of certain scenes than in the reconstruction of the narrated material, though certain differences in the order or importance of episodes are significant.

What differs then from one version to the other? The referential details occasionally added in the second version are not the most important divergence. The essential difference lies in a change of point of view or perspective. This change is evident in the treatment of historical and political questions related to the French Revolution. It acts as well upon the representation of others and of the self. The past becomes gloomy in the second version, the rewriting seems to give consistency to the "tempérament mélancolique" (melancholy temperament) that the writer attributes to himself in the preface of 1797.

In writing, then rewriting his first trip to Paris between 1789 and 1796, Casanova cannot escape the clashes between memories and the historical present. With very few exceptions, and no more than the *in-depth* representation of time, does the Venetian use the pile-up of temporalities, the collisions between recollected periods and the present of writing. However, the account of his encounter with the France of Louis XV depends upon perception, upon the present of revolutionary events. The changes that affect this perception between 1789–90 and 1795–96 govern a number of differences that pass between the two versions. The autobiographer reconfigures certain events of his past; the memorialist modifies his evocation of kings and the monarchy.

The most spectacular modification consists of the deletion of a passage, five pages long in the manuscript, devoted to Louis XVI and to the people. In the first version, its starting point is the contrast between the delight of the people after the birth of *Madame la Dauphine* and "ce que cette même nation fait contre son roi" (Laffont, 1:796) (what the very same nation is doing against its king [3:166]) at the time of the writing. A

long "harangue historique" (Laffont, 1:802) (historic harangue [3:169])
by Louis XVI, which Casanova declares "literally true," paints a pitiless
portrait of the monarch as a lazy king too happy to be removed from
power, then follows a satire of the "people," a collective, violent, irra-
tional entity, quick to let itself be manipulated by demagogues without
scruples: "tout peuple est une union de bourreaux" (Laffont, 1:804)
(every people is a union of executioners [3:170]) in Casanova's assessment. The unresolved historical questions concern a doubtful change of
attitude of Louis XVI and a hypothetical counter-revolution. The second
version deletes all references to Louis XVI and sums up the comments
on the people in a few lines:

Les fêtes que j'ai vues à l'occasion de cette naissance me font réfléchir
à ce que c'était que l'amour tant vanté de la nation française à ses rois.
J'ai entendu plusieurs personnes dire que ce que les Français firent, et
poursuivent à faire pour gagner leur liberté, démontre qu'ils en sont dignes.
Ceux qui leur font cet éloge entendent parler de leur bravoure. Mais cette
bravoure à quoi l'ont-ils employée? C'est comme si l'on disait que les seuls
assassins méritent la souveraineté de toute la terre. (Laffont, 1:801)

The celebrations that I saw on the occasion of this birth make me think
of what the ever-praised love of the French nation to its kings was. I heard
several persons say that what the French did, and continue to do to gain
their freedom, demonstrates that they are worthy of it. Those who sing
them these praises heard of their bravery. But to what end have they applied
this bravery? It is as if one said that only murderers merit sovereignty over
the entire earth.

The "people" become the "French," the "executioners" in power turn
into "murderers" in action: the Revolution confirmed the fears of the
Venetian actors' son whose pretentions to a aristocratic lifestyle and "tro-
pisme nobiliaire" (nobiliary tropism)[3] never falter. Other places in the
second version testify to this: after praising "la beauté du grand chemin
ouvrage immortel de Louis XV" (Laffont, 1:709) (the beauty of the high-
road, the immortal work of Louis XV [3:121]) in the second version
Casanova added a venomous relative subordinate clause: "que la canaille
ennemie des rois ne s'avisera pas d'abattre actuellement" (Laffont, 1:709)
(that the riffraff, enemy of kings, will not currently dare to destroy). In
the same way, both versions recognize the abuses of the monarch's despotism, but in the first one it is preferred to the "despotisme d'un peuple

toujours effréné, féroce, indomptable qui s'attroupe, pend, coupe des têtes et assassine ceux qui n'étant point peuple osent dire leur avis" (Laffont, 1:710) (despotism of an always unbridled, ferocious, untameable people that gathers, hangs, cuts off heads and kills those who, not being of the people, dare to give their opinion); and in the second version, to "une anarchie générale, un empire effréné d'une canaille roi, qui sûre de l'impunité se porte à tous les excès" (Laffont, 1:709) (general anarchy, an unbridled empire of the rabble, reigning as a king, who, certain of its impunity, overindulges in every excess).

Casanova deletes the long sermon that pours scorn upon Louis XVI: the death sentence of the king inspired more indulgence or diminished his acrimony. All happens more or less as if the historical present made the ad hominem charge less pertinent. Altogether, the king no longer appears except during a critique of parliaments that he was wrong to recall: "quand la philosophie pense à cette faute, elle est tentée de dire que le trop bon Louis XVI mérita dans ce moment-là la mort. Mais son bourreau ne devait jamais être sa nation. C'était la foudre qui devait le punir" (Laffont, 1:805) (when philosophy reflects upon this fault, it is tempted to say that the overly good Louis XVI deserved death at that moment. But his executioner should never have been his nation. It was lightning that should have smitten him). The judgment is hardly more obliging, but it is dispatched in only two sentences: Louis XVI's moral portrait no longer matters in order to apprehend the historical present, to demonstrate its presence.

In the manner of Louis XVI, from one version to another, certain major historical figures disappear or fade, in particular during the transition between the Parisian stay and the return to Venice. The portrait of August III and the praise of the Count of Brühl, written during the trip to Dresden in the first version (Laffont, 1:894), are deleted in the second. As well, Casanova removes the fictive discourse where Maria-Theresa of Austria explains in a despotic tone her severe policy on amorous pleasures and the persecution of prostitutes (Laffont, 1:904–5). If the portrait of Emperor Franz-Joseph is present in both versions, that of Joseph II is reduced to a paragraph in the second, while it extends over two pages in the first. Each of these deletions calls for singular analysis, but it is difficult to be insensitive to their overall effect, the textual effacement – total or partial, depending on the case – of historical figures in the foreground of monarchic Europe. The reconfiguration of the past would be thus elaborated on one hand by the progressive specification of *Histoire de ma vie*, the life story, as R. Démoris put it, of "un individu non historique *en tant que non historique*" (non-historic individual *as non-historic*);[4]

and on the other hand by the disappearance of the old world after 1789. Louis XVI's address is replaced by the evocation of Monsieur de Marigni and of Monsieur de Sersale, whom Casanova knew and appreciated: the monarch's fictive speech gives way to two portraits, which, though less illustrious, involve the writer's affectivity, perhaps a certain image of himself as well. Both M. de Marigni and Monsieur de Sersale died young. The first was "doux, très aimable en compagnie, bienfaisant, modeste, et aimant le sexe et la table … il mourut avant l'âge de quarante ans" (Laffont, 1:801) (gentle, very likeable in company, beneficent, modest and a lover of women and table pleasures), and "he died before his was forty years of age," as did his sister and his daughter "avant l'âge de la puberté" (before the age of puberty): "toute cette famille mourut" (all this family died), laments the Venetian. As for M. de Sersale, a "noble napolitain de la première classe" (Neapolitan noble of the first class), he died "pour s'être trop livré aux plaisirs de Vénus n'ayant pas encore l'âge de cinquante ans" (Laffont, 1:803) (for having indulged too much in the pleasures of Venus, not yet at the age of fifty years). In the second version, often more sombre, the motifs of the end and of loss thus come back within a more personal, individualized universe, no longer as threats, but as a realized and pervasive reality.

The memorialist's perspective and the organization of the story itself can be affected by his historical present: this element allows reflection on the difference in Casanova's treatment of his stay at Fontainebleau, in particular during his first visit to the Court and the encounter with Juliette "La Cavamachia" (the dry-cleaner), a famous Venetian courtesan. I had the opportunity recently[5] to analyse modifications to the description of Louis XV's appearance: the first version celebrates Louis XV's handsome head, nicely set plumb on his neck, and combines a reflection on majesty with the description; the second version erases both considerations, the former probably to avoid a cruel or tasteless ironic effect following the death of Louis XVI, the latter, one might hypothesize, because of its political irrelevance around 1795–6. More broadly, the first version organizes two distinctly separate moments: the visit to the Court (Laffont, 1:776–82), then the encounter with Juliette, whose destiny Casanova summarizes in advance (Laffont, 1:782–6). In this version, the Venetian reports a single visit where the scenes related to the spectacle of the monarchy follow on: he catches sight of the king and the royal family going to mass, then a dozen ugly ladies perched on high heels; a little later the king appears again, crossing a gallery with M. d'Argenson; finally, Casanova attends the queen's supper and hears an exchange with the count of Lowendähl about a chicken fricassee, an exchange empty of content, but meaningful by what it shows of the monarchic ceremony. The second version interrupts the narrative of the visit to the Court with that of meeting Juliette and isolates the reminiscence of the queen's supper. Both versions contain a satire of the vanities of Court life, probably more emphasized in the second one, given the deletion of the admiring reflection on majesty. By shifting the anecdote of the queen's dinner and adding several lines on Juliette's name changes, the second version authorizes a comparison between the seductive but stuffy monarchic ritual and the lively theatricality of a courtesan capable of changing her identity according to need: "Les friponneries de cette espèce sont charmantes, et il n'y a que les sots qui puissent les trouver malhonnêtes. Je regardais Juliette comme une comédienne qui portait de droit les différents noms qui étaient attachés aux différentes farces qu'elle jouait en Europe" (Laffont, 1:787) (Impishness of this sort is charming, and only fools can find it dishonest. I saw Juliette as an actress who rightfully carried different names, which were attached to different farces that she played around Europe). The first volume of *Histoire de ma vie* gives a derogatory physical portrait of Juliette. Here she has become an accomplice and almost a double of the Venetian, through the use of a pseudonym, consubstantial with the theatrical and ludic conception of identity that *Histoire de ma vie* never ceases to legitimize and represent. The mention of the genre "farce" in itself is far less significant than the theatrical metaphor. The mirroring of successive, provisionally adopted identities is a resolutely euphoric counterpoint to the contortions of ugly courtesans and to the ambivalences of the monarchical spectacle, seductive by its theatrical essence, but also degraded by what, within it, is intractable[6] and not lacking threatening shades: all the humour Casanova can muster is needed to laugh at and make laughable this ceremony in which a war leader judges a chicken dish with the same tone that he would use in a court martial to condemn a man to death. In the first version, written in 1789–90, Louis XV's beauty and royal majesty counterbalance all the ugliness of the Court; in the second version, a comparable role is reserved for the pleasurable impostures of a courtesan, and to the happy mobility of a reinvented identity that corresponds with circumstances.

In the end, the historical present has a tendency to modify the representation of the past beyond the treatment reserved for historical figures. Let us read Casanova's remark about his dazzling social integration in the Paris of Louis XV. The first version sets an opposition between a general framework and an exception that manifests itself in thrilling infatuation between the Venetian and Paris: "Ceux qui disent que tous les étrangers qui vont à Paris s'ennuient au moins les premiers quinze jours, disent vrai, car pour se faufiler il faut le temps. Pour ce qui me regarde je sais qu'en vingt-quatre heures je me suis vu déjà occupé, et sûr de m'y plaire" (Laffont, 1:740) (Those who say that all foreigners who go to Paris remain bored for at least the first two weeks, speak truly, for it takes time to make one's way in. For my part, I know that in twenty-four hours I was already kept occupied and was sure that I would enjoy myself there [3:137]). The second version no longer opposes "the foreigners" and "Casanova," but the past and the present: "Voilà de quelle façon les étrangers se faufilaient à Paris dans ce temps-là: actuellement c'est fini. Me souvenant de cette ville, je frissonne" (Laffont, 1:743) (that was the way foreigners worked their way into Paris at that time: now it is finished. Remembering that city, I shudder). The Venetian's own exception becomes a general law whose new extension declares the absolute rupture between yesterday and today, between the Paris of Louis XV and that of the revolutionary decade.

The second version is thus characterized by a more frequently dark tone. The motifs of aging and of death are found there more often. Erotic representations, in the broad sense, are sometimes more explicit, in particular during the scene of the Hôtel du Roule where Casanova describes his night of love and the candlestick manoeuvres of a certain bacchanal, let down by Patu's impotence: this "tableau," absent from the first version, redoubles the amorous ardour of the Venetian. In the same movement, these representations become more sombre, and the theme of amorous disenchantment takes up more space. The text appears to project on the first Parisian stay worries absent from the first version and more characteristic of the three final volumes of the manuscript, after the London crisis triggered by La Charpillon.

On the way to Paris, Casanova plays the role of a "third," according to a recurrent amorous scenography.[7] Thanks to a slit in a door or in a wall, he watches the frolicking of Cattinella and the Count Ostein,[8] an "énorme machine" (Laffont, 1:686) (enormous bulk [3:110] of Germanic provenance. The scene is not exciting in either version. In the first, however, Casanova witnesses "démonstrations de tendresse qui ne faisaient aucun honneur ni à l'un ni à l'autre des personnages qui en étaient les sujets" (Laffont, 1:686) (demonstrations of love, which did no honor to either of the persons who were concerned in them [3:111]); in the second, he recounts "plaisirs amoureux qui déshonoraient la nature" (Laffont, 1:689) (amorous pleasures that dishonour nature). The deterioration is clear. It is just as significant that the Count Ostein embodies a possible anticipation of an aged and has-been Casanova – a preoccupation absent from the first version: "Je m'humiliais pensant qu'il pouvait m'arriver devenant gras et vieux de ressembler un jour à ce Comte d'Ostein" (Laffont, 1:689) (I felt humiliated thinking that it could happen to me one day to become blubbery and old enough to look like that Count Ostein). It is difficult not to read a sort of projection here, by anticipation, of how later in his narrative, after the liaison with La Charpillon, and even then only fitfully, the Venetian stages the body's aging and the deterioration of erotic drive.

Moreover, the reference to aging contaminates several characters. In the second version, Casanova writes about the Empress Maria-Theresa, who was beautiful and conscious that "elle ne cessa de l'être qu'en vieillissant; mais y a-t-il quelque chose au monde que la vieillesse ne détruise?" (Laffont, 1:919) (she did not cease to be so until she was old, but is there anything in the world that age does not destroy?). In Turin, on the way to Paris, Casanova gets excited by the beauty of the city, of the women in general, and the duchesses of Savoy in particular: "J'ai trouvé à Turin tout également beau, la ville la cour, le théâtre, et les femmes toutes belles en commençant par les duchesses de Savoie" (Laffont, 1:688) (I found everything just as beautiful in Turin, the city, the Court, the theatre, the very beautiful women, beginning with the duchesses of Savoy). The second version reiterates this judgment, but nuances it immediately by invoking old age and misfortune: the duchesses of Savoy, continues Casanova, "me parurent faites pour l'amour. Apparence trompeuse, car elles étaient destinées à être venues au monde pour végéter, prier Dieu, vieillir, et mourir. C'est l'affreuse destinée de presque toutes les filles des rois" (Laffont, 1:693) (seemed to me made for love. A misleading appearance, for they were destined to come to the earth to vegetate, pray to God, get old and die. It is the horrible destiny of almost all daughters of kings). The comment on princesses' misfortunes verges on a verbal screen: the significant element there is rather the reference to illusion and to aging. A passage deleted from the second version has the same effect. In it, Casanova sings the praises of carnal pleasures, the table, and fickleness: "Songeons que le plus précieux de tous nos partages est le plaisir, et que si l'inconstance nous en procure, nous avons tort et nous ne devenons que des vrais ingrats lorsque nous en faisons la satire" (Laffont, 1:685) (Let us bear in mind that the most precious of all our shares is pleasure, and that if fickleness brings us pleasure, we are wrong and we become quite ungrateful when we satirize it). Its disappearance from the second version can be interpreted as a tendency towards gloominess.

Such is the case, as well, with the increased amorous disenchantment. In the first version, the author's love for a Milanese dancer smitten by another man is only useless. The young girl's indifference allows Casanova to at least take pleasure "in the beauty of her eyes." The second version adds several disenchanted sentences that transform the dancer's indifference into aggressive conduct toward Casanova: "Pour parvenir à lui plaire j'ai fait des bassesses: je l'ai célébrée dans des vers; je l'ai préférée à une autre qui valait mieux qu'elle; mais tout en vain: cette fille *aliis benigna* s'obstina à me mépriser" (Laffont, 1:923) (To succeed in pleasing her, I stooped to anything: I extolled her in verses; I preferred her to another who was better than she; but all in vain: this girl *aliis benigna* persisted to scorn me). Similarly, the second version of the liaison with La Vesian twice reiterated his fear of being fooled in love, a theme that is absent from the first version. After having met the young girl, Casanova declares himself "porté à lui être utile, et ayant grande peur d'en être la dupe" (Laffont, 1:825) (inclined to be useful to her, and having great fear of being fooled by her). The theme returns in her portrait: "Si elle m'avait vanté son courage, si elle avait fait parade de vertu j'aurais eu peur d'être dupe" (Laffont, 1:827) (If she had bragged to me about her courage, if she had paraded her virtue I would have been afraid to be fooled). The past conditional tense expresses less a non-actualized possibility in the time of the story than the contamination of the episode, albeit in the hypothetical mode, through an unhappy amorous scenario, already announced in the past, in Angela's severities, but more and more menacing following the voyage in England.

In contrast, the second version contains the story of an amorous liaison that is absent in the first. During the Viennese stay, Casanova meets an "accomplished beauty of twenty to twenty-four years." We do not know her name, which is no surprise for the Venetian. More peculiar is her designation – unique and constant throughout the text – by the generic term of "La Fraïla," a Casanovian phonetic transcription, of "Fräulein" (young lady). The story occupies the place left empty by the deletion of Maria-Theresa's speech and the portrait of Joseph II. It substitutes again a private adventure for the representation of great men and women of Europe. In counterpoint to the contagion by anticipation of amorous disenchantment, Casanova offers the story of light and happy liaisons. La Fraïla is a ghostly silhouette, almost disembodied; the amorous narrative has a schematic tinge, or even a generic feeling: the sequence consists of a meeting in a house where Casanova lodged, and a game of cards; attention is on the economic situation of the belle (whom the Venetian saves from losing money), followed by several funny anecdotes and obstacles that are far from insurmountable (a lost address, religious scruples that necessitate waiting till the end of Lent to make love), some preliminary fondling during a carriage ride, finally full amorous satisfaction, which is all the more delectable as Casanova had the time to desire her without the fear of being fooled. The amorous story is in sum simply sketched; it nuances, however, the general darkening in the second version.

This version further develops certain comical traits studied by Erik Leborgne.[9] Black humour appears in the evocation of the tragic destiny of the ambassador Mocenigo, summed up in the first version: "M. de Mocenigo était d'un caractère fort doux, il aimait le jeu, et il perdait toujours, il aimait les femmes, et il était malheureux parce qu'il ne savait pas prendre le bon chemin. Deux ans après son arrivée à Paris il devint amoureux de Madame de Colande, elle lui fut cruelle, et l'ambassadeur de Venise se tua" (Laffont, 1:796) (M. de Mocenigo was completely unassuming; he loved gambling, and he always lost; he loved women, and he was unsuccessful because he did not know how to go about it. Two years after he came to Paris he fell in love with Madame de Colande; she would have none of him and the Venetian Ambassador killed himself [3:166]). The second version lingers upon the ambassador's suicide and widens into a comparison with that of Chamfort, which introduces the historical present and the laughter of black humour:

Cet ambassadeur Mocenigo devint amoureux de Madame de Colande qui lui fut cruelle, et pour se distraire il s'adonna au jeu, et perdit de très grosses sommes. Il devint mélancolique, et il se tua vers la fin de la seconde année de son ambassade; mais il choisit une mauvaise mort. Il donna de la tempe contre la hauteur d'appui de la cheminée de marbre. Il n'expira que trois jours après. Je ne sais pas comment un homme qui ne sait pas comment il faut s'y prendre pour se donner la mort puisse se résoudre à se tuer. Le suicide du malheureux Chamfort me fait toujours rire. (Laffont, 1:799)

This Ambassador Mocenigo fell in love with Madame de Colande who was cruel to him, and to distract himself he gave himself to gambling, and lost very large sums. He became melancholic, and he killed himself at the end of the second year of his embassy; but he chose a bad death. He struck his temple against the ledge of the marble chimney; he did not die until three days later. I do not know how a man who doesn't know how to go about it can make the decision to kill himself. The unfortunate Chamfort's suicide always makes me laugh.

Chamfort attempted to kill himself in 1793 while threatened with arrest, and he mutilated himself without succeeding; he died several months later. Mocenigo's suicide shows a contextual resemblance with the London episode in *Histoire de ma vie*, but its narrative occupies a prime space in a brief series of failed suicides that comes out of black humour, the "challenge to death" and the "discursive strategy" enabling the author to make a taboo thought laughable.[10]

There is no more than a "real" Casanova – if we conceive of the real as a stable and ascribable identity – from an editorial point of view, a definitive and unquestionably preferable edition of the first stay in Paris. Perhaps one never tells the same story twice, and nothing leads us to believe that the last narrative version is the most accomplished. The editorial tradition would have us choose the last text that the author retained. It is a possible and sensible choice, but a choice like any other. The publishing house Laffont reprints the two versions side by side, a configuration to which I gave some thought, because of the break it makes with habitual reading practices. It seems legitimate to me because it invites distancing oneself from the idea of a definitive text, facilitates the perception of the most massive modifications and of small but significant variations, and makes the work of writing and rewriting palpable. The existence of the two versions is in itself a fact of the autobiographical "text" where manifestations of the historical present and the passage of time can be read, counterbalanced by the praise of pleasure (even if it is crossed out), the amorous story and humour: happiness and melancholy mixed.[11]

NOTES

1 Casanova, *Histoire de ma vie*, ed. Jean-Christophe Igalens and Erik Leborgne, "Bouquins," 3 vols. (Paris: Laffont, 2013). (In this chapter, all citations in French come from this edition. As the English translation by Trask is based on the first version, the citations from the second version have been translated by the editor.)

2 See "Introduction" of this volume, n14.

3 According to Alain Viala's expression in *Naissance de l'écrivain. Sociologie de la littérature à l'âge classique* (Paris: Editions de minuit, 1985).

4 René Démoris, "Introduction," in Casanova, *Mémoires (1744–1756)* (Paris: Garnier-Flammarion, 1977), xix.

5 Jean-Christophe Igalens, "Le Roi de France et la religieuse de Murano. Réflexions sur les régimes du portrait dans l'*Histoire de ma vie* de Casanova," in *Les Portraits dans les récits factuels et fictionnels de l'époque classique*, ed. Marc Hersant and Catherine Ramond, 315–28 (Amsterdam: Brill-Rhodopi, coll. "Faux titre," 2019).

6 On the subject of a comparable reaction of Casanova before the attire of the emperor of Austria, see Casanova, *Histoire de ma vie* (Laffont, 1:917) and our analysis in "Casanova, écrivain" (Laffont, 1:vii–lxv).

7 On this subject, see Michel Delon, "Le tiers," *Revue des sciences humaines*, 271 (July–September, 2003): 43–53.

8 Casanova erroneously writes Holstein, according to the editor's note in the English edition.

9 See Jean-Christophe Igalens and Erik Leborgne, "Introduction" (Laffont, 2:xxv–xxxvi); and Erik Leborgne, *L'Humour noir des Lumières* (Paris: Classiques Garnier, 2018).

10 Igalens and Leborgne, "Introduction" (Laffont, 2:xxxiii). The analysis of black humour in these pages is due to Erik Leborgne.

11 Text translated by William Hamlet, and revised by the editor.

Chapter Nine

Casanova, from Man to Myth

MICHEL DELON

The word *myth* is often a hackneyed term, and so we should start by asking whether we can rightfully speak of a "Casanova myth." Pierre Brunel proposes three criteria in his definition of a myth.[1] A myth recounts, explains, and reveals. A story unfolds, linked to primary forces and with meaning in mind. Heroes – whether warlike or civilizing, in love or in revolt, bearing religious, national, or human values – are all marked for myth. They embody a collective destiny that exceeds their own persons. They are magnified by the high stakes of their adventures that transform mere existence into a destiny. But to what might an adventurer – who was born in Venice, under a republic that would not survive him, and who died in Bohemia under an empire destined to shatter a century later – lay claim? Throughout his life he wavered between *le rouge et le noir*, a religious or a military career, between social successes or amorous seductions, political or literary projects, expressing himself in Italian and then in French – only to be forgotten for many years by literary histories on both sides of the Alps. He may be associated as much with the new Enlightenment ideas as with the principles of the Old Regime. No established group seems to have laid exclusive claim to him, nor does he seem to have been taken up by any national cultural tradition, except perhaps by a Europe that is still striving to define itself institutionally, but that could recognize itself in this figure that exists beyond borders and fixed identities.

Casanova hints at the possibility of a triangulated continent, its corners being Venice, Paris, and central Europe, *ein Mitteleuropa* whose capital would be Vienna or Prague: the Venice of colour and carnival, the Paris of the rococo and libertines, the Vienna or Prague of music. The triangle is of another kind as well: the updating of the memory of antiquity in the Renaissance, French-style classicism, and the aspiration to a new romantic culture.

For many years, people wanted to read Casanova's memoirs as merely a guide to being the perfect seducer or as a European *Kama Sutra*. Readers found in his pages the good humour of a hedonist who makes the most of life and who seizes every unexpected opportunity. On occasion people have gone so far as to turn the *History of My Life* into a catalogue of pleasures, likening it to Don Juan's or Don Giovanni's list. If there is a myth here, it is that of the Latin lover's triumphant virility, of an omnipotent phallus free of all of puritan prohibitions. This fantasy exasperated Fellini, who caricatured this pretension through the character of a hung-up and made-up male and the emblematic mechanical doll. But the reality of the *History of My Life* reveals a considerably subtler sexual euphoria, which unfurls between the young man's first founding failure in Padua and a disastrous passion for La Charpillon in London, and that feeds on the sexual ambiguity that cloaks transvestites and castrati. Documentation on the conditions in which Casanova wrote his memoirs in Dux reveals that he invented this euphoria as a kind of literary therapy to combat the melancholy of old age and the failings of virility. The myth became one of masculinity that is both in search of willing and complicit partners and in dialogue with another sex, which is not limited to a simple physiological definition. Casanova was thus raised to the level of Don Juan – and the opposition of the two figures quickly became commonplace. In an essay written in 1949 and re-edited in 1985, Félicien Marceau contrasts the two men as mirror images of each other: "Don Juan is Spanish, Casanova is Italian.... The former is from the seventeenth century, the latter from the eighteenth."[2] Don Juan loves women for what they signify, Casanova for the pleasure he shares with them.

The Venetian has also been identified with the joyful *saraband* of the carnival, its masks and its festivities. This intoxication is all the more captivating for being under threat and ephemeral – at once individually under threat and historically ephemeral. Casanova may have presented himself as an individual up against the full might of the Inquisition in a republic that jailed him, yet his biography remains intimately linked to his city's fate. He developed the oral account of his escape from the notorious Leads, then put pen to paper, editing the written version in a place and time of loss and nostalgia. He first lost the security he had enjoyed as a young man at the senator Bragadin's expense when he escaped in the autumn of 1756. He then lost the familiarity of a known world for a second time in January 1783 when the scandal caused by one of his pamphlets made him once again persona non grata in the lagoon. He composed the *History of My Life* in exile and after the loss of the Old Regime, which had been brought low by the French Revolution and its aftershocks across Europe. The Venetian carnival was invented both to ward off the collapse of a republic that disappeared with Casanova and to deny the disappearance of an aristocratic model that henceforth belonged to the past. This invention was a tourist advertisement for a town whose commercial foundations had crumbled and a compensatory reverie with which to idealize the now-vanished aristocratic spending.

For 150 years, this character's success was founded on the German and French rewritings of the original manuscript, on adaptations, and on editors' textual tampering. Literary critics were aware of the discrepancy between these essentially fanciful versions and the authentic one, locked up and inaccessible in the safe of the Brockhaus publishing house. One had to wait until 1960 to read a *History of My Life* that approximated the original, and until 2010 to see with one's own eyes the author's idiosyncratic way of writing, free of the scansion of the text that was imposed by Brockhaus in the nineteenth century. The long uncertainty about the authentic text and the aura of opacity surrounding it set people dreaming about the character behind it. Into the gap between what was known and what was not, there stepped fiction. Sade, Casanova's contemporary and like him a largely posthumous author, similarly acquired a mythic dimension following the destruction of several of his manuscripts. Imagining what might have been has caused anxious musing. The inability of their contemporaries and then of posterity to grasp their work in all its reality encouraged authors to rewrite it.

Casanova's life could become a myth all the more easily because with his memoirs he provided the first version of a tale – a fleeting and uncertain version – and because this life is portrayed as a fight against time, old age, and all the coercive forms of power, and as a search for a fragile, hypothetical meaning. Just as his individual existence was governed by the rhythm of the great events of the continent's history, so the myth's flowering is linked to key historical moments. Is it not significant that three major works inspired by the figure of the Venetian are exact contemporaries of each other, albeit in different countries? Apollinaire's *Casanova, comédie parodique* in French, Arthur Schnitzler's *Casanova's Homecoming* in German, followed by Marina Tsvetaeva's play *The Sisters or Casanova in Spa* and her two Russian plays or, as she preferred to call them, dramatic poems, *An Adventure* and *The Phoenix* – all these were written from 1918 to 1919, at the end of the First World War, in the agony of an old Europe that did not withstand the massacres and the Russian Revolution.

Apollinaire's parodic comedy adapts the Bellino episode: it begins as night falls and ends as day breaks in winter; it plays on misunderstandings and mistaken identities during the night. The isolated park at dawn seems to offer little more than a melancholy decor, but the revelation of Bellino's true sex, his transformation into Bellina, and the formation of the loving couple resonate defiantly against the collective tragedy. In the style of the *Ballets russes*, this is provocative affirmation of what was to become the Roaring Twenties. The assonance of *cor*, *corps*, and *cœur* transform love into music and change morals into aesthetics.

> BELLINA: Entends le cor qui sonne,
>   Qui sonne au fond des bois.
>   Prends mon cœur, je le donne
>   À qui connaît ma voix.
> CASANOVA: J'entends le cor qui sonne,
>   Qui sonne au fond des bois.
>   Je prends ce cœur qu'on donne
>   Pour la première fois.[3]

> BELLINA: Hear the horn that sounds / That sounds from the deepest forest / Take my heart, I give it / To the one who knows my voice.
> CASANOVA: I hear the horn that sounds / That sounds from the deepest forest / I take this heart you give / For the very first time.

Casanova's Homecoming stages the Venetian on the eve of his return to the lagoon after an absence of eighteen years. He falls for a young woman who rebuffs him. He can spend the night with her only by assuming her lover's identity, by buying this embrace from him, and by fooling him. In the small hours, the imposture is revealed. Lorenzi, the young officer who was able to sell his mistress to pay off his debts, suddenly recovers a sense of honour; he challenges Casanova to a duel and is killed by him. The old seducer, once irresistible, confronts the limits of his power. He kills his double, the rejuvenated image of himself, at the very moment he betrays his own youth by submitting to the Inquisition in order that he might return to his homeland. The homecoming does not mark a second youth – it signals its definitive loss. However, in the wake of Hugo von Hofmannsthal, Arthur Schnitzler did not confine himself to this cynical tale. A few months later he created a play that summons up a younger, less sombre Casanova, who conforms more closely to the stereotype of the seducer.[4] One may observe that from Hofmannsthal to Schnitzler and Tsvetaeva, the changing figure of the Venetian requires two different texts from the creators who appropriate him for themselves.

Marina Tsvetaeva dreamt up a first dramatic poem in which the hero is twenty-three and then thirty-six years old, and a second in which he rails against his seventy-five years: "What am I? Nothing. What was I? Everything?"[5] To enhance the beauty of this final portrait, the poet shifts Casanova's death from 1798 (the real year of his demise) to the very end of the century. The librarian of Dux is nothing more than a "terrible and gracious skeleton"; he wears a violet morning coat, red-heeled shoes, "on the thin line that separates grandeur from the grotesque." "At any moment he could crumble into dust. But, as he waits, he is the very expression of the eighteenth century. The final hour of the year 1799. The new year, the storm that howls."[6] A century and an *art de vivre* both come to a close. At the very moment that the First World War ends, Casanova is caught in an eternal and impossible youth, then in an old age that reaches a sublime form, and he accepts death.

Apollinaire's character sings:

Je suis Casanova
L'amant joyeux et tendre
Je dis à l'Amour: va,
Il va sans plus attendre
Cueillir le cœur des belles,
J'en ai des ribambelles…
Don Juan
Était tragique et triste
Ainsi qu'un chat-huant.

Longue est la liste
De celles qui moururent pour lui,
Mais moi je ne fais pas de victimes
Je suis le plaisir et non l'ennui
Je commets des péchés, non des crimes.
Je suis gai, tendre et charmant
Je suis le meilleur des amants
Car j'aime légèrement.[7]

I am Casanova / The joyous tender lover / I say to Cupid "Go" and he goes straight away / to pluck beauties' hearts / I have handfuls of them / … Don Juan was tragic and sad / Like a barn owl / Long is the list / Of lovers who

> died because of him, / But I don't make any victims / I am pleasure and
> not boredom / I commit sins not crimes. / I am gay, tender and charming
> / I am the best of lovers / For I love lightly.

Arthur Schnitzler's seducer does not love "lightly." He represents the most Don Juanesque and possessive version of the man whom we might consider an anti-Don Juan. His character is a crook who steals a night of passion from the young Marcolina and finds himself face-to-face with the betrayed woman. Marcolina

> was standing by the foot of the bed contemplating Casanova with unutterable
> horror. Her glance instantly recalled him to his senses. Involuntarily he
> stretched out his arms towards her with a gesture of appeal.... Neither
> was able to look away from the other. His expression was one of rage and
> shame; hers was one of shame and disgust.... what he read in Marcolina's
> countenance was not what he would a thousand times rather have read
> there; it was not thief, libertine, villain. He read only something which
> crushed him to earth more ignominiously than could any terms of abuse ... –
> old man![8]

Marina Tsvetaeva's poet is neither Apollinaire's idealized lover nor Arthur Schnitzler's libidinous old man. He casts into the fire the thousand love letters he has kept and finds himself faced with a final apparition, Franziska, "salamander and child, visionary and innocent, thirteen years old." She embodies the youthful spirit or the principle of adventure. Before vanishing into the storm, the old man slips a ring onto the sleeping child's finger and kisses her lips. He attains with her a loving relationship without possession. Apollinaire's "joyful and tender lover" contrasts with Arthur Schnitzler's handsome old man; the man who kills the young lover and rapes Marcolina is incompatible with the sublime old man who kisses the youthful Franziska's lips before disappearing into the snow. Such breadth of interpretation characterizes a figure who is increasingly severed from all biographical reference, thereby embodying the man who battles with the passage of time: the time of the body that weakens and collapses, the time of history that transforms societies through slow alterations or by violent jolts. Casanova embodies the incessant negotiation with time, from denial to acceptance.

Some twenty years later, the Hungarian novelist Sándor Márai wrote *Conversations in Bolzano.* He concentrates on the fugitive from the Leads, who has arrived in the Austrian town, escaping the Venetian police. He is never named. He is the stranger, the traveller. The very title of the story does not bear the name *Casanova*. "His reputation preceded him like a herald announcing his name. The prelate had already sent word to the police chief that morning, requesting the force to send the notorious guest on his way."[9] Such expressions are repeated: "There was something dubious even about his name, as if it were not really or entirely his own."[10] The novel tells of the encounter between the individual and his character, between the unnamed fugitive and the myth that he has already become. During his first night at the hostelry in Bolzano, he is watched through the keyhole by the young servant girl, then by all the women drawn there by rumour. What are they looking to see? He sleeps spread-eagled, as if he had been crucified. "His face was serious and ugly. It was a masculine, lacking beauty and grace, the nose large and fleshy, the lips narrow and severe, the chin sharp and forceful, and the whole figure small-framed and a little tubby, for in sixteen months in jail, without air or exercise, he had put on some weight."[11] This is not the body of a seductive fop; it has not escaped the burdens of time, fatigue, and aging. The character is a prisoner of his past, of an old seduction, and of a duel that should have ended in the death of one of the two men. He is confronted by the old count of Parma, whom he once tricked and who now wishes to avenge himself by killing not the man, but his legend. The former lovers, the countess and the adventurer, meet again, masked, for a single night that proves to them that the past cannot be repeated. And the following day, the traveller sets off, condemned to move on and to live transiently. He has not only fled the Leads – he never stops fleeing.

Conversations in Bolzano was published in 1940, when Europe was once again sinking into war. Much later, once the war was over, when Hungary had turned socialist and he himself had emigrated to the United States, Sándor Márai speculated about the two dates that had changed the course of his country's history: 12 March 1938 (the *Anschluss*), and 31 August 1948 (the date of his and his family's departure from Hungary). He recalled the creation of *Conversations in Bolzano*, written when German jackboots thundered across Austria:

At the time, I was writing a book about Casanova and I was engrossed in the universe of this adventurer who was like someone straight out of a novel. I was reading books about the *Settecento*. My mind was then as full of all that I'm writing about today as it was of Casanova's personality and period; but

at that moment, I had not written a single word about it. I preferred to write
about Casanova. Perhaps it was a mistake, guilty negligence, but that's how
it was, I could not do otherwise. I would be out walking and thinking of
Casanova and, at the same time, of Hitler, who was marching in Vienna, just
a hundred kilometres west of the Buda Hills.[12]

The figure of Casanova has a double function: first, to occasion a nos-
talgic withdrawal to an art of living and an art of writing that evoke the
Settecento; second, to encourage an acceptance of life and history as flight
and roaming. Is this nostalgia for vanished refinement or consciousness
of the tragedy of human and collective experience?

Casanova is a myth of modernity, defined as the mourning for all
transcendence. Apollinaire's parodic comedy closes with a final couplet
marking the departure of the itinerant acting troupe. The carnival has
come to an end, and reality comprises good and bad elements alike:

Allons, Bohémiennes!
Mettons-nous en chemin.
Les plaisirs et les peines
S'épouseront demain.

Let us go, Bohemian girls! / Let us take the road / The pleasures and the
    pains / Will come joined tomorrow.

Marina Tsvetaeva also conceives the denouement of *The Phoenix* as the
final departure of the librarian of Dux, a final wrench so that he might
remain true to his ideal of fleetingness. On his journey, she has him take
a volume by Ariosto, the model of heroic chivalry. In Sándor Márai's
work, the anonymous traveller dictates to the Count of Parma a letter in
which he refers to a great love for a woman: "Nothing but You and for
ever." This love is admitted yet endlessly deferred, experienced in the
profundity of the moment yet never for any length of time. Eternity is
thus nothing more than a way of making the transitory sacred. Balbi, the
monk who escaped from prison with Casanova, serves him as a secretary
and as a burlesque double. Like Sancho Panza, he refuses his master's
delusions and, having made a fair copy of the letter destined for the
Count of Parma, he "fell to loud, full-bellied laughter."[13] Just like the
curious glances from the women of Bolzano, this burlesque counterpoint
endows the Old Regime adventurer, now transformed into a traveller of

modernity, with a mythic grandeur, as he waits for cinema – the very art of modernity – to seize his figure and explore its contradictions.[14]

NOTES

1 *Dictionnaire des mythes littéraires*, dir. Pierre Brunel (Paris: Éditions du Rocher, 1988), 8–9.

2 Félicien Marceau, *Casanova ou l'anti-Don Juan* (Paris: Gallimard, 1985), 146.

3 Guillaume Apollinaire, *Œuvres poétiques* (Paris: Gallimard, 1965), 1020, 1023. Translation by the editor.

4 Both Hugo von Hofmannsthal and Arthur Schnitzler staged a forty-year-old Casanova, the former in a comedy, *The Adventurer and the Singer* (1899), the latter in this novel, written in 1918. See Carina Lehnen, *Das Lob des Verführers. Über die Mythisierung der Casanova-Figur in der deutschsprachigen Literatur zwischen 1899 und 1933* (Paderborn: Igelk Verlag, 1982), 217–32.

5 Marina Tsvetaïeva, *Romantika* (Paris: Gallimard, 1998), 269.

6 Tsvetaïeva, *Romantika*, 312–13.

7 Apollinaire, *Œuvres poétiques*, 972.

8 Arthur Schnitzler, *Casanova's Homecoming*, trans. E. and C. Paul (New York: Thomas Seltzer, 1928), 171–2.

9 Sándor Márai, *Conversations in Bolzano* (London: Viking, 1992), 7.

10 Márai, *Conversations in Bolzano*, 24.

11 Márai, *Conversations in Bolzano*, 19.

12 Sándor Márai, *Ce que j'ai voulu taire* (Paris: Albin Michel, 2014), 91.

13 Márai, *Conversations in Bolzano*, 294.

14 Translated by Thomas Wynn.

Chapter Ten

Fellini's Casanova: The Story of a Man Who Was Never Born

CHRISTOPHER B. WHITE

For the major part of his long career in the film industry, Federico Fellini avoided using literature as a basis for his work and tended to draw inspiration from a combination of personal experience and a particularly vivid imagination. Out of twenty-four projects he directed, including feature-length movies, episode films, and productions for television, only four were based on literary works, and all can be said to depart considerably from the source materials.[1] *Fellini's Casanova* (1976) was no exception, and the film perplexed a number of critics and spectators at the time of its release in large part because of its distance from the *History of My Life*. As Fellini biographer and film critic Tullio Kezich aptly cautions, "In order to understand the movie, one needs perhaps to first try and forget the historical figure and the legend of Casanova."[2] Federico had trouble getting through Giacomo Casanova's lengthy memoirs, and he grew to detest the Venetian pleasure-seeker while preparing for the project he had initially agreed to undertake after signing a contract with producer Dino De Laurentiis in 1971. Instead of adhering to Casanova's portrayal of his life in the text, Fellini assimilated him into the body of his own work, using Casanova to revisit themes from previous films. He conceived of his protagonist as an extreme version of the idle provincial youth in *I vitelloni* (1953) and the sex-starved adolescent fascists in *Amarcord* (1973), an insufferable blowhard who was "traumatized by the fact that sexuality was crucified as a major sin" by the Catholic Church and who shared the "exaggerated appetite for all that is feminine" manifested by many of the male characters populating Fellini's movies.[3] With the aid of his crew in Teatro 5 of Cinecittà, Fellini channelled his loathing of Casanova into a dark, funereal work that shatters the myth of the man best known for his enviable powers of seduction.

In his autobiographical collection *Making a Film,* Fellini argues that it is impossible to directly transpose a work of art from one medium to another: "Cinema-literature: it's an approach that usually springs from polemical relationships, misplaced priorities, and fabricated dependencies. Each work of art resides in the dimension in which it was conceived and expressed; transferring it, moving it from its original language to a different one, means cancelling it, denying it."[4] Fellini disliked the limitations to creativity that accompany a faithful adaptation of a literary work, and as a result his film adaptations are all very loosely based on their sources. In "Toby Dammit," for example, Fellini's segment of the episode film *Spirits of the Dead,* the director and his collaborators shifted the time period and location of Edgar Allan Poe's short story "Never Bet the Devil Your Head" from nineteenth-century America to modern Rome and transformed the protagonist into a troubled British actor visiting the Eternal City for an award ceremony. It should therefore be no surprise that Fellini chose to stray from the *History of My Life.* The tone of the film and the portrayal of the protagonist were ultimately more closely related to the director's hatred of the text and the events surrounding the production of the movie than to the contents of the *History of My Life.*

Fellini firmly believed that the circumstances behind the creation of a movie are fundamental to it and determine the character of the finished product: "There are no events, opportunities or elements that can be considered completely irrelevant to the film. Everything's a part of the film."[5] In the case of *Casanova,* the movie passed from one producer to another: first Dino De Laurentiis, then Andrea Rizzoli; it finally ended up in the hands of Alberto Grimaldi, as the result of a host of issues, from disagreements over the choice of the male lead and over the shooting locations to concerns over the budget. Sutherland became ill during shooting, strikes in the Italian film industry in 1975 temporarily halted production, and at one point a box of film negatives mysteriously went missing. The movie took two and a half years to make, and, in the words of Frank Burke, it "was one of the most difficult projects Fellini undertook in his four-decade career as a filmmaker."[6] *Fellini's Casanova* reflects this unusually long and tortuous shooting process and the director's struggle with the text that provided the basis for his movie.

Although Fellini had been talking about making a film about Casanova for years, he had never read the memoirs when he signed the contract with De Laurentiis in 1971.[7] De Laurentiis believed that the movie was destined to become "a box-office dream," but "for Fellini it became a nightmare."[8] When he started working on the project, he discovered that he detested *The History of My Life*, and in an interview Federico told Costanzo Costantini that he felt Casanova's writings were "just an ocean of paper, more tedious and depressing than a phone book."[9] To facilitate the task of sifting through all of the material, Fellini divided the reading with screenwriters Bernardino Zapponi and Tonino Guerra, and, according to Fabrizio Borin, he wrote denigrating comments about the man he nicknamed "lo stronzone" (the asshole) in the margins of his personal copy of the memoirs.[10] A quotation from *Making a Film* establishes his attitude toward the text and explains how the idea for the film arose:

> I waded through the limitless paper sea of *History of My Life*, that arid listing of an abundance of events stored with statistical rigor as if they'd been inventoried, a pedantic, meticulous, peevish record that doesn't even contain many embellishments, and irritation, non-involvement, disgust, and boredom were the only variations of my depressed, dispirited state of mind.
>
> This refusal, this revulsion, was what suggested the meaning of the film.
>
> That's how I came up with the idea of telling the story of a man who was never born, the adventures of a zombie, a mournful marionette without personal ideas, feelings, or viewpoints; an "Italian" imprisoned in the mother's womb, buried there inside to dream about a life he never really lived, in an emotionless world inhabited only by forms that take shape in volumes, perspectives marked by chilling, hypnotic repetition. Empty forms that gather and dissipate, the allure of an aquarium, a sort of amnesia like the ocean depths where everything is completely flattened and unfamiliar because there's no penetration or human familiarity.[11]

Fellini translated his opinion about the text into the aesthetic and structural makeup of *Casanova*. He and his colleagues made use of muted colours, heavy shadow, and bitter symbolic environments consisting of dark water, ice, and wind to create what he called "an abstract and informal film about "the 'absence of life.'"[12] Concerning the structure of the film, Tullio Kezich observes that "there is no logical progression or real narrative connections."[13] Referencing a distinction Umberto Eco makes in *The Open Work*, John Stubbs explains that Fellini typically adopts the "open form" over a traditional linear narrative, and this is certainly true of *Casanova*.[14] The film contains characters and events that derive from the memoirs, with scenes that take place in Paris, Forlì, London, Parma, Württemberg, and Dux in Bohemia, but the studio sets that stress cinematic artifice, Fellini's signature grotesques and layered compositions, and symbols that call to mind previous films such as *La strada* (1954) and *La dolce vita* (1960) signal to anyone familiar with Fellini's work that the movie is more closely related to the director's cinematic universe than to the world Casanova depicts in his writings.[15]

One of the first steps Fellini took in debunking the myth and incorporating the Casanova character into his own cinematic world was choosing Donald Sutherland, a slender, fair-haired Canadian actor who conflicted with the traditional conception of the Latin lover. Fellini felt that Casanova was "a stereotype," "a façade," and "a meaningless universality,"[16] and he attributed the legendary seducer's popularity in Italy to the harmful effects of a conservative Catholic upbringing on Italian men. The director explained this connection during an interview for the television documentary *E il Casanova di Fellini?* (So what happened to *Fellini's Casanova?*): "Under the daily shadow of gripping sexual frustration, it was practically destiny that the Italians gave birth to the legend of a man who conquers everyone. After years, centuries even, of the misogynistic xenophobic teachings of the Catholic Church, the Latin male has built up such a paralyzing heated longing for woman that he remains a perpetual adolescent, an individual incapable of growing up."[17]

Fellini's cinema is populated by laughable, bungling seducers, vulgar adolescents obsessed with voluptuous ladies, sophomoric grown men leering at passing women, and soldiers eagerly waiting in line at state-sanctioned brothels; these characters are meant to be the products of Catholic repression, a topic Fellini's movies frequently engage with. Fellini made Giacomo Casanova part of this lineage of stunted male figures and likened him to the would-be seducers who "built up Casanova as their precursor."[18]

Fellini stated that when choosing actors, he sought out "expressive, distinctive faces that say everything about themselves as soon as they appear on screen" and that he "[tended] to highlight everything that can point out the person's psychology with makeup and costume."[19] The dark sunglasses that the shady swindler Oscar wears in *Nights of Cabiria* (1957) are a straightforward example from one of his earlier films. The accentuated body hair and the massive pink boil that Fellini added to Titta's father, Aurelio, to stress the patriarch's irascibility in *Amarcord* are a more grotesque illustration of this feature of Fellini's movies, which stems from his experience as a caricaturist prior to working in the film industry.[20] Fellini carefully planned the primary characteristics of Casanova in his preliminary drawings, and Donald Sutherland spent hours in makeup each morning before shooting in order to conform to Fellini's conception of the character.[21] Fellini gave the actor a pronounced chin and nose, a shaved forehead that alters his hairline, and personally oversaw the drawing on of the protagonist's eyebrows.[22] In reference to his idea of Casanova, Fellini stated that he sought a specific symbolic countenance: "I want a character who is still unborn, still in the placenta."[23]

Along with the desire to make Casanova resemble a child in utero, there is also a more bawdy rationale behind Donald Sutherland's unique appearance in the film. Casanova's raised hairline and prominent forehead, his predilection for clothing that looks like long johns or undergarments, and the unnatural, rigid posture he frequently assumes in the film suggest that Fellini intended to ridicule his protagonist by making him resemble a phallus. The comparison becomes especially clear when Casanova wakes up prior to preying on the anemic Annamaria and abruptly and unnaturally pops up from the bed, during one of a series of flashbacks during his internment in the Leads.[24] Fellini reinforces the comparison by juxtaposing Casanova with phallic objects throughout the film, from the mechanical bird that serves as a metronome for his sexual encounters (*uccello*, or "bird" in Italian, is a colloquial term for penis) to the upright statue in the court in Rome where the copulation contest takes place. Fellini playfully transforms the mythical man who was known for his sexual exploits into a walking erection.

Fellini overturns the idea of Casanova as a skilled seducer by making a number of his conquests questionable and many of his partners grotesque. While in his prison cell, Casanova fondly thinks back on what he defines as "rendezvous with alluring, fascinating women," but the couplings often involve unsightly figures, including a sex-crazed hunchback with a freakishly long tongue, an aged Madame d'Urfé with missing teeth, and a mute robotic doll. His monotonous bedroom routines are performed to the tune of the gilded mechanical bird that stresses the futility of his relentless lovemaking. Furthermore, as Frank Burke has noted, Casanova takes three women (Annamaria, Romana, and Rosalba) without their full consent, thus calling into question his integrity.[25]

Casanova's ridiculous dialogue in the film further undermines his legendary ability to cajole women into bed. For example, Casanova compliments Annamaria on her beauty by saying, "I thought you were Diana, the moon goddess become mortal." His clichéd attempts at seduction often sound more like the words of Fernando Rivoli, the pathetic *foto-romanzo* actor who unsuccessfully attempts to take advantage of a young newlywed in *The White Sheik* (1952), or the feeble pick-up lines of the protagonists of *I vitelloni* than those of a skilled womanizer.

The similarity between Casanova and characters from previous films is intentional, for Fellini envisioned his protagonist as "an old *vitellone*" or "a braggart Fascist," terms that link Casanova to Alberto and the other indolent young men living off their families in *I vitelloni* and to the permanent adolescence Fellini associated with fascism in *Amarcord*.[26] The representation of Casanova as a child in utero harks back to the juvenile *vitelloni*, in particular Alberto, whose head is tightly wrapped in a scarf that makes him look like a swaddled infant in the famous *lavoratori* (workmen) sequence of the 1953 film.[27] Fellini likens Casanova to the adolescents in *Amarcord* through a humorous reference to the masturbation scene that takes place inside a rocking automobile in a garage. In *Amarcord* the boys fantasize about the local beauty Gradisca and the buxom *tabaccaia* (tobacco vendor); in *Fellini's Casanova* the protagonist pleasures himself frenetically in the back of a carriage while singing the praises of Paris and calling out, "Descartes, Voltaire, oh how I love you!"

William Van Watson provides an interesting link between Fellini's film about Rimini in the 1920s and the uterine or aquatic theme that the director chose to make central to *Casanova*. Although it is common knowledge that *Amarcord* is *romagnolo* and translates as "I remember," Van Watson offers a unique interpretation of the term that suggests the director may have intended a secondary meaning of the title that refers to the puerility he associated with the inhabitants of Rimini during the fascist era: "The Latin roots of the Italian verb '*ricordare*' etymologically encode both the umbilical *cord* and its function as extension of the mother's heart or '*cuore*' in Italian ... '*amare*' in Italian means 'to love,' so ... the title would roughly translate from Italian as 'to love the umbilical.'"[28] In *Making a Film*, Fellini explains that with *Amarcord* he intended to explore "the psychological, emotional manner of being a fascist: a sort of blockage, stopping development at the adolescent phase."[29] Fellini believes that the failure to grow up and assume responsibility leads to the need to seek out external sources of authority; fascism is one among many possibilities, and Fellini also points to the church and the mother in *Amarcord*.[30] The *mammoni*, or mamma's boys, in *Amarcord* and *I vitelloni* might all be said to "love the umbilical," and if Fellini intended Casanova to be read as a more extreme form of *vitellone*, then the natural place for him would be the womb.

Fellini establishes the aquatic or uterine theme in *Casanova* in the opening credits by pairing a shot of the surface of the water with a soundtrack that includes music from a glass harp, and the motif recurs at various points throughout the film. The scene in which Casanova goes inside the belly of the great whale, or *mouna,* at the carnival in London is one of the most obvious examples, as the man beckoning passers-by to step inside directly refers to the cavern as "the warm, welcoming womb." Numerous dark, cramped spaces, from the jail cell in the Leads to the interiors of the carriages Casanova uses throughout his travels, contribute to a feeling of enclosure unlike any found in Fellini's other works. Fellini stresses his perception of Casanova as the "man who was never born" by placing Giacomo in the fetal position in three separate shots in his jail cell in the Leads, an idea that Fellini came up with during the planning stage, as evinced by a preliminary drawing that depicts Giacomo curled up in a dark, round, uterine environment.[31] When Casanova decides to attempt suicide while in London, his chosen method is to drown himself in the dark water of the River Thames, further reinforcing the film's aquatic motif.

The lugubrious atmosphere and unique studio sets in *Fellini's Casanova* can also be attributed to the director's interest in art history. Fabrizio Borin argues that *Casanova* is the Fellini film "most inspired by painting," and he explains that the work of the Venetian painter Pietro Longhi has had a major influence on the representation of the eighteenth-century on film.[32] In *Exhibition of a Rhinoceros at Venice* (1751), one can identify clothing styles and the colour palette Fellini employs in the various courts he visits around Europe, touches of colour on the costumes paired with a preponderance of what Borin refers to as "crepuscular tones."[33] In *Federico Fellini: Painting in Film, Painting on Film,* film scholar and art historian Hava Aldouby offers a convincing study of Fellini's frequent use of "art-historical referencing" in a group of films made between 1965 and 1976: *Juliet of the Spirits,* "Toby Dammit," *Fellini Satyricon, Fellini's Roma,* and *Casanova.* She identifies the Swiss symbolist painter Arnold Böcklin's *Isle of the Dead* series (1880–6) as an influence on the visual presentation of the Isoletta di San Bartolo, where Casanova stands with a candle awaiting the arrival of Maddalena, the French ambassador's lover.[34] The isolated protagonist on the desolate shore serves as an appropriate prelude to one of many couplings that bring Casanova no closer to a greater understanding of life or a meaningful relationship. Fellini looks to the Böcklin series and works by other unique artists, such as Giorgio De Chirico's *The Enigma of the Oracle* (1910), as inspiration for the set design to create the otherworldly atmosphere of *Casanova.*

Although Fellini was a disciple of Roberto Rossellini, who made his early films on location in keeping with the neorealist tradition, during the latter half of his career he spent the majority of his time in the studio, a testament to his preference for imaginative productions over realism. In an interview with Giovanni Grazzini, Fellini states that he was unmoved by natural sights, and that "a beautiful landscape, a sunset, the primordial grandiosity of the mountains, the silence with which snow falls, only affect me if I manage to reproduce them in Cinecittà, in the studio, messing around with silk fabrics and light filters."[35] The passing of the Rex in *Amarcord,* the substitution of painted replicas for real people and animals, the maritime battle at the conclusion of *And the Ship Sails On,* and the prominent garbage-bag sea in *Casanova* are all memorable examples of Fellini's celebration of cinematic artifice and the creative potential of the studio. Aldouby appropriately labels *Casanova* "Fellini's most expressly artificial film";[36] while *Amarcord* and *Fellini Satyricon* contain a handful of scenes that were filmed outdoors in natural light, *Casanova* was made entirely inside Cinecittà, a decision that helped the director achieve the gloomy atmosphere he was looking for.

In the director's notes for *Fellini Satyricon,* Fellini indicates that he and the cinematographer Giuseppe Rotunno were aiming for a painterly aesthetic, "a film made up of fixed, immobile frames, without dollies or other movements of the camera."[37] The cinematography in *Casanova* also consists primarily of static shots, a creative decision that helps showcase the distinctive set design and elaborate mise en scène in the film's various studio environments. One of few exceptions to the tendency to use a stationary camera appears during the scene in which Casanova first finds himself alone with Rosalba, the life-size mechanical doll he meets in Württemberg, and this switch in shooting technique marks a pivotal moment in the film.[38] The camera assumes the protagonist's point of view in a dolly shot as he slowly walks toward Rosalba, reflecting Casanova's fascination with the mechanical figure and offering the viewer a glimpse into the protagonist's psyche. In a discussion of the film with Costanzo Costantini, Fellini expresses his belief that someone who continually engages in sexual activity "without tenderness and any real sense of intimacy," "as mere repetition, physical activity, gymnastic display," as Casanova does throughout the course of the film, "can see a woman only as an object."[39] Therefore, in Fellini's estimation, the ideal partner for his protagonist is an automaton.

The conclusion of the film, the dream sequence set in a wintry Venice, is one of the most striking segments of *Fellini's Casanova,* and it serves to reinforce the film's central themes. Now an old man working as the librarian in the castle of Dux in Bohemia, the elderly protagonist envisions the robotic doll he encountered in Württemberg and twirls with her on the surface of the frozen canal, an appropriate summary of a life spent mechanically copulating without establishing meaningful relationships with any of his countless partners. The mysterious figurehead that briefly emerges from the canal and then plunges back down into the depths at the beginning of the film reappears below the ice in the conclusion as a symbol of the inscrutability of women for Casanova. The presence of his ghoulish mother in a gilded carriage seated next to an ever-smiling pope recalls themes raised in *Amarcord*, namely the repressive attitudes of the family and the church, those external authority figures that Fellini believes are essential to the gestation of a stereotypical "Italian" like Casanova. The dance with the "man who was never born" and Rosalba in the movie's final sequence conforms perfectly to Fellini's vision in *Making a Film*: "It's an abstract and informal film about the 'absence of life.' There are neither characters nor situations; there are no introductions, developments, or catharses. It's a frenetic, pointless mechanical ballet, like an electrified waxworks museum."[40]

Casanova was one of Fellini's least successful projects, most likely because, in the director's words, "spectators ... entered the theater with their own movie in mind, which they would've liked to see confirmed on screen."[41] But Fellini did just what viewers should have expected from him: he moulded Casanova's memoirs to fit his own peculiar take on the famous eighteenth-century adventurer. The director's distaste for Casanova resulted in a dark, otherworldly film that both draws from Fellini's previous projects and explores new territory. In defence of his movie, Fellini called it his "best film, the clearest, the most meticulous, and the most complete from a stylistic standpoint."[42] Some spectators and critics may have disagreed at the time of its release, but the boat crossing the garbage-bag sea, the carnival with the giantess Angelina and her diminutive companions, and Casanova's dance on the ice with Rosalba the mechanical doll remain undeniably some of the finest sequences in the cinema of Federico Fellini.[43]

NOTES

1   Aside from *Fellini's Casanova*, "Toby Dammit" in *Spirits of the Dead* (1968) draws from the short story "Never Bet the Devil Your Head" by Edgar Allan Poe, *Fellini Satyricon* (1969) is based on the work by Petronius, and *The Voice*

of the Moon (1990) is inspired by *Il poema dei lunatici* (The lunatics' poem), a novel by Ermanno Cavazzoni.

2 Tullio Kezich, *Federico Fellini: His Life and Work* (New York: Faber and Faber, 2006), 325.

3 Liselotte Millauer, "Federico Fellini: Great Half-and-a-Half Movie Director," in *Federico Fellini: Interviews*, ed. Bert Cardullo (Jackson: University Press of Mississippi, 2006), 184.

4 Federico Fellini, *Making a Film*, trans. Christopher B. White (New York: Contra Mundum, 2015), 158.

5 Fellini, *Making a Film*, 266–7. For Fellini's comments on the gestation of his movies, see chapter 13 (248–67).

6 Frank Burke, *Fellini's Films: From Postwar to Postmodern* (New York: Twayne, 1996), 223.

7 Kezich, *Federico Fellini*, 318.

8 Paul Schwartzman, "Fellini's Unlovable Casanova," *New York Times*, 6 February 1977.

9 Federico Fellini, *Conversations with Fellini*, ed. Costanzo Costantini (San Diego: Harvest, 1995), 93.

10 Fellini, *Conversations with Fellini*, 43.

11 Fellini, *Making a Film*, 275–6.

12 Fellini, *Making a Film*, 276.

13 Kezich, *Federico Fellini*, 326.

14 John C. Stubbs, *Federico Fellini as Auteur: Seven Aspects of His Films* (Carbondale: Southern Illinois University Press, 2006), 4, as well as 1–36 for Fellini's narrative form and signature style.

15 In *La strada*, the snowy, desolate mountain landscape reflects Gelsomina's despair following the death of the Fool; *La dolce vita* begins and ends with enigmatic symbols that can be likened to the figurehead that emerges from the canal in *Casanova*.

16 Schwartzman, "Fellini's Unlovable Casanova," 3.

17 Quoted in Kezich, *Federico Fellini*, 321.

18 Kezich, *Federico Fellini*, 321.

19 Federico Fellini, *Making a Film*, 255.

20 See Fellini's drawing of Aurelio in Pier Marco De Santi, *I disegni di Fellini* (Rome: Laterza, 2004), 122.

21 See De Santi, *I disegni di Fellini*, 144–202.

22 Fabrizio Borin, *Casanova* (Palermo: L'Epos, 2007), 48.

23 William Van Watson, "Fellini and Lacan: The Hollow Phallus, the Male Womb, and the Retying of the Umbilical," in *Federico Fellini: Contemporary Perspectives*, ed. Frank Burke and Marguerite R. Waller (Toronto: University of Toronto Press, 2002), 80.

24   DVD 28:35.

25   Burke, *Fellini's Films*, 228.

26   Kezich, *Federico Fellini*, 319; qtd. in Hollis Alpert, *Fellini: A Life* (New York: Marlowe, 1986), 252.

27   *I vitelloni*, DVD 1:40:40–1:41:36.

28   Van Watson, "Fellini and Lacan, 85.

29   Fellini, *Making a Film*, 242.

30   Fellini, *Making a Film*, 242–3.

31   De Santi, *I disegni di Fellini*, 143; DVD 21:17; 21:36; 25:50.

32   Borin, *Casanova*, 45–6.

33   Borin, *Casanova*, 47.

34   Hava Aldouby, *Federico Fellini: Painting in Film, Painting on Film* (Toronto: University of Toronto Press, 2013), 111–30; DVD 6:32–7:26.

35   *Federico Fellini: Interviews*, 114–15.

36   Aldouby, *Federico Fellini*, 11.

37   Fellini, *Making a Film*, 167.

38   DVD 2:6:28–2:6:40.

39   *Conversations with Fellini*, 95.

40   Fellini, *Making a Film*, 276.

41   Fellini, *Making a Film*, 277.

42   Fellini, *Making a Film*, 277.

43   For excerpts from a number of reviews of *Fellini's Casanova* written by a variety of Italian and French critics, see Claudio G. Fava and Aldo Viganò, *I film di Federico Fellini* (Rome: Gremese, 1987), 150–2.

Contributors

Raphaëlle Brin is associate professor of French language and literature at the University of Kyoto (Japan). Her PhD thesis, "'A Man of No Consequence': Writing Strategies and Ambiguities of the Auctorial Figure in Casanova's Work (between 1752 and 1798)," addresses the adventurer's complex relationship with the notions of *authority* and *auctoriality*, and aims to investigate his writing strategies and their effect, both in his philosophical and autobiographical works. She is the editor of a collective volume *"Écrire à tort et à travers": Casanova* (Paris: Classiques Garnier, 2016).

Bruno Capaci is associate professor at the Alma Mater Studiorum University of Bologna, where he teaches Didactic of Italian Literature and Rhetoric, and Italian Literature. Among his publications are several monographs on Casanova: *Le impressioni delle cose meravigliose. Giacomo Casanova e la redenzione imperfetta della scrittura* (The impressions of wonderful things: Giacomo Casanova and the imperfect redemption of writing, Venice, 2002); *Giacomo Casanova. Una biografia intellettuale e romanzesca* (Giacomo Casanova: An intellectual and romantic biography, Naples, 2009); and *Giacomo Carissimo ... Lettere delicate e deleterie a Giacomo Casanova* (Dear Giacomo ... Delicate and deleterious letters to Casanova, Bologna, 2019).

Michel Delon, professor emeritus of literature at Sorbonne Université, columnist at the *Revue des deux mondes*, was chair of the French Society for the Study of the 18th Century (2003–9). Among his works: scholarly editions of Diderot, Sade (for Gallimard's Pléiade), *L'Idée d'énergie au tournant des Lumières, 1770–1820* (1988), *Dictionnaire européen des Lumières* (translated as *Encyclopedia of the Enlightenment,* Routledge, 2001), *Le savoir-vivre libertin* (2000), *Les Vies de Sade* (2007), *Le Principe de délicatesse. Libertinage et mélancolie* (2011), *Le XVIIIe siècle libertin, de Marivaux à Sade* (translated as *The Libertine: The Art of Love in Eighteenth-Century France,* 2013), *Diderot, cul par-dessus tête* (2013), *Sade un athée en amour* (Paris, 2014) and, on Casanova, *Histoire de ma vie* (2011), *Casanova à Venise, des mots et des images* (2013), *Album Casanova* (2015), and *Casanova. Mes années vénitiennes* (2018).

Clorinda Donato holds the George L. Graziadio Chair for Italian Studies at California State University, Long Beach, and directs the Clorinda Donato Center for Global Romance Languages and Translation Studies. She works on eighteenth-century knowledge transfer in encyclopedic compilations, and on gender in medical and literary accounts. Recent publications include "Fanny Hill Now," a special issue of *Eighteenth-Century Life* (co-edited in 2019 with Nicholas Nace), *The "Encyclopédie Méthodique" in Spain* (Oxford University Studies in the Enlightenment, 2015), co-authored with Riccardo Lopez; *Gender, Science and Sensationalism in Eighteenth-Century Italy and England: The Life and Legend of Catterina Vizzani* (Oxford University Studies in the Enlightenment, 2020) and *John Fante's* Ask the Dust: *A Joining of Voices and Views,* co-edited with Stephen Cooper (Fordham University Press, 2020).

Jean-Christophe Igalens, associate professor of literature at Sorbonne Université, counts among his past and upcoming publications *Casanova. L'écrivain en ses fictions* (Paris, Classiques Garnier, 2011); a new scholarly edition of Casanova's *Histoire de ma vie,* in collaboration with Érik Leborgne (Paris: Robert Laffont, 3 vols., 2013–18), as well as two edited volumes: *Casanova/Rousseau: lectures croisées* (Paris: Presses de la Sorbonne Nouvelle, 2019) and, in collaboration with Fabien Gris, *Casanova à l'écran* (Rennes: Presses Universitaires de Rennes, 2020).

Mladen Kozul, associate professor of French at the University of Montana, specializes in Enlightenment studies, intellectual history, cultural studies, gender studies, Mediterranean studies, social and cultural theory, film, and media. In addition to numerous articles, among his books on topics in French literature, thought, sexuality and cultural history of the Enlightenment, are *Discours antireligieux français du XVIIIe siècle, du curé Meslier au marquis de Sade,* in collaboration with Patrick Graille (2003), *Le Corps dans le Monde, récits et espaces sadiens* (2005), *Le Roman*

Véritable: stratégies préfacielles au XVIIIe siècle, in collaboration with Jan Herman and Nathalie Kremer (2008), *Le Corps érotique au XVIIIe siècle: amour, péché, maladie* (2011), and *Les Lumières imaginaires. Holbach et la traduction* (2016).

Pierre Saint-Amand teaches the literature and philosophy of the French Enlightenment at Yale University, where he is the Benjamin F. Barge Professor of French. His books include *Diderot: Le Labyrinthe de la relation* (1984), *The Libertine's Progress: Seduction in the Eighteenth-Century Novel* (1994), *The Laws of Hostility: Politics, Violence, and the Enlightenment* (1996), and more recently, *The Pursuit of Laziness: An Idle Interpretation of the Enlightenment* (2011). He has edited two libertine novels: *Thérèse philosophe* (2000) and *Confession d'une jeune fille* (2005) for Gallimard's Pléiade collection.

Malina Stefanovska is professor of French and francophone studies at the University of California, Los Angeles, and has held visiting positions at the University of Lausanne and the University of Tours. She specializes in seventeenth- and eighteenth-century autobiography, memoirs, and other non-fictional narratives. Among her published work: *Saint-Simon, un historien dans les marges* (1998), *Factions et passions: la politique du cardinal de Retz* (2007), *Space and Self in Early Modern European Cultures* (co-edited with David Sabean, 2012), *Littérature et politique. Factions et dissidences de la Ligue à la Fronde* (co-edited with Adrien Paschoud, 2015), and *Récits de vie et pratiques de sociabilité (1680–1850),* (co-edited with Marie-Paule De Weerdt-Pilorge, 2020).

Chantal Thomas is a scholar of eighteenth-century French literature. She studied with Roland Barthes in Paris, and taught literature in a number of American universities, before working at the Centre National de la Recherche Scientifique (CNRS). She is the author of over twenty scholarly books of fiction and non-fiction, a number of which have been translated into English: among them are *Casanova, Un voyage libertin,* (1985); *Casanova, La passion de la liberté,* (co-edited with Marie-Laure Prévost, 2011); *The Wicked Queen: The Origins of the Myth of Marie Antoinette* (trans. by Julie Rose, Zone Books, 1999), *Farewell, My Queen* (trans. by Moishe Black and George Braziller, Simon & Schuster, 2003; Weidenfeld & Nicolson, 2004); *The Exchange of Princesses* (trans. by John Cullen, Other Press, 2014), *Memories of Low Tide* (trans. by N. Lehrer, Pushkin Press, 2019). She won the Prix Femina for her novel *Farewell My Queen*

(2002), adapted as a film by Benoit Jacquot, and later received the Roger-Caillois and Prince de Monaco prizes for her entire work. She also works as a screenwriter.

Christopher B. White is an Italianist, film scholar, and visual artist from Pittsburgh, Pennsylvania. He holds a doctorate in Italian from the University of California, Los Angeles, and has taught at Oberlin College, the University of Arizona, and Ohio University. He published in *Journal of Italian Cinema and Media Studies, Italica,* and *World Film Locations: Florence.* He also translated, annotated, and wrote the introduction to *Making a Film* by Federico Fellini, the authoritative collection of the director's autobiographical writings and comments on cinema. In addition to all things Fellini, his research interests include postwar Italian cinema and culture, the *commedia all'italiana* (Italian style comedy), and the history of film censorship in Italy.

Index

Abramovici, Jean-Christophe, 20

Academy of Fisticuffs (Accademia dei Pugni), 73

Academy of the Comfortable (Accademia degli Agiati), 73

Academy of the Defective (Accademia de' Diffetuosi), 73

Academy of the Restless (Accademia degli Inquieti), 73

Adventure, An (Tsvetaeva), 143

Adventurer and the Singer, The (Hofmannsthal), 144–5, 149n4

Aldouby, Hava: *Federico Fellini: Painting in Film, Painting on Film*, 156–7

Alembert, Jean le Rond, d', 5

À Léonard de Snetlage (Casanova), 12n12

Amarcord (film by Fellini), 150, 153, 155, 157–8

Amphitryon (Molière), 91, 103, 103n1

And the Ship Sails On (film by Fellini), 157

Ange Goudar, Pierre: *Chinese Spy*, 98

Anti-Justine (Rétif de la Bretonne), 34n19

Apollinaire, Guillaume, 9, 17; *Casanova, comédie parodique*, 143–4, 146, 148

Arbuthnot, John: *Essay Concerning the Effect of Air on Human Bodies*, 78

Argens, Jean Baptiste de Boyer, Marquis d', *Thérèse philosophe*, 11n1

Ariosto, Ludovico, 148

Augsburger, Marie Anne Geneviève (Auspurger), 53n28

August III of Poland, 132

Autre et le frère, L' (Beaurepaire), 76

Avanturos (Prince de Ligne), 126

Aventures du chevalier de Faublas, Les (Louvet), 34n19

Balletti, Manon or Nena (Maria Maddalena), 36–49, 51nn1–2, 51–2n4, 52n5, 53n25

Balletti, Silvia Benozzi, 5, 37–8, 44–5, 53n23, 106

Bal masqué de Giacomo Casanova, Le (Roustang), 65n1, 119n9

Barthes, Roland, 3

Beaurepaire, Pierre-Yves, 72; *L'autre et le frère*, 76

Beccaria, Cesare, 79

Belchase convent, 44, 46

Bernardin de Saint-Pierre, Jacques-Henri, 6, 12n13

Berne, 8, 71, 74–84

Bernier, André (ed. with Donato and Luesebrink): *Jesuit Accounts of the Colonial Americas*, 88n1

Bernis, François-Joachim de Pierre de, 5, 37

Bianchi, Giovanni: *Breve storia della vita di Catterina Vizzani*, 84–5, 90n19

Blondel, Jacques François, 36, 42, 52n5

Blondel, Jean Battiste, 36

Böcklin, Arnold: *Isle of the Dead* series (paintings), 156

Boerhaave [Boerhave, Boherave], Herman, 78, 80–1; *De viribus medicamentorum*, 63, 65

Bordeu, Théophile de, 63

Bordoni, Giovani, 85

Borin, Fabrizio, 152, 156

Boucher, François: *Girl Reclining* (painting), 115

Boulainvilliers, Mlle de. *See* Augsburger, Marie Anne Geneviève (Auspurger)

Breve storia della vita di Catterina Vizzani (Bianchi), 84–5, 90n19

Brin, Raphaëlle, 7, 10, 17–34

Brockhaus, F.A., Publisher, 143

Brockliss, Laurence (with Jones): *The Medical World of Early Modern France*, 66n10

Brühl, Heinrich, Count of, 132

Brunel, Pierre, 141

Burke, Frank, 151, 154

Buschini, Francesca, 51n2

Caffé, Il (periodical), 79

Cahusac, Louis de: *Zoroastre*, 99

Capaci, Bruno, 7, 10, 35–53

Casanova (Flem), 11n2

Casanova (Temerson), 11n2

Casanova (Thomas), 11n2

Casanova, comédie parodique (Apollinaire), 143–4, 146, 148

Casanova, Francesco Giuseppe, 5

Casanova, Giacomo

—compared to: Don Juan, 91, 14; Gorani, 88–9n4

—contemporary memoir writers, 73

—correspondence: with Haller, 78; with women, 7–8, 35–53

—education and knowledge: chemistry, 92; finance and exchange, 96; intellectual aspirations, 5; Kabbalah, 94, 98; literary ambition and egotism, 48, 123; mathematics and accounting, 95–6; sexual science, 82–5; tutored by Crébillon, 12n4, 76, 106, 121

—escape from Leads prison. See under *History of My Life* (Casanova)

—financial affairs, 95–8

—ideas and beliefs: ethics of love, 17–20, 30, 32; Freemasonry, 72–7; the French Revolution, 9; imposture, 50; marriage, 36, 39–41, 44–5; religion, 7; women, 50

—interests: Italian academic sociability, 73; medicine, 5–8, 10, 55–6, 66nn8–9; periodical literature, 79; philosopher's stone/ elixir of life, 80–1; poetry, 86; theatre, 45; women, 99

—legacy: the "Casanova myth," 7–10, 17, 26, 54, 141–9, 153–4; conflicted status and legacy,

6, 10, 141; embodiment of the
Enlightenment, 10, 36, 88, 141
—physical and emotional
characteristics: age and physical
capacities, 124, 136, 142; "fear
of women," 54–5; instability in
identity, 10; marginalization, 6;
melancholic temperament, 4,
9, 45–6, 130, 137, 142; physical
appearance, 36–7, 45; self-
fashioning, 8; use of mercury, 8,
91, 93–4
—relationships: adaptation
to European sociability, 71;
connections to the culture of his
times, 6–7, 10; failed engagement,
41–3, 47–8; failure in society, 126
—roles: adventurer and witness of his
century, 3–4; broker and mediator,
98; educator-philosopher and
mentor "Longin," 48–9; fiction of
illegitimate birth, 118n6; foreign
national, 112, 135; librarian for
Count Waldstein at Dux, 6, 49, 145,
148, 158; pretentions to aristocratic
lifestyle (nobiliary tropism), 131,
139n3; storyteller and listener, 45,
51; trade facilitator, 95
—scholarship about, 6–7, 9, 12n15
—visits to Paris, 9, 105–19, 120–6
—works: *À Léonard de Snetlage*, 12n12;
Di aneddoti viniziani militari, 12n8;
autobiographical abstract, 48;
collaboration on libretto of *Don
Giovanni*, 6, 91; *Confutazione della
storia del governo veneto*, 12n8, 40;
contribution to Ange Goudar's
Chinese Spy, 98; *Examens des* Études
de la Nature, 12n13; *History of
My Life* (see *History of My Life*

[Casanova]); *Icosameron*, 6, 12n10,
57–63, 66n12, 92–3, 96, 99; *Istoria
delle turbolenze*, 12n8; *Lana Caprina*,
5, 12n9, 99; medical treatises,
66n8; *La Moluccheide* (play), 12n6,
53n24; parody of Racine, 99; *Le
philosophe et le théologien*, 12n11;
Le Polémoscope, 12n6; *Précis de ma
vie*, 48; *Rêve. Dieu. Moi*, 12n11;
rewriting of novels by Mme de
Riccoboni, 99; *Soliloque d'un
penseur*, 50; *Solution du problème
déliaque*, 12n7; for theatre, 45; *Les
Thessaliennes*, 12n6; translations
of Cahusac, Homer, and Voltaire,
99; writing and translations,
5–6, 12nn5–6, 99; *Zoroastro* (play),
53n24
Casanova, the Seduction of Europe
(Ilchman, Dickerson, and Michie,
eds.), 6, 13n16
Casanova's Homecoming (Schnitzler),
143–6, 149n4
Casanova's Women (Summers), 90n16
Castiglione, Baldassare: *Il Libro del
Cortegiano*, 86
Catholic Church, 79, 150, 153
Cavazzoni, Ermanno: *Il poema dei
lunatici*, 158–9n1
Chinese Spy (Ange Goudar), 98
Choiseul, Étienne-François, duc de, 5
Ciaccheri, Giuseppe, the Abate, 85–6
Cleland, John: *An Historical and
Physical Dissertation on the Case of
Catherine Vizzani*, 90n19
Clément, Charles-François, 36
Comédie Italienne (Italian theatre),
36, 45, 107, 120
*Comédie médicale de Giacomo Casanova,
La*, 65–6n6

Confessions (Rousseau), 4, 122
*Confutazione della storia del governo
  veneto* (Casanova), 12n8, 40
Conversations in Bolzano (Márai),
  146–8
conversazione (conversazioni), 8, 72, 74,
  85–7, 89n7
Corilla Olimpica *(Poetessa)* (Maria
  Maddalena Morelli), 86–7
Corinne, ou l'Italie (Staël), 87
Cornelys, Teresa. *See* Imer, Teresa
  (later Cornelys)
Costantini, Costanzo, 152, 157
Crébillon, Claude Prosper-Jolyot de
  (son), 122; *La nuit et le moment*,
  121; *Le sopha*, 121
Crébillon, Prosper-Jolyot de (the
  Elder), 5, 12n4, 33n6, 39, 76,
  121–5; *Lettres de Ninon de Lenclos*,
  52n13; *Rhadamiste et Zénobie*, 106

dall'Orto, Giovanni, 88–9n4
Da Ponte, Lorenzo, 91
De Chirico, Giorgio: *The Enigma of the
  Oracle* (painting), 156
De Laurentiis, Dino, 150–1
Delon, Michel, 7, 9–10, 140n7,
  141–9; *Le savoir-vivre libertin*, 52n20
Démoris, René, 132
De Santi, Pier Marco: *I disegni de
  Fellini*, 159n20
De viribus medicamentorum
  (Boerhaave), 63, 65
Di aneddoti viniziani militari
  (Casanova), 12n8
Dickerson, C.D. (with Ichman
  and Michie, eds.): *Casanova, the
  Seduction of Europe*, 6, 13n16
Dictionnaire Universel de Médecine, 64–5
Diderot, Denis, 5

Die Alpen (Haller), 78
Die Göttingische Gelehernte Anzeigen, 78
Di Sangro, Raimondo, Prince of San
  Severo, 78–9, 81
disegni de Fellini, I (De Santi),
  159n20
Di Trocchio, Federico (with Forleo):
  Giacomo Casanova e le ostetriche, 66n8
dolce vita, La (film by Fellini), 153,
  159n15
Donato, Clorinda, 7–8, 10, 71–90;
  (ed. with Bernier and Luesebrink):
  Jesuit Accounts of the Americas, 88n1
Don Giovanni (Mozart), 6, 91
Don Juan (Molière), 91
Don Juan (Tirso de Molina), 91
Doria, Alessandra, 90n13
Dubois, Madame, 90n16
Dux (Dushcov), 6, 35–50, 51–2n4

Eco, Umberto: *The Open Work*, 152
Ecossaise, L' (Voltaire), 99
Edelstein, D. (with Matytsin, eds.):
  Let There Be Enlightenment, 13n17
E il Casanova de Fellini? (television
  documentary), 153
Elements of Physiology (Haller), 78
Emch-Deriaz, Antoinette: *Tissot*,
  67n18
Encyclopédie, 5, 21, 63–4, 67n19
Encyclopédie d'Yverdon, 79
Enclyclopédie méthodique de Padoue,
  89n7
Enigma of the Oracle, The (painting by
  De Chirico), 156
Enlightened Pleasures (Kavanagh),
  33n9
Enlightenment: encyclopedic spirit,
  4; relationship with religion,
  13n17; "revisionist" scholarship,

13n17; sociabilities and networks,
3–4, 7–8, 10
*Essay Concerning the Effect of Air on
Human Bodies* (Arbuthnot), 78
Estratto della letteratura europea,
79, 90n14
Examens des Études de la Nature
(Casanova), 12n13
*Excerptum totius Italicae nec non
Helveticae literaturae*, 79, 90n14
Exhibition of a Rhinoceros at Venice
(painting by Longhi), 156

Farussi, Zanetta, 45
Fava, Claudio G. (with Viganò): *I film
di Federico Fellini*, 160n43
*Federico Fellini: Painting in Film,
Painting on Film* (Aldouby), 156–7
Federico Fellini as Auteur (Stubbs),
152, 159n14
Felice, Fortunato Bartolomeo, de
78–80, 90n13
Félicia ou mes fredaines (Nerciat),
108–9
Fellini, Federico, films: *Amarcord*, 150,
153, 155, 157–8; *Fellini Satyricon*,
156–7, 158–9n1; *Fellini's Casanova*,
10, 17, 142, 150–9, 160n43; *Fellini's
Roma*, 156; *I vitelloni*, 150, 155;
Juliet of the Spirits, 156; *La dolce
vita*, 153, 159n15; *La strada*, 153,
159n15; *Making a Film*, 151–2, 155,
158, 159n5; *Nights of Cabiria*, 153;
And the Ship Sails On, 157; *Spirits
of the Dead*, 151, 158–9n1; "Toby
Dammit" (film segment), 151,
156, 158–9n1; *The Voice of the Moon*,
158–9n1; *The White Sheiks*, 155
film di Federico Fellini, I (Fava and
Viganò), 160n43

Findlen, Paula, 85
Flem, Lydia: *Casanova*, 11n2
Fleming, John V., 72–3
Fontainebleau, 133
Fontenelle, Bernard Le Bovier de, 5
Forleo, Romano (with Di Trocchio):
Giacomo Casanova e le ostetriche,
66n8
Foucault, Michel: *La Volonté
de savoir*, 108
Fragonard, Jean–Honoré: *Le Verrou*
(painting), 122
Franz-Joseph, emperor of Austria,
132, 140n6
Frederick II, 24
Freemasonry, 8, 72–7, 95, 97
French Revolution, 9, 129–40

Gage, Jennifer Curtiss, 118n2,
119n11
Galeazzi, Giuseppe, 79
Galen, 67n18
Galiani, Ferdinand, 5
Giacomo Casanova e le ostetriche (Forleo
and Di Trocchio), 66n8
*Giacomo Casanova und die Medizin des
18. Jahrhunderds* (Hermann),
66n8
Girl Reclining (painting by
Boucher), 115
Giroud, Françoise, 17
Goldoni, Carlo: *Pupilla*, 45
Goldzink, Jean: *Le Vice en bas
de soie*, 11n1
Gorani, Giuseppe (Joseph), 79; *Histoire
de ma vie*, 88–9n4; *Mémoires pour servir
à l'histoire de ma vie*, 73; *Mémoires
secrets et critiques des cours*, 73
*Göttingische Anzeigen von gelehrten
Sachen*, 78

Graffigny, Françoise de, 5
Grand dérèglement, Le (Wald
    Lasowski), 11n1
Grazzini, Giovanni, 157
Grenier, Marco, ed. (with Leeflang):
    *Lettres de Manon Balletti à G.
    Casanova*, 51–2n4, 53n25
Greuze, Jean-Baptiste, 122
Grimaldi, Alberto, 151
Guerra, Tonino, 152

Haller, Albrecht von, 5, 56, 79–81,
    89n11; *Die Alpen*, 78; *Elements of
    Physiology*, 78
Hamlet, William, 140n11
Hartmann, Pierre, 33n6
Hermès (Serres), 94, 98
Herrenschwand, Johann Friedrich
    von, 5
Herrmann, Sabine: *Giacomo Casanova
    und die Medizin des 18. Jahrhunderds*,
    66n8
Hippocrates, 67n18, 80
Histoire de Juliette, L' (Sade), 121
Histoire de ma vie (Gorani), 88–9n4
Histoire des deux Indes (Raynal), 71
Histoire du viol (Vigarello), 34n15
*Historical and Physical Dissertation on
    the Case of Catherine Vizzani, An*
    (Cleland), 90n19
History of My Life (Casanova)
—characters: abbé de Bernis, 59–60,
    64, 97; Angela, 137; Armellina, 61;
    August III, 132; Barbaruccia, 100;
    Bellino/Teresa, 85, 144; bishop of
    Martorano, 103; the bride, 25–7;
    Cardinal Acquaviva, 96; Cardinal
    S.C., 100; Carlino Bertinazzi, actor,
    109–10; Cattinella, 135; C.C., 130;
    Chamfort, 139; Charlotte, 125;
    Chevalier de Württemberg, 111;
    Ciaccheri, 86; Claude-Pierre Patu,
    lawyer and poet, 107; Clementina,
    60–1, 66–7n14; Corallina, 110–
    12; Countess Ambrosio, 60–1;
    Count of Brühl, 132; count of
    Lowendähl, 133; count of Saint-
    Germain, 97; Count Ostein, 135–6,
    140n8; Damiens, 29; Demetrio
    Papanelopoulo, 97–8; duc de
    Clermont, 89n8; duchesses of
    Savoy, 136; Emilie, 61; Esther,
    42; François, 29; Franz-Joseph,
    Emperor, 132; Giovanni Bucchetti,
    96; Goudar, 21, 30; Greek
    merchant, 92, 103; Henriette,
    41, 49, 100–2, 118, 119n10, 123,
    125, 129; Hungarian officer,
    100–2, 119n10; Joseph II, 132,
    137; Juliette La Baret, later actress
    l'Anglade, 97; "La Cavamachia,"
    courtesan, 133–4; La Charpillon,
    18, 21, 30–3, 47–8, 135–6, 142;
    La Fraïla, 137–8; La Vesian, 137;
    Louison O'Morphy, "O-Morphi,"
    "Helen," 113–15; Louis XV, 112–
    15, 131, 133–5; Louis XVI, 130–3;
    Lucie, 25–7; M. d'Argenson, 133;
    M. de Beauchamp, tax collector,
    106; M. de Chavigni, 80; M. de
    Marigni, 133; M. de Mocenigo,
    138–9; M. de or Signore Bragadin,
    senator, 94, 98, 124, 142; M.
    de Sersale, 133; M. Felix, 80;
    Malipiero, 30; Maria Fortunata,
    86; Maria-Theresa, archduchess of
    Austria, 132, 137; Mario Balletti,
    112; marquise de G., 100; M.D.O.,
    banker and ship-owner, 99; Milanese
    dancer, 137; Mlle de la M –, 22–3

(*see also* Balletti, Manon or Nena [Maria Maddalena]); Mlle Le Fel, 107–8; M.M., 49, 59–60, 64, 97, 130; M.M. (the second), 19–20, 60; Mme de Boufflers, 122; Mme de Colande, 138; Mme de la Caillerie, landlady, 109; Mme de Pompadour, 112–13; Mme Dubois, 81–2, 90n16; Mme d'Urfé, 93, 96, 99, 122–4, 154; Mme Pâris, 116; Mme XXX, 22–4, 29; Monsieur de la Rochebaron, 75, 89n8; Pantalon, actor (Carlo Veronese), 110; Pasiano, 26; Patu, 135; Pauline, 49, 96; Pistoi, 86; Pochini, pimp, 97; prince de Courlande, 93; prince of Monaco, 110–12; Queen Marie, 114; Schmid, 80; Signora Querini, 101; Silvia, 43, 106 (*see also* Balletti, Silvia Benozzi); Stratico, 87; Teresa Imer, later Tranti or Trenti, Pompeati, and Mrs. Cornelys, 97; Thérèse, servant, 30, 122; Tireta, 22–4, 29; Voiture, 39
—compared to: *Icosameron*, 57; novel by Nerciat, 108; novel by Rousseau, 115–17, 122
—film adaptation, 150–60
—literary devices and styles: aging and death motifs, 135–6; assumed identities, 99; Bildungsroman, 105; black humour, 138–9, 140n10; *comédie humaine*, 45; *comédie marivaudienne*, 46; confessional 24; conversational, 72; "feminist" reading, 17; gallant metaphors, 28; heroic or military metaphors, 25; *humeur*, 39; irony, 24; *lettre badine*, 39; memoir/autobiography, 12n3, 35–53; moments of theatre, 45; myth of modernity, 10, 148; neo-humoral model, 56, 62, 64–5, 67n15; parody, 22; pecuniary motif, 96–7; reconfiguration of the past, 132; seduction by narration, 100; the social gaze, 26; solicitation of the reader's complicity, 28; theatrical metaphor, 134; theme of Paris, 125; translation/mediation, 100–2; voluntary forgetfulness, 125
—literary influences: 10, 94, 122
—manuscript: organization, 129–40; original 6–7, 9, 143
—representations: age and physical capacities, 124, 136, 144–6; amorous disenchantment, 135–7; cheating and hoaxes, 99–100; children, 108–9, 114, 119n9; *coquetterie*, 39; cross-cultural encounters, 72; elements of Venetian carnival, 142–3; erotic, 59, 135–6, 140n7; eroticization of breastfeeding, 61–3; escape from Leads prison, 5, 37, 45, 94, 123, 130, 142, 146–7, 156; European sociabilities, 8, 71–90; failed engagement, 43; the French people, 130–1; gift exchanges, 103; historical figures, 132, 137; history and memory, 129–40; impotence, 62; Italian *conversazione*, 85–7; justice system, 21, 26, 32; laughter and violence, 26–33; libertine, 3, 7–10, 19, 24–5, 33n9, 108–126; masquerade, 101; mechanisms of exchange, displacement, and substitution, 62; medical imagery of the body, 56, 65n6, 66n9; memory lapses, 10, 130; network of contacts, 97, 104n5; *officiers du*

roi, 36, 51–2n5; paternity, 109–10, 117, 119n9; phallic power, 23, 34n18; majesty and monarchy, 134; notable people, 5; Paris, 5–9; sexual ambiguity, 54–67; sexuality, 84; sexual violence, 17–34; suicide, 32, 138–9; undifferentiation of the body, 7, 54–67; villainy, 27; visits to Paris, 105–26, 129–40; visit to Berne, 74–84; visit to Fontainebleau, 133; visit to Orsara, 92–3; visit to Pisa, 87; visit to Rimini, 84–5; visit to Siena, 85–7
Hofmann, Friedrich, 67n18
Hofmannsthal, Hugo von: *The Adventurer and the Singer*, 144–5, 149n4
Hölzle, Dominique: *Le Roman libertin au XVIIIe siècle*, 11n1
Homer, 99

Icosameron (Casanova), 6, 12n10, 57–63, 66n12, 92–3, 96, 99
Igalens, Jean-Christophe, 10–11, 19–20, 33n8, 129–40; edition of *History of My Life*, 7, 9
Ilchman, F. (with Dickerson and Michie, eds.): *Casanova, the Seduction of Europe*, 6, 13n16
Imer, Teresa (later Cornelys), 97
Isle of the Dead (paintings by Böcklin), 156
Istoria delle turbolenze (Casanova), 12n8

James, Robert: *Medical Dictionary*, 62
Jesuit Accounts of the Colonial Americas (Bernier, Donato, and Luesebrink, eds.), 88n1
Jesuits, 71, 88n1

Jeu de l'amour et du hasard, Le (Marivaux), 38
Jones, Colin (with Brockliss): *The Medical World of Early Modern France*, 66n10
Joseph II, Holy Roman Emperor, 132, 137
Julie ou La Nouvelle Héloïse (Rousseau), 9, 115–17, 126
Juliet of the Spirits (film by Fellini), 156

Kavanagh, Thomas M.: *Enlightened Pleasures*, 33n9
Kezich, Tullio, 150, 152
Kihli-Sagols, Didier: *La Comédie médicale de Giacomo Casanova*, 65–6n6
Kozul, Mladen, 7–8, 10, 54–67

Laclos, Pierre Choderlos de: *Les Liaisons dangereuses*, 121
Lana Caprina (Casanova), 5, 12n9, 99
Laqueur, Thomas, 55–6
Leborgne, Erik, 138, 140n10
Leeflang, Marco, 35; (ed. with Grenier) *Lettres de Manon Balletti à G. Casanova*, 51–2n4, 53n25
Lejeune, Philippe, 42
Lettere di donne a Giacomo Casanova (Rava, ed.), 51n3, 53n25
Let There Be Enlightenment (Matytsin and Edelstein, eds.), 13n17
Lettres de Manon Balletti à G. Casanova (Leeflang and Grenier, eds.), 51–2n4, 53n25
Lettres de Ninon de Lenclos (Crébillon), 52n13
Liaisons dangereuses, Les (Laclos), 121
libertine literature, 11n1, 17, 34n11, 120–6, 124. See also under *History of My Life* (Casanova)

Libro del Cortegiano, Il (Castiglione), 86

Ligne, Charles Joseph, Prince de: *Avanturos*, 126

Lilti, Antoine, 72

Loiselle, Kenneth, 72

Londen, Robert: *The World We Want*, 13n17

Longhi, Pietro: *Exhibition of a Rhinoceros at Venice* (painting), 156

Louis-Courvoisier, Micheline, 66n9

Louis XV, 45, 112, 130–5

Louis XVI, 130–3

Louvet, Jean-Baptiste: *Les Aventures du chevalier de Faublas*, 34n19

Luesebrink (ed. with Bernier and Donato): *Jesuit Accounts of the Colonial Americas*, 88n1

Making a Film (film by Fellini), 151–2, 155, 158, 159n5

Mallarmé, Stéphane, 95

Márai, Sándor, 9; *Conversations in Bolzano*, 146–8

Marceau, Félicien, 142

Maria-Theresa, archduchess of Austria, 132, 136–7

Marivaux, Pierre Carlet de Chamblain de, 5, 45–6; *Le Jeu de l'amour et du hasard*, 38

Martin, Christophe, 34n11

Matytsin, A. (with Edelstein, eds.): *Let There Be Enlightenment*, 13n17

Medical World of Early Modern France, The (Brockliss and Jones), 66n10

Mémoires et Aventures d'un homme de qualité (Prévost), 71, 88n1

Mémoires pour servir à l'histoire de ma vie (Gorani), 73

Mémoires secrets et critiques des cours (Gorani), 73

Mengs, Anton-Raphael, 5

Mercury/Hermès/Mercurio, 8, 91–104

Michie, Th. (with Ichman and Dickerson, eds.): *Casanova, the Seduction of Europe*, 6, 13n16

Mill, James, 65n1

Molière: *Amphitryon*, 91, 103, 103n1; *Don Juan*, 91

Moluccheide, La (Casanova), 12n6

Monconseil, Marquise de, 44, 46

Montesquieu, 99

Morelli, Maria Maddalena. *See* Corilla Olimpica *(Poetessa)* (Maria Maddalena Morelli)

Mozart, Wolfgang Amadeus: *Don Giovanni*, 6, 91

Naissance de l'écrivain (Viala), 139n3

Nattier, Jean-Marc, 36–7

Nerciat, André-Robert Andréa, de: *Félicia ou mes fredaines*, 108–9

"Never Bet the Devil Your Head" (Poe), 151, 158–9n1

Nietzsche, Friedrich, 123

Nights of Cabiria (film by Fellini), 153

Nouvelle Héloïse, La (Rousseau). See *Julie ou La Nouvelle Héloïse* (Rousseau)

Nuit et le moment, La (Crébillon), 20, 121

Onanisme (Tissot), 67nn17–18

Open Work, The (Eco), 152

Oulipian writing, 99

Panzutti, Countess Agnese Arcuato, 79

Papanelopoulo, Demetrio, 97–8

Paracelse, 66n10

Petronius, 158–9n1

Philosophe et le théologien, Le (Casanova), 12n11

Phoenix, The (Tsvetaeva), 143, 148

Pilloud, Severine, 66n9

Poe, Edgar Allan: "Never Bet the Devil Your Head," 151, 158–9n1

poema dei lunatici, Il (Cavazzoni), 158–9n1

Poinsinet, Antoine-Alexandre-Henri, 5

Polémoscope, Le (Casanova), 12n6

Pompadour, Jeanne-Antoinette Poisson, Marquise de, 36, 45, 112

Pope Benedict XIV, 79

Précis de ma vie (Casanova), 48

Prévost-d'Exiles, Antoine-François, abbé de (known as Prévost), *Mémoires et Aventures d'un homme de qualité*, 71, 88n1

Pupilla (Goldoni), 45

Quadrille of Gender, The (Roustang), 54–5, 62, 65n1, 118n6

Racine: *La Thébaïde ou les frères ennemis*, 99

Ramsay, Andrew Michael, 73–4

Ravà, Aldo, ed.: *Lettere di donne a Giacomo Casanova*, 51n3, 53n25

Raynal, Guillaume-Thomas François: *Histoire des deux Indes*, 71

regard froid, Le (Vailland), 121

Rétif de la Bretonne, Nicolas: *Anti-Justine*, 34n19

Rêve. Dieu. Moi (Casanova), 12n11

Rhadamiste et Zénobie (Crébillon), 106

Riccoboni, Marie Jeanne, 99

Rimini, 71, 84–5

Rizzoli, Andrea, 151

Roggendorff, Cécile de, 35, 48–9, 51nn1–2

Roman libertin au XVIIIe siècle, Le (Hölzle), 11n1

Romantika (Tsvetaeva), 145–6

Rossellini, Roberto, 157

Rotunno, Giuseppe, 157

Rousseau, Jean-Jacques, 3, 118; *Confessions*, 4, 122; *Julie ou la nouvelle Héloïse*, 9, 115–16, 123

Roustang, François: *Le Bal masqué de Giacomo Casanova*, 65n1, 119n9; *The Quadrille of Gender*, 54–5, 62, 65n1, 118n6

Sade, Marquis de, 8, 18, 29, 33, 34n19, 124, 143; *L'Histoire de Juliette*, 121

Saggio alfabetico d'istoria medica e natural (Vallisneri), 83

Saint-Amand, Pierre, 7–8, 10, 105–19

Salomon's clavicula, 98

Samaran, Charles, 37

savoir-vivre libertin, Le (Delon), 52n20

Schmidt zu Rossan, Friedrich Samuel, 80

Schnitzler, Arthur, 9; *Casanova's Homecoming*, 143–4, 146, 149n4

Schopenhauer, Arthur, 123

Serres, Michel: *Hermès*, 94, 98

sexual and gender identity, 7; ambiguity of, 54–67, 142; castrati, 142; fluidity in, 85; hermaphroditism, 82–4; heterosexuality, 54; homosexuality, 24; lesbianism, 82; "one-sex" and "two-sex" models of, 55–6; transposition of gender, 117; transvestitism, 142

sexuality: celibacy, 79, 90n13; effects
of the church on, 150, 153, 158;
effects of the family on, 158; erotic
imagination, 8; impotence, 29;
libido of libertine, 8, 43, 54; of men,
25; permanent adolescence, 153,
155; promiscuity, 105–19; sexually
transmitted diseases, 8, 91–3;
"sexual myth," 8, 17; of women, 7
sexual violence, 7, 17–34;
consequences, 17, 20, 23, 25, 27,
29, 32, 33; discourse on rape, 18,
20–6, 34n11, 34n17; and laughter,
26–9; the problem of consent,
20–6, 34n11, 154; question of
proof, 20, 34n15; sodomy, 23–4,
29; use of a "molesting chair," 21,
31–2, 34n19
Sisters or Casanova in Spa, The
(Tsvetaeva), 143
Soliloque d'un penseur (Casanova), 50
Solution du problème déliaque
(Casanova), 12n7
Sopha, Le (Crébillon), 121
Spirits of the Dead (film by Fellini),
151, 158–9n1
Sprüngli, Daniel, 80
Staël, Mme de: *Corinne, ou l'Italie*, 87
Stefanovska, Malina, 7–8, 91–104
strada, La (film by Fellini), 153,
159n15
Stubbs, John C.: *Federico Fellini as
Auteur*, 152, 159n14
Stuber, Martin, 89n11
Summers, Judith: *Casanova's Women*,
90n16
Sutherland, Donald, 151, 153–4

Temerson, Katherine: *Casanova*, 11n2
Thébaïde ou les frères ennemis, La
(Racine), 99

Thérèse philosophe (Boyer d'Argens),
11n1
Thessaliennes, Les (Casanova), 12n6
Thomas, Chantal, 7, 9–10, 105,
120–6; *Casanova*, 11n2
Tirso de Molina: *Don Juan*, 91
Tissot (Emch-Deriaz), 67n18
Tissot, Samuel-Auguste André David,
66n9; *Onanisme*, 67nn17–18
"Toby Dammit" (film segment by
Fellini), 151, 156, 158–9n1
Trask, Willard, 11, 139n1
Tronchin, Théodore, 56
Tscharner, Vincenz Bernhard von,
78–9
Tsvetaeva, Marina, 9; *An Adventure*,
143; *The Phoenix*, 143, 148;
Romantika, 145–6; *The Sisters or
Casanova in Spa*, 143
Typographical Society of Berne, 78

Urfé, Jeanne Camus de Pontcarré,
marquise de, 37

Vailland, Roger: *Le regard froid*, 121
Vallisneri, Antonio: *Saggio alfabetico
d'istoria medica e natural*, 83
Van Watson, William, 155, 159n23
Venel, Gabriel-François, 63–4, 67n19
Verri, Pietro, 79
Verrou, Le (painting by
Fragonard), 122
Viala, Alain: *Naissance de l'écrivain*,
139n3
Vice en bas de soie, Le (Goldzink), 11n1
Viganò, Aldo (with Fava): *I film de
Federico Fellini*, 160n43
Vigarello, Georges, 18–19, 21; *Histoire
du viol*, 34n15
Vila, Anne C., 65n1
Vitali-Volant, Maria G., 88–9n4

vitelloni, I (film by Fellini), 150, 155
Vizzani, Catterina, 84–5
Voice of the Moon, The (film by Fellini),
    158–9n1
Voisenon, Claude-Henri de Fuzée,
    abbé de, 5
Volonté de savoir, La (Foucault), 108
Voltaire, 5, 79; *L'Ecossaise,* 99

Wald Lasowski, Patrick: *Le Grand
    dérèglement,* 11n1
Waldstein, Ferdinand Ernst Gabriel,
    Count von, 6, 48
Waldstein, Maria Anna Theresa,
    Countess von, 48
White, Christopher B., 7, 10, 150–60
White Sheik, The (film by Fellini), 155
Wilbur, Richard, 103n1
Winckelmann, Johan Joachim, 5
Withers, Charles, 72, 74, 90n21
women: breastfeeding, 63; critique,
    30, 123; dressing in men's clothing,
101–2, 118; erotic emancipation,
18–19, 22; freedom of, 40;
gynecocracy, 117; inscrutability,
158; men's fear, 54–5; misogyny,
123, 153; moodiness, 39–40;
moral reputation, 87; as mothers,
158; objectification, 18, 28, 157;
physiology, 82–4; as poets, 86–7; as
property, 21; release of anxieties,
20, 34n10; roles, 85–6; theories
about thinking, 6; unequal
treatment, 79; victimization, 26
World We Want, The (Londen), 13n17
Wynn, Thomas, 149n14
Wynne, Giustiniana, 37

Yale French Studies, 11n1

Zapponi, Bernardina, 152
"Zenobie, Madame." *See*
    Roggendorff, Cécile de
Zoroastre (Cahusac), 99

THE UCLA CLARK MEMORIAL LIBRARY SERIES

1. *Wilde Writings: Contextual Conditions,* edited by Joseph Bristow
2. *Enchanted Ground: Reimagining John Dryden,* edited by Jayne Lewis and Maximillian E. Novak
3. *Culture and Authority in the Baroque,* edited by Massimo Ciavolella and Patrick Coleman
4. *Ritual, Routine, and Regime: Repetition in Early Modern British and European Cultures,* edited by Lorna Clymer
5. *Momigliano and Antiquarianism: Foundations of the Modern Cultural Sciences,* edited by Peter N. Miller
6. *Monarchisms in the Age of Enlightenment: Liberty, Patriotism, and the Common Good,* edited by Hans Blom, John Christian Laursen, and Luisa Simonetti
7. *Thinking Impossibilities: The Intellectual Legacy of Amos Funkenstein,* edited by Robert S. Westman and David Biale
8. *Discourses of Tolerance and Intolerance in the European Enlightenment,* edited by Hans Erich Bödeker, Clorinda Donato, and Peter Hanns Reill
9. *The Age of Projects,* edited by Maximillian E. Novak
10. *Acculturation and Its Discontents: The Italian Jewish Experience between Exclusion and Inclusion,* edited by David N. Myers, Massimo Ciavolella, Peter H. Reill, and Geoffrey Symcox
11. *Defoe's Footprints: Essays in Honour of Maximillian E. Novak,* edited by Robert M. Maniquis and Carl Fisher
12. *Women, Religion, and the Atlantic World (1600–1800),* edited by Daniella Kostroun and Lisa Vollendorf
13. *Braudel Revisited: The Mediterranean World, 1600–1800,* edited by Gabriel Piterberg, Teofilo F. Ruiz, and Geoffrey Symcox
14. *Structures of Feeling in Seventeenth-Century Cultural Expression,* edited by Susan McClary
15. *Godwinian Moments,* edited by Robert M. Maniquis and Victoria Myers
16. *Vital Matters: Eighteenth-Century Views of Conception, Life, and Death,* edited by Helen Deutsch and Mary Terrall
17. *Redrawing the Map of Early Modern English Catholicism,* edited by Lowell Gallagher
18. *Space and Self in Early Modern European Cultures,* edited by David Warren Sabean and Malina Stefanovska
19. *Wilde Discoveries: Traditions, Histories, Archives,* edited by Joseph Bristow

20. *Jesuit Accounts of the Colonial Americas: Intercultural Transfers, Intellectual Disputes, and Textualities*, edited by Marc André Bernier, Clorinda Donato, and Hans-Jürgen Lüsebrink
21. *Skepticism and Political Thought in the Seventeenth and Eighteenth Centuries*, edited by John Christian Laursen and Gianni Paganini
22. *Representing Imperial Rivalry in the Early Modern Mediterranean*, edited by Barbara Fuchs and Emily Weissbourd
23. *Imagining the British Atlantic after the American Revolution*, edited by Michael Meranze and Saree Makdisi
24. *Life Forms in the Thinking of the Long Eighteenth Century*, edited by Keith Michael Baker and Jenna M. Gibbs
25. *Cultures of Communication: Theologies of Media in Early Modern Europe and Beyond*, edited by Helmut Puff, Ulrike Strasser, and Christopher Wild
26. *Curious Encounters: Voyaging, Collecting, and Making Knowledge in the Long Eighteenth Century*, edited by Adriana Craciun and Mary Terrall
27. *Clandestine Philosophy: New Studies on Subversive Manuscripts in Early Modern Europe, 1620–1823*, edited by Gianni Paganini, Margaret C. Jacob, and John Christian Laursen
28. *The Quest for Certainty in Early Modern Europe: From Inquisition to Inquiry, 1550–1700*, edited by Barbara Fuchs and Mercedes García Arenal
29. *Entertaining the Idea: Shakespeare, Philosophy, and Performance*, edited by Lowell Gallagher, James Kearney, and Julia Reinhard Lupton
30. *Casanova in the Enlightenment: From the Margins to the Centre*, edited by Malina Stefanovska

www.ingramcontent.com/pod-product-compliance
Lightning Source LLC
Chambersburg PA
CBHW030403180625
28310CB00013B/85/J